PRAISE FOR *KINGDOM OF CHARACTERS*

"Rigorous and engaging . . . Languages, as this book makes clear, convey worlds."
—*The New York Times*

"A lively and insightful history of the intersection of China's information technology systems and its language revolution. The book is a richly documented, riveting, and scholarly rigorous transnational account of how Chinese evolved from a hard-to-learn script entrenched in the beleaguered Middle Kingdom in the nineteenth century to a global language in the twenty-first century."
—*Science*

"This is where the author is at her best: she brings to life the individuals who gave their all to solve China's problems with language technology, even as political and social turmoil was raging around them." —*The Guardian* (London)

"Stimulating." —*Nature*

"Fascinating . . . While focusing on the Chinese script, the book ultimately tells a story of much broader importance and furnishes the reader with a sense of the obstacles that China had to overcome to 'join' the modern world."
—*Financial Times*

"A fascinating book" —*The Economist*

"Essential reading for anyone interested in Chinese language or modern Chinese history." —*Library Journal*

"In *Kingdom of Characters*, Jing Tsu introduces us to a cast of unforgettable figures. She tells an essential story of modern China: a country at once transformed and yet deeply traditional."

—Peter Hessler, author of *Oracle Bones* and *River Town*

"Jing Tsu wears her erudition lightly and gives us a fascinating and moving story. It shows the passionate struggle of generations of pioneers. It's a story of desperate strife, unflagging dedication, and, ultimately, triumph."

—Ha Jin, author of *Waiting* and *War Trash*

"Seldom have I read a book about modern China so informative, revelatory, and enjoyable."

—Simon Winchester, author of *The Professor and the Madman* and *The Man Who Loved China*

"An absolute joy to read. This stunning, meticulously researched book is the detective story of Chinese characters. Jing Tsu has seamlessly fused the craft of the linguistic historian with the artistry of the storyteller—including cliff-hangers." —David Crystal, author of *How Language Works* and *The Stories of English*

"A deeply engaging and revealing narrative of the Chinese language in modern times. Meticulously researched and beautifully written."

—David Wang, Edward C. Henderson Professor of Chinese and Comparative Literature, Harvard University

"Tsu's humanistic, big-picture sensibility makes an otherwise obscure thread in the history of information technology vivid and compelling." —*Booklist*

"An engaging, relevant work that delves into the linguistic past in order to predict China's future success in the world." —*Kirkus Reviews* (starred review)

"An immersive history of the effort to transform the written Chinese language's vast and complex set of characters into a modern communication technology . . . Tsu sheds light on the intriguing interplay between Chinese language and politics. Sinophiles and language buffs will be fascinated."

—*Publishers Weekly*

"Interesting and very readable." —*Asian Review of Books*

"Pioneering" —*Physics World*

"I was more than delighted to read Jing Tsu's incredibly fascinating book. . . . [It] may be as prophetic as it is historical." —*The Scotsman* (Edinburgh)

KINGDOM OF CHARACTERS

THE LANGUAGE REVOLUTION THAT MADE CHINA MODERN

JING TSU

RIVERHEAD BOOKS
NEW YORK

RIVERHEAD BOOKS
An imprint of Penguin Random House LLC
penguinrandomhouse.com

Script and character illustrations by Naiqian Wang and Stephanie Winarto.

The Library of Congress has catalogued the Riverhead hardcover edition as follows:

Names: Tsu, Jing, author.
Title: Kingdom of characters : the language revolution that made China modern / Jing Tsu.
Description: New York : Riverhead, 2022. | Includes bibliographical references and index.
Identifiers: LCCN 2021017006 (print) | LCCN 2021017007 (ebook) |
ISBN 9780735214729 (hardcover) | ISBN 9780735214743 (ebook)
Subjects: LCSH: Chinese characters—History—20th century. |
Chinese language—Writing—History—20th century. |
Chinese language—Modern Chinese, 1919–
Classification: LCC PL1171 .T776 2022 (print) | LCC PL1171 (ebook) |
DDC 495.11/1—dc23/eng/20211110
LC record available at https://lccn.loc.gov/2021017006
LC ebook record available at https://lccn.loc.gov/2021017007

First Riverhead hardcover edition: January 2022
First Riverhead trade paperback edition: January 2023
Riverhead trade paperback ISBN: 9780735214736

Printed in the United States of America
2nd Printing

BOOK DESIGN BY MEIGHAN CAVANAUGH

To David

CONTENTS

Evolutionary theory says that the inferior shall be gotten rid of. . . . We must then start with the Chinese script.

—LI SHIZENG (1907)

If the Chinese script does not go, China
will certainly perish!

—LU XUN (1936)

Computers are finally able to process Chinese!
Long live square characters!

—CHEN MINGYUAN (1980)

INTRODUCTION

F
ew contemporary societies take their writing culture as seriously as China. The oldest living language spoken by the most
people, at the same time ancient and modern, Chinese is currently used by more than 1.3 billion people—not counting those
around the globe who learn it as a second language. Its written form
has remained largely unchanged since it was first standardized more
than 2,200 years ago. By comparison, the number of letters in the
Roman alphabet fluctuated until the sixteenth century, when the letter
"j" split from "i" and completed the twenty-six-letter set.

Chinese heads of state are probably the only political leaders in the
world who can still be seen demonstrating their cultural prowess at
official occasions, in their case by dashing off a few characters or auspicious phrases with an ink brush. Deng Xiaoping was reputedly a bit
shy, but his immediate predecessor and onetime rival, Hua Guofeng,
devoted his late life to the practice, and former president Hu Jintao was
fond of displaying his penmanship in public. Mao's calligraphy still sits

prominently on the masthead of the country's official newspaper, the *People's Daily*, and recent computerized handwriting analysis showed that Xi Jinping's style is remarkably similar. Such showmanship not only serves as a daily reminder of the leader's legitimacy but also reinforces the importance of a cultivated skill that has been the hallmark of China's ruling elite since the time long before nations. Calligraphy, in fact, is one of the few practices of the Chinese tradition that survived the country's twentieth-century revolt against its feudalistic past.

It's hard to imagine an American president or European head of state opening an official state ceremony or visit with a show of penmanship. But in the Chinese context, literacy means something more than just knowing how to read and write. It has traditionally signaled many things: the mark of being steeped in the classics and wisdom of the ancients; a meditative craft through which to cultivate a higher self; an elite medium through which to express one's inner character, thoughts, and emotions.

Deciphering Chinese is not only an insider's art; it has also been a cross-continental pursuit. For more than four centuries, devoted followers of the Chinese language in the West have tried to peer into the secrets behind its ideographic capture of reality, speculating about its provenance and complex physical structure. Extravagant claims and theories met with enthusiastic reception in seventeenth- and eighteenth-century Europe and twentieth-century America. Kings, clerics, adventurers, scholars, modern poets, and theorists of language were drawn to its strangeness and exceptionality, looking for a key to unlock its secrets through grammar and compositional laws. Sixteenth-century Jesuit missionaries labored to learn it, seventeenth-century savants were fascinated by it, and eighteenth-century Sinologists fetishized it.

How an entire civilization outside of Christendom evolved to have a writing system as complex and massive as the Chinese script has been an enduring linguistic mystery for outsiders. This inquiry poorly masks a deep suspicion: How can a people who read and write in characters ever think the way we do? Even in the late twentieth century, views like this were touted by Western experts in different fields. Alphabetic thinking, social theorists would say, explains the advent of the scientific revolution in the West. A modern theorist of networks and the digital age sees the alphabet as a conceptual technology that forms the bedrock of Western science and technology. A scholar of ancient Greece saw the signs much earlier at the fount of Western civilization, where "the alphabetic mind" was responsible for all the West's accomplishments. Joseph Needham, a renowned British historian of Chinese science, spent his life's work defending scientific inventions in ancient China against claims like these, but he also recognized that the Chinese language remained the greatest barrier for Westerners to understanding the minds of the Chinese. It is China's first and last Great Wall.

The Opium War of 1839 to 1842 marked the beginning of a new course for China. During a series of crises and confrontations with the Western world that would keep China in an inferior position well into the early years of the twenty-first century, the demise of the Chinese script was foretold by many. Still, the Chinese were hesitant to accept the prospect of a future without their written language. They saw how the Chinese language, like the empire, might not be viable in a modern world increasingly transformed by various branches of Western science and new modes of electricity-powered communication, beginning with the telegraph. But the Chinese language had been the fundamental building block of China's cultural universe. So rooted was the script in the country's history and institutions over the millennia that it was difficult for the Chinese to consider abandoning it. From the grassroots to the highest level of the modern state, intellectuals, teachers, engineers, everyday citizens, eccentric inventors, duty-bound librarians, and language reformers embarked on one of the most extraordinary revolutions of the millennium in search of a solution. That is the subject of this book. The rude awakening of Western cannons firing at the gates; a teetering empire and the last throes of the imperialistic order; an urgency to modernize taken into overdrive by a new political ethos—all these shifts compelled the Chinese to embark on a parallel course: to get their language on the same footing as languages using the Western alphabet.

BRIDGING THE CHASM between two radically different scripts and systems of language seemed impossible at times, and the onus was mostly on the Chinese to modernize—or, what amounted to the same thing for most of the twentieth century, to westernize. The scale of the transformation was daunting. This important process lies at the core of China's modern identity, but the burden of this assimilation may be hard to imagine for those who have not experienced it. Languages make worlds. Those who attempt to cross over into one that is different from their own often experience the same hesitation, doubt, and uncertainty China did as a nation. To gain entry into a language, one has to cross several thresholds.

Six months before my family emigrated from Taiwan to the United States, my mother started teaching us English. My siblings and I, then ages nine to twelve, learned its basic alphabet on ruled pages in spiral notebooks—which we had never seen before. I was ecstatic to find out that there were only twenty-six letters. The inside edge of the top joint of my middle finger had grown a thick callus from gripping the pencil every night, tracing the complicated contours of written Chinese characters in square-ruled practice books. Alphabet letters' simple curves and lines were much easier to reproduce on paper, compared to the thousands of characters that had been drilled into our heads in school. Under my mother's expectant eye, we practiced the English alphabet as diligently as we did Chinese calligraphy, using imported BIC pens that landed hard and easy on paper instead of the soft ink brushes with hairy tips that were nearly impossible for a nine-year-old to control with patience. I adjusted my habits of writing—from going right to left and vertically to left to right and horizontally. "D" was easy, "Q" my favorite—because their lowercase versions were the least like their uppercase selves. The sticks and lines became habitual, and we quickly graduated to cursive. My father had hoped I would one day become a journalist like the NBC anchorwoman Connie Chung, then the first professional Chinese American woman seen nightly on screen in every household in the United States. English, it seemed, was the only thing that stood between me and my conquest of American network television.

The determined effort to learn English was overkill, it turned out. My siblings and I learned to write the alphabet letters in no time. It was, to use an English idiom that took me many years to get right, a walk in the dark (park). There was just one problem: I had no feeling for the Western alphabet. I strained to relate to its form, despite the ease of picking it up. The written form was strangely empty of expressiveness, and the sounds attached to the letters felt arbitrary and emotionally flat without the tonal fluctuations of Chinese—the sounds I was born into.

After arriving in Monterey Park in Los Angeles, an enclave known as "Little Taipei," English remained foreign despite learning it in context. My elementary school was full of Asians I had never seen before—Vietnamese, Cambodian, some Japanese and Korean. No one spoke English except in English class, where we struggled to move our tongues and mouth muscles in unnatural ways.

Every stage of English was a new experience. Bit by bit, how I made sense of the world through language changed. The transformative moment came in college, where the stakes of analyzing and thinking in English grew greater. "Critical thinking"—that unique acrobatics of the mind that is often taken as the universal and only acceptable set of thought procedures in making coherent, logical arguments—made me realize how decisively I had to leave Chinese behind in order to immerse myself in English and know it from the inside. I never had to think so hard in dogmatic ways in Chinese to arrive at sense-making. The two language worlds did not accord; they clashed. Chinese had a prior claim to every experience that was expressive, intuitive, and creative to me, while English felt like a corrective device that straightened and twisted me to fit a new mold. It was not enough to just master writing, reading comprehension, and vocabulary. To think in English, I had to breathe and live a worldview that was expressed and constructed in that language.

For the Chinese language to survive adapting to the Western alphabet, it had to do a lot more. Luckily, an equivalent journey from English to Chinese isn't necessary to follow this story, but it does help to bear in mind a few essential points about Chinese ideographic writing. It is fundamentally unique, distinct from any other writing system in the world, and it is built from individual dots and lines that form clusters of patterns with a distinct contour. There are six basic properties of the Chinese script that are distinct from the Roman alphabet and the focal points of its modern transformation into a technology.

First of all, a *character* is a written unit that bears meaning. It is roughly equivalent to what we mean by a word in English, but—as we shall see—also more and less than that. Characters often appear in pairs to convey a full sense, and each character carries only one syllable. Characters are known by many different names, some more disputed than others: logographs, pictographs, semantograms, pictograms, sinographs, and—what the Chinese call them—*hanzi* ("Han characters," named after the dynasty that first standardized them). Like an alphabetic word, a character indicates both meaning and sound, though to a different degree of direct correlation and emphasis. While written

Chinese was for a long time described as pictographs—one of its more misapplied names—no more than 3 percent of characters are historically pictorial or properly ideographic. Even for that small quantity of characters, it is a bit of a stretch to say they depict objects the way pictures do, because script is an agreed-upon system of symbols that represents, rather than captures, reality. The character 日 is not really a spitting image of the sun, which is round rather than rectangular in shape, and 山 might strike you more as the top of a pitchfork unless someone tells you that it is a pictorial representation of "mountain." I use "character" and "ideograph" interchangeably in this book as a reminder of how misnomers like these nonetheless carried the authority of truth in their own times.

Second, characters are made up of *strokes*—continuous lines of any length, including dots, that are the basic elements in the composition and writing of an ideographic character. Strokes are written in a specific order established by the practice of calligraphy: left to right, top to bottom. Though the number of stroke types varies depending on the purpose, eight have been considered fundamental. The character 永, "eternity," has been used for pedagogic purposes to teach these strokes

Eight calligraphic strokes in the character "yong."

because it happens to embody all eight: dot, horizontal, vertical, hook, rising, downward left slant, downward right slant, folding.

When you look at a character, it is clear that the strokes are not randomly thrown together. Most characters are made up of distinct parts, smaller clusters of intersecting strokes that are sometimes simple characters themselves. A *component* refers to those parts that, when combined with other clusters of stroke patterns, form a more complex, stand-alone character.

A particular component that is shared by and recurs in other characters has historically been given a weightier, unique status. This special part is known as a "radical." Like "character," the name "radical" has also been contested. Some consider it misleading, because a radical is not the root of a character in the way English has root words; it is not a stem to which prefixes and suffixes can be attached. Also known as "semantic classifiers" or "indexers," radicals are used to organize and categorize characters, as in a dictionary.

Finally, Chinese is a tonal language, which means the same syllable can be sounded at different pitches, or *tones.* Because characters carry only one syllable, tones evolved to help differentiate between characters that have the same syllable and are pronounced the same way. But there are limits to what tones can do, with the result that there are a lot of *homophones* in Chinese—characters that not only share the same pronunciation but also, less frequently, share the same tone. Depending on a region's dialect, tones also change.

Behind the grand narratives of great powers and national humiliation that occupy the contemporary understanding of China's encounter with the West is a deeper entanglement of their script worlds. The Chinese have gone to extremes to develop and to become modern on their own terms. Key to this path was tapping into the global communications infrastructure, from telegraphy to typewriters and computers, built in the Roman alphabet's image. In a dramatic series of language skirmishes and clever one-upmanships, of unexpected feats and crushing failures, Chinese and foreigners wrestled, struggled, and threw in their lot with the future of the Chinese script. At a time of major political and social upheavals inside and outside China, their words, ideas, and deeds exerted pressure on the center of history from the fringe. Across four centuries and spanning three continents, native speakers and foreigners alike have been engaged in a singular, shared pursuit: to crack the Chinese code in order to modernize its script. Behind every written character that can be learned and used today stands a group of human characters who went to extraordinary lengths to make sure that could happen. With no guidance other than their obsessive love for the Chinese language, their ambition opened up a world of discovery and revolution—and bold, perilous adventure.

ONE

A MANDARIN IN REVOLUTION

(1900)

UNIFYING THE NATIONAL TONGUE

I t was the first spring of the twentieth century. The red pines were in bloom and the snow was still capping Mount Tai when a Buddhist monk reached the northeastern shores of the Chinese Empire, undetected at dusk. Arriving at the port of Yantai, he stepped off the boat in the early evening shadows, hearing the sounds of flutes and men singing above the din of the docks. Lights from British battleships, patrolling their newly occupied territory, swept the headlands at regular intervals. He proceeded with haste along the coastline. Concealed inside his dusty robe was a document that would change the Chinese-speaking world forever.

Those who spotted the monk as he traveled by foot in the days to come would never have sensed anything so extraordinary. The man seemed commonplace enough. He had a broad nose and sunken cheeks, and his scowling eyes matched the downward arc of his lips. The rather humorless face possessed a quiet dignity, with a long goatee pointing down like a compass needle. It was the sort of face that age would lend roundness, but not necessarily kindness. If there was anything noteworthy about the monk it was that, if you talked with him, he might sound a little prickly for someone who had supposedly pledged a life of spirituality, devoid of mortal passions. This tone sprang from a deep sense of thwarted ambition.

Worn and unwashed, Wang Zhao was, in fact, only disguised as a monk. He was using a pseudonym, and when asked about his journey he'd reply that he had just arrived from the remote outpost of Taiwan. The island was distant enough from the locals' knowledge to be a credible cover. For centuries pirates had gathered on the island while trolling the South China Sea. Hiding in the crevices of its jagged landscape, they shared the mountainous no-man's-land with indigenous headhunting tribes and political castaways. Then Japan seized it as its first colony in 1895, after an easy victory over China in the First Sino-Japanese War. It was a haven for uninvited guests, safe beyond the reaches of Chinese law.

Wang had actually been hiding out in Japan. A wanted fugitive for the past two years, he carried a hefty bounty on his head. The Empress Dowager Cixi, who effectively ruled the Qing dynasty, had personally ordered his arrest on charges of treason. But his desire to go home eclipsed his fear of capture. His plan was to make his way into the Shandong Province and then zigzag up to the northern port city of Tianjin, his hometown. He dozed in open fields during the day and walked up to fifteen miles each night under the stars, traveled light and stayed off main roads. A cotton sack, two Buddhist ceremonial props and instruments, and a red-lacquered iron scepter were all that he carried to maintain his cover. He could always ask for alms, or food and water, at the next village. He despaired a little at times. The craggy paths got so steep and rocky that he had to stop every few steps to catch his breath. He wheezed while mustering the will to cross the mountain range that stretched out like an endless graveyard. There was hardly any sign of life—not even a blade of grass—during these long interludes, imbued with the grayish sunlight of windy days. It would have been a long and arduous trip under any circumstances. For a wanted outlaw, the journey was nothing less than perilous.

Wang purposely didn't carry Western-style leather baggage, so as not to arouse any xenophobic sentiments among the locals he encountered. Shandong was the epicenter of the growing unrest known as the Boxer Rebellion, named for the distinct martial-arts fighting style of the peasant insurrectionists. With sashes cinching their waists and cloth wrapped around their heads, the Boxers also believed in magic, claiming a bulletproof invincibility against their enemy, and harbored a hatred for Westerners. In recent months they had torn up railroad tracks and electric cables—noxious evidence of foreign intrusion—and left destruction in their wake.

Wang had never aspired to be on the wrong side of the law. Far from it; he was a true Confucian mandarin, loyal to the imperial court, and had never missed a day's roll call at the Forbidden City. He had simply advocated for change at a time when many of his colleagues either still slumbered in China's past glories or cried out for revolution. Wang had been one of the rallying voices for the reform movement in 1898, which came to be known as the Hundred Days Reform, a reaction to the growing sense that China was at a dangerous crossroads. To protect his country from being overrun by foreigners or crumbling under outdated practices, Wang supported constitutional reform, overhauling education, building a national industrial base, modernizing the army and the postal system, updating the national civil examinations system, and rooting out inefficiencies in the empire's unwieldy bureaucracy. But he stopped short of suggesting the dismantling of the millennia-old empire.

Although China's last dynasty—the Qing—would hold on for nearly another decade and a half, it was clear to those like Wang that China desperately needed to figure out a new way to exist in the twentieth century. Maintaining the status quo was an ineffectual foreign policy, and, what's more, it was no longer feasible. The West was in the East to stay—if not physically with soldiers on every street, then intellectually with its new ideas flooding in. There was no turning back the clock. China was part of the world. But could it adapt and reassert itself in changing times?

The Chinese language seemed to be a major impediment to the country's adaptation. At negotiation tables with foreigners, the Chinese were unable to find easy equivalents for loaded concepts like "rights" and "sovereignty" and were seen as barbaric and inferior by their counterparts. On the streets, the Chinese spoke hundreds of dialects of various major languages like Cantonese and Mandarin, despite all sharing one written script. So decisive was the role of language that U.S. president John Quincy Adams, observing the Opium War of 1839–42 from afar, had noted that the fight was over not chests of opium and unfair trade but words and their meanings. If China couldn't communicate with the rest of the world, it was because China was also struggling to communicate within its borders.

Little did Adams know that language would become a matter of life and death for China in the modern age and a central weapon for ensuring China's survival as a nation. Wang himself embodied this effort to rise again: he was trying to lift himself out of his own infamy the same way his country was attempting to rebound from humiliation. The pamphlet he had tucked in his robes for the journey back home held China's linguistic destiny. The old empire was on the brink of major change, rattled and shaken to its foundations by decades of internal problems and tumultuous encounters with other nations. The Chinese universe and the Chinese language were about to undergo an irreversible transformation. Wang was determined to plant himself in the middle of the action.

CHINA WAS IN TURMOIL in 1900. Anxiety pervaded the land. An early example of what would come to be known as the Map of National Humiliation began circulating in the late nineteenth century. It depicted the different foreign powers, presented as their popular avatars, carving out their share of the country. The Russian bear lurked in the Amur basin, inching its way down from Mongolia and Manchuria, while Japan's imperial sun guarded its new foothold in the northeast. In the south, the British bulldog and the French "frog" flanked the coastal provinces, their rivalry spilling into Indochina, while a formidable American bald eagle was about to roost over the Philippines and the Pacific.

More than a half century after five treaty ports were forced open to the West during the First Opium War, various foreigners had bombed, pillaged, and cut deep into China's market. Greed for power and resources in a rich, enclosed part of what was then known as the Far East lured Westerners to its shores, as they extended their national rivalries outside Europe. The Chinese, unaccustomed to the barbarians' worldview but too complacent about their own, paid a steep price for the unwelcome guests. At the dawn of the twentieth century, Chinese hatred for foreigners was high. People seethed when mentioning the "foreign devil," and a series of popular revolts (the Boxer Rebellion among them) flared up across the empire, nearly crippling it. Rumors spread like wildfire, drawing on the earlier hostility toward the propagation of Christian thought. It had been said that Western missionaries sodomized Chinese children and gouged out their eyes; they murdered the women and destroyed the crops. While many stories were fabrications, new evidence of racial discrimination and exploitation lent them legitimacy. Abroad, the Chinese Exclusion Acts (the first of which passed in

Tse Tsan Tai, *The Situation in the Far East*, Hong Kong, July 1899. The map, a precursor to a popular genre known as the Map of National Humiliation, was widely reproduced in books and leaflets as a warning to the Chinese populace.

1882 and the last of which was not repealed until 1943) made sure that Chinese labor would remain free and cheap, and the laborers themselves would not have a path to citizenship. Even in China, certain public areas under foreign jurisdiction were off-limits to the Chinese.

During the pivotal decades leading up to the 1898 movement, many conscientious Chinese saw the world being increasingly divided into two groups: the winners and the losers. Newspapers reported on how ancient civilizations like Persia, Egypt, and India were collapsing, one by one, under the force of Europe's rise. Vietnam, China's erstwhile tribute state and linguistic kin, was engaged in a struggle against the French; the Boers were fighting the British in the Transvaal as settlers against colonizers; the Pacific was becoming a new world stage, as America consolidated its reach across Hawaii, Guam, and the Philippines. Failure to resist one's oppressors led to losing the right to use one's mother tongue. Poland had been severed from its own language when the Russians imposed theirs after quelling the insurgency in 1864; in China stories of Polish slaves circulated in journals and newspapers as cautionary tales.

In addition to failed diplomacy, reforms, and persistent corruption, the Qing court's inability to address large-scale poverty and famine further eroded the empire. Social unrest—among not only the Boxers but also religious sects and minorities like the Taipings and the Muslims in northwestern China—was rife. Swaths of northern and northeastern China suffered the worst series of droughts, famines, and plagues in more than a century. At the same time, the population had expanded threefold by the mid-nineteenth century, further straining scarce resources. Missionaries reported desperate peasants tearing out the cotton filling of their clothes or scraping the bark from trees to eat; some even resorted to cannibalism, consuming the corpses of loved ones—including children. The growing number of peasant rebellions starting in the 1860s blighted the countryside.

There were plenty of reasons to worry about China's future in the early twentieth century. But as some court officials and pundits wrote in newspapers and policy analyses, it was not too late for China to save itself. The 1898 reform movement, led by Kang Youwei and his disciple Liang Qichao, brought together a clique of scholars and officials who proposed ways of altering and improving governance, education, and defense. Wang Zhao fell under this category. Progressive and sometimes Western-friendly in their outlook, the reformers advocated moderate institutional and policy changes that would help return China to a more stable footing, especially in the wake of the disastrous military defeat in the Sino-Japanese War. That defeat prompted many Chinese to take a sober look at not only China's technological backwardness but also its internal decay. A number of officials and intellectuals traveled to Europe and America as envoys, students, and emissaries of the empire, marveling at electric lights and telegraphs, coal-fed locomotives and public trolleys, practical education and political systems, and cultures that prized individual freedom and modernization. While headlines fanned fears and raised specters of the foreign devils as the root of all evil, cooler-headed observers pointed out that the reasons for the country's decline did not ultimately lie with outsiders. Something else was wrong. Rectifying it would require seeing things inside China with a clear eye. The 1898 movement forced those in power to consider abandoning the China-centered worldview and embrace important aspects of Western learning.

Kang Youwei, a clever Confucian from Guangdong, had greater political ambitions at court. He tried to play members of the imperial family against one another. Liang Qichao, a precocious upstart from the same province, followed his teacher's tactics before rising to be a thought leader in his own right. They had the twenty-six-year-old Guangxu Emperor's sympathetic ear, and the young ruler even implemented some of their proposed changes, showing his readiness to stand up to his powerful aunt. But it did not take long for the Empress Dowager to suspect that the reforms would directly curtail her power. She halted them, ordered the participants' arrests, and forced the emperor into isolation in the Forbidden City. Fearing for his life, Wang fled to Japan.

The Empress Dowager may have stamped out the 1898 movement, but the impulse for reform had already taken hold. Of all the pillars of tradition that began to crack under new scrutiny—from foot binding and feudalism to Confucianism—the Chinese writing system came under especially scathing attacks. Western views on the Chinese language played a role in spreading this attitude. The Chinese script, once revered, celebrated by its people, and practiced by neighboring cultures, now seemed clumsy and backward. The philosopher G. W. F. Hegel had banished it from the consideration of history, because "the nature of the written language in itself is a great hindrance for the development of the sciences." It was seen as inherently incompatible with logic and inhospitable to abstract thinking. Just preparing to speak it entailed a permanent, menacing disfiguration of one's face. "Their teeth are placed in a different manner from ours," the bishop of Dromore, Thomas Percy, observed with the cold curiosity of a surgeon. "The upper row stands out, and sometimes falls upon the under lip, or at least on the gums of the under row, which lies inward; the two gums scarce ever meet together, like those of Europeans." The sound that then came out was even worse: "It [is] a kind of cry fetched from the hollow of the stomach; of which it is difficult to give an exact idea in speaking only to the eyes."

Others closer to home also confirmed that the Chinese language was unfit—even onetime users. China's neighbor and recent colonizer Japan began to reduce the number of Chinese characters in its lexicon and experimented with Romanization—distancing itself from a character-dominant writing system and admitting that the West, with its alphabetic languages, was superior. It was clear to the Chinese themselves, too, that their writing system stood in the way of modernization. Instead of facilitating China's entry into the world, it was an impediment. The world was increasingly connected by telegraphy and other forms of standardized communication built on a central premise: a language was made up of twenty-six phonetic letters that, when added together, created words, and these words, when read aloud, sounded most of the time as if they were a perfect sum of their parts. The disadvantage of not having a Roman alphabetic language was evident.

Some feared that the aged Chinese civilization was perhaps too old to reinvent itself. More alarming than its level of difficulty were the growing opportunity costs of keeping such a writing system alive in classrooms and beyond. The practice of cool, abstract reasoning formed the bedrock of modern disciplines like mathematics, physics, and chemistry. If China wanted to level the playing field—to learn the secrets of the West's wealth and power—then language was the key to accessing that knowledge. The Chinese script was the gateway through which translations and the imported new knowledge must pass.

Even learning the Chinese script, some Chinese educators soon worried, wreaked havoc on the body. Fanned by the recent introduction of Western anatomy, especially of the brain and the nervous system, people began to fear that long-term exposure to rote learning made one lose intelligence. The fear of mental exhaustion soon created a mass market for health remedies like Dr. Yale's (Ailuo) Brain Tonic and Dr. Williams' Pink Pill for Pale People for anyone from students to businessmen. Peddled by a marketing genius, Huang Chujiu of Shanghai, Ailuo Brain Tonic—which came with the English name of "Yale" because Huang thought a foreign name made it more fancy—was a sensational bestseller across the country, and was still available for purchase in certain back-alley pharmacies until recent times. Sold alongside jars of traditional herbs and roots in Chinese apothecaries, these remedies were part of a personal everyday arsenal to combat the pressures of modernity.

The Chinese script was not just tangential to this historical change; it seemed as though it stood for everything that was wrong with China—so much so that some began to wonder whether the writing system should continue to exist. Anarchist Wu Zhihui sounded one of the first alarm bells: "No amount of change can alter the fact that the Chinese script is bizarre-looking and weird in form; it assumes a thousand shapes and is nearly impossible to differentiate—all because it is fundamentally flawed. That is why we believe it is only a matter of time before it is abolished." Wang vowed to save China from this desperate situation. With a phonetic script system for a unified national language hidden in his robe, he was determined to pull China back from the precipice of ruin.

BORN IN 1859, the last year of the Second Opium War, Wang came from a family of military loyalists who achieved distinction not through noble birth but dedicated service. His grandfather, a formidable horse archer, had fought valiantly in the First Opium War in the 1840s. A legend on the battlefield, he earned even more praise for his sense of loyalty and equality. He trained his men with draconian discipline but fought alongside them like a brother. When he finally fell in combat, his sash and boots stained with blood, it was from a British bullet to the head that pierced his painted helmet. His men delayed their own escape in order to retrieve his body from the enemy. They died in the attempt, and Grandfather Wang's body was mutilated as additional punishment—severed limb from limb, sliced and then diced. For his bravery he was posthumously given the greatest imperial honor, and his family was consoled with wealth and recognition.

Wang's father committed suicide when Wang was young, leaving him largely to the paternal care of his uncle. Wang made himself into a scholar and proved his distinction not on the battlefield but at the imperial court. Climbing up its ladder of bureaucracy, he found a good, solid niche as an overseer at the Board of Rites, the office in charge of the court's ceremonies and rituals. His grandfather had dabbled in calligraphy and verse making, and while he was a far cry from Du Fu or Li Bo, China's greatest poets, Grandfather Wang had impressed the importance of learning on his grandson before his death. Wang easily inhabited the same literary persona as his grandfather. In private, he often relieved his distress in heartfelt, if at times platitudinous, lines of poetry. While in exile in Japan, he sought out the company of local scholars and intellectuals and wrote copiously about his experiences in 246 poems. He saw himself as a melancholic poet-patriot:

> In grief I passed through the old country and familiar
>   mountains,
> Biting was the cold wind that brushed against the shores.
> The heavy burden on my shoulders was the weight of the
>   heavens.
> In the shadows of the overlap peaks there I was—one lone
>   monk.

As he traveled through the rugged countryside that spring of 1900, his feet swelled with blisters and his robe stiffened with dried sweat mixed with dirt. It was not the solace of poetry but the discipline of a soldier that kept him going. The lone monk did not look like your average Confucian scholar. By the time he was a young man he was already known for his tough constitution. He trained in the open air, honing his martial-arts skills wearing nothing but shorts and a sleeveless shirt, even during the winter months. Friends and neighbors remembered his physical strength, but even more so his sense of justice and righteousness. They often repeated the story of when Wang came upon a young scribe who was down on his luck; he saw the poor lad, hunched over his ink brush and makeshift table, selling his calligraphy for a paltry sum on the street corner in the freezing cold. He treated the young man to a hot meal and, upon learning that he was trying to become a scholar and take the civil exams, generously offered him a hefty sum of money so that he could finish his studies. Common lore has it that the grateful beneficiary repaid Wang's kindness years later, once he had succeeded in life.

Now on his way back, Wang was well outside the comforts of the court. The simple folks he met on dirt paths and country roads were poor and uneducated. The general rate of literacy among men was less than 30 percent, and as low as 2 percent for women. Wang saw what ignorance could do—and he knew that the peasants needed to learn how to read if they were ever to better their lives. While he pitied them, he could not help but find their boorish manners as uncouth as their lack of good sense. The pages of his travel diary carry a tone of disapproval: he scoffed at coarse and superstitious commoners, who blamed the poor harvest on the curse of the modern railroads that the Germans introduced into the region to build their seaside colony in Qingdao.

Wang endured the bravado of the village savants, who pounded their cups of ale on the tavern tables while offering unsolicited prophecies. The recent winter freeze, they pronounced, and the hundreds of lives it claimed, was the first of greater calamities to come. Enthralled by their fortune-telling rhetoric, the more gullible peasants were convinced that the 1898 reform movement had actually been successful and that a revolution had taken place, with Kang now ruling the empire. News did not travel quickly or accurately in these parts of the country. Whenever he lost patience with such baseless country banter,

Wang cut the conversation short by feigning a sudden deep meditation, striking his hollow wooden prop and chanting a Buddhist sutra to its thump. His concern for the poor masses was not at odds with the view of the scholar gentry: only enlightenment and modern education could save China's untutored souls. Importantly, he believed, this was not an existential but a practical problem—for which there were tangible solutions. Solutions he could offer.

The task of saving China with literacy had kept him focused. While in exile, he completed his vision for its salvation: a thin document titled *Mandarin Combined Tone Alphabet*. This was the thread-bound pamphlet he kept tucked away in his robe. With it, he intended to help China's masses of poor peasantry rise, building a common bridge of communication and understanding that extended even to the foreigners they hated. Wang set out to revitalize both the language and its people. He wanted to use the Chinese language to achieve one goal in the modern era: unity. Using sixty-two elemental parts derived from Chinese characters he had scribbled by hand to represent sounds, he created a phonetic notation system for indicating how whole characters could be read aloud.

Chinese characters were usually learned by sight rather than by sound, relying heavily on visual and tactile recognition. The only way for children to remember their shapes and strokes was to laboriously trace every character, stroke by stroke, over and over again. And this learning process took years, if not most of one's lifetime. The patience necessary for learning Chinese characters had developed writing into a contemplative art form that conferred great prestige on its adult practitioners. Wang was part of a small group of forward-looking language reformers who took a pragmatic approach to speeding up the whole endeavor. They tried to improve the Chinese script's capacity to indicate sound by creating a separate system of simpler sound-indicating character parts. Wang cast the problem in remarkably democratic terms:

The Chinese language is the first written script ever created . . . the first to unveil the essence and secrets of the universe, and is far superior to the language of any other nation. Though the scripts of other nations are shallow, however, their citizens can learn them quickly, because the words are written exactly as they sound, and sound just as they are written. . . . Through this important medium, political doctrines are thereby shared and made as one, while divergent views connect and communicate with one another. . . . In our country, however, you cannot find a single person out of one hundred who knows and understands what is written or the deeper meaning behind it. If you asked someone, at the end of his diligent study—which may drag on for decades—what did you learn? He would say that he learned how to recognize the Chinese characters. . . . Nine out of ten never move past this point. Of those who manage to get over the initial hump, another nine out of ten people do only a bit better than that before giving up as well. The educated elite and the masses thus inhabit two entirely separate worlds. The commoners have no real means of acquiring a general knowledge in order to grasp politics, geography, the appropriate relations between those who govern and those who are governed, or whether China is waning while the rest of the world is on the rise, or vice versa.

By drastically reducing the time and labor required to learn the complicated script, Wang was attempting to address a problem that had stood in the way of the East and West comprehending each other since the days of the Dominican and Jesuit missionaries' first arrival in the sixteenth century. Back then, the missionaries used Latin letters to sound out every Chinese character they were trying to learn and memorize. The Western alphabet was the only tool they had to record the strange sounds they heard on the streets as they tried to interact with the locals. The Romanization schemes they produced were uneven in quality, neither systematized nor standardized and only useful locally. Because of the hundreds of different dialects across China, what was transcribed in the narrow alleys of Beijing did not work in the ports of Guangdong, the same way a transcription of what people in Paris were saying would be incomprehensible to those in Madrid.

Wang published the first version of his book with a Chinese overseas student group while still in Tokyo. The few Chinese officials who traveled to Japan and discovered it appreciated the ingeniousness of the idea, but there weren't enough of them to lend it sizable support. Looking to the relative success of Japan's literacy experiments in the untamed lands of Taiwan, they grew confident that the Mandarin Alphabet could do one better. When Wang returned to China, it was with great expectations and even greater uncertainty. Could he successfully create a new way for his people to communicate? Those handwritten scribbles on thin leaves of rice paper, wrapped securely inside his robe, offered a complete system of phonetic transcription based on one unified tongue. If adopted on a wide scale, it could increase literacy, cut down the time it took to write in Chinese, and make it easier to learn to speak it.

China had always harbored great linguistic diversity: the empire was vast, containing multitudes. In the earliest study of regional dialects, a scholar, Xu Shen, in the first century took on the mammoth task of surveying the different forms of everyday speech. This early lexicographer worked for twenty-seven years, listing around nine thousand entries, based on interviews with soldiers and officials who had gathered in the capital from all corners of the empire—and the survey was still far from complete. In the latter half of the nineteenth century, aware of the successful replacement of Latin with national vernaculars in Europe, Chinese officials grew even more worried by the deep divisions between their spoken languages and the written form. Alphabetic languages were lauded as the trains and automobiles of modernity, while the Chinese script trailed behind as the rickety oxcart. The inefficiency was glaring. People living in the northern provinces could not communicate with those from the south; officials from the capital assigned to the countryside likened the experience to traveling to a foreign land. They themselves relied on a court dialect for official communication just to get their jobs done, like distributing famine relief or taking the census. That officials' language came to be known as Mandarin.

Mandarin was not the language of the common people, many of whom got by with simple math and used their thumbprint to sign sales slips or contracts, barely knowing how to recognize or write the characters. For the majority of the population to have no access to written language was, to people like Wang, a tremendous handicap that prevented the Chinese from progressing. The language barrier rose above all other concerns as the most urgent and palpable consequence of China's backwardness in everyday life.

For Wang, the strategy was simple: first, help people recognize and notate their own speech—*exactly as it sounded*—in writing, then help them communicate with one another across dialectal, regional, and possibly national divides. Ideally, one writing system would do the job. He believed his Mandarin Alphabet was destined to be the standard of modern Chinese for all of China. The question was whether China was ready for it.

It was late May. Wang had been on the road for almost two months, as weary as he was dirty. His hometown of Tianjin was about to be occupied by foreign powers, already advancing under the pretext of subduing the Boxers, so he had been heading straight there. But first he looped down south to Shanghai to visit an old supporter. The Baptist missionary Timothy Richard was one of the most influential Westerners in China at the time, a devout man who harbored a deep affection for China and published a report in 1884 that recommended the establishment of higher education institutions in the capital of every province. He was deeply invested in resolving China's social and political problems and one of the few outsiders attuned to the country's language question. Sympathetic to the 1898 reform, he urged the court to adopt an alphabetic system of writing instead of sentimentally clinging to the cumbersome character system. A trusted friend of the Chinese Empire when few foreigners were trusted at all, he had become an influential spokesperson for progressive Western views. When the 1898 reform failed, he helped its leaders Kang and Liang escape.

Wang no doubt went to him for advice. By the time of his visit to Richard, Wang had parted on hostile terms with Kang and Liang. Early on in the movement, they seemed to have been on the same side. The reformers agreed that the unification of speech and script was key to China's survival as a nation. Kang had imagined collecting all spoken languages of the world into a spherical sound hall, where scholars and linguists could come to sample and study languages as one would the ancient and rare species displayed in a museum. Liang took up the cause of earlier proposals—before Wang's—and argued for the importance of a Chinese linguistic revolution.

Six months after Wang fled to Japan, the alliance cracked. Wang gave a tell-all interview to a Japanese newspaper, exposing Kang's distortion of the intrigues at the court. He called out Kang and Liang for stealing his personal letters and accused them of being "quack doctors who kill their patients" rather than able-minded leaders. Just to make his feelings clear, Wang pronounced, "If I could, I'd finish them off with my own bare hands." Despite having a fine ear for the sounds of Chinese script, Wang was not known for his tact or subtlety.

As Wang waited in Richard's office at the Society for the Diffusion of Christian and General Knowledge among the Chinese—the first organization in China to introduce Western publications—he must have felt he was coming back a different man. Richard was there when the reform happened—and failed. While still a minor official at the Board of Rites, Wang had taken his advice about establishing a Ministry of Education as China's first step toward building a modern education system, where a modernized Chinese language would be taught. Richard had previously proposed an alphabet system, essentially borrowing from the Western alphabet, but Wang was hoping for an indigenous phonetic solution that would appeal more to the Chinese. It was no doubt prudent to test the waters with a trusted ally.

Richard agreed to receive him, and Wang was shown to the back room. Wang did not give his name but asked instead whether Richard recognized him. It would have been hard for even his family to do so: at the age of forty-one, having narrowly escaped execution once and still risking capture, he must have appeared older than his age, weathered in his threadbare robe. But Wang came bearing a personal message. There must have been a half dozen different ways for him to explain where he had been and what he was up to. But he first had to reveal who he was in a way that matched the urgent secrecy of his mission. Without speaking, he extended one hand, palm up, and traced out two Chinese characters with the other—first "Wang" and then "Zhao," in the way that Chinese literati would communicate with and honor one another with calligraphy. What he conveyed in silence was nonetheless clear: Wang was back.

The 1898 Reform was quashed in deed—along with Kang Youwei— but not in spirit. With or without Richard's help, Wang would reassume the reformist cause and bring about the Mandarin language revolution he had intended. We know that, after the meeting with Richard, he went to see Lao Naixuan, a prominent figure in the late-nineteenth-century Chinese script and education reform movement. Wang was trying to figure out what could be salvaged of the original reformist ideas and how to make his comeback. He was still working on the draft of his Mandarin Alphabet and needed the input of leaders like Lao. And he needed to find a place to regroup and rest.

When he finally arrived in Tianjin, Wang sought out a distant family relative, Yan Xiu, a member of the powerful scholar gentry and a civil examinations official who had a quiet residence on the east side of the city. Wang took refuge in Yan's house for the next year or so, no doubt the most peaceful period he'd had since before the Hundred Days Reform. As he strolled in Yan's courtyard and sat on the garden stools behind miniature mountains of rock, he mulled over possible allies among those who had some power at court. In October 1901, he finally ventured back to Beijing, the capital from which he had fled three years before. When he arrived, the city looked different; it was like flesh marked by a fresh scar. The Boxers whom Wang had come across in the countryside in Shandong had advanced into the capital in June of the previous year. The Empress Dowager had reversed her suppressive tactics against them in order to help redirect their hatred to the foreigners who were living in the Forbidden City. Armed with lances and swords, the Boxers burned down churches and railroad stations and looted the foreign district just east of Tiananmen Square. A Protestant missionary on-site captured the harrowing scene: "Awful sights were witnessed. Women and children hacked to pieces, men trussed like fowls, with noses and ears cut off and eyes gouged out."

Fifty-five days of chaos, killings, and destruction were more than the rest of the world could handle: Italy, the United States, France, Austria-Hungary, Japan, Germany, the United Kingdom, and Russia

joined forces, marched into the capital, and forced the Boxers into submission. Incapable of putting down its own rebellion as the violence
spun out of control, imperial China lost what little credibility it had in
the eyes of the world—and its own people. China was forced to agree
to pay the foreign states an indemnity of 450 million taels of fine silver
(about U.S. $9.1 billion today). Beijing was divided up into eight areas
of foreign occupation, and the foreign legation quarter was purged of
Chinese residents and much expanded to become a special zone of states
within a state. It was a new low in China's humiliation.

As Wang entered the Forbidden City, the core of the ancient capital,
he must have mourned the city's diminished splendor. The imperial
center would have sprawled out before him as he entered at the Eastern
Gate. Because of its proximity to the imperial palace, the area near the
gate swarmed with officials and statesmen who had business at the
court. Everyday life on the streets was restless with vendors, onlookers,
rickshaws, foreigners, and diplomats. Everyone had some business and
ambition to fulfill in the heart of the imperial center, and Wang was
no different.

He was there to see Li Hongzhang, a powerful minister and viceroy.
Li had been the governor general of the capital province for a quarter
century. He had seen China through its most dramatic clashes with
various Western powers and dozens of internal unrests. He had a seat
at every major negotiating table—the treaty that ended the Second
Opium War in 1860; the signing of the Yantai Treaty with the British
in 1876, which subjected China to unequal terms; the Treaty of Shi-
monoseki in 1895, which ceded Taiwan to Japan; and, most recently,
the Boxer Protocol in 1901 with the Eight Powers who occupied Beijing
to quell the peasant rebellion. It was a delicate balancing act for Li, who
had to smooth over relations with foreign aggressors but also wanted to
strengthen China against the West. He was the embodiment of China's

diplomatic statesmanship as much as Richard was a conduit of Western learning. Li could be an important ally for Wang at the court.

Wang didn't know it, but Li's health was declining steadily: in less than a month, the greatest statesman of China's closing dynasty would pass away. Wang was disappointed when Li sent his closest personal aide to greet him in the well-decorated front room. Wang felt he deserved the ear of the great Li himself; a personal assistant was not the audience he had hoped for. As soon as they sat down for tea, the conversation started going in the wrong direction. Wang later recalled the aide demanding, "My dear sir, having come all this way, back from overseas, you must have returned with a grand strategy to save our empire. Please disclose it to me, and I shall pass it on to the Minister."

Wang brushed off the very idea of resolving all of China's problems with a single solution, but did offer his opinion:

> The greatest disadvantage of our good empire is that our four hundred million people do not have the power of knowledge. . . . What is the use of talking "grand strategy" when two hundred thousand of our anointed elite scholars cannot match the effectiveness of, for instance, Japan's commonly educated multitude of fifty million? The Chinese government must prioritize primary school education among the lower-class masses . . . it is urgent that we create a script that can allow the different tongues to communicate, to make speech and script as one.

The aide took offense at Wang's answer. He made a quick snide comment and let it be known that he suspected Wang was holding back: "These words do not sound like the ones you would speak. You must be harboring some grand scheme but do not deign to share it with someone of a lower rank such as myself." Wang's reaction was as swift as it was short: *What a fool!* He had to restrain himself from pounding on the pearl-inlaid wooden table and left in a huff. Maybe his Mandarin Alphabet was doomed to be ignored. Li had been his last chance. Defeated, he returned to Tianjin. He hid himself away at Yan's house—and worked.

WANG MAY HAVE BEEN BACK HOME, but he felt no relief from exile. He could not calm his mind enough to enjoy the quietude of Yan's refuge. The sight of ink paintings of lone human figures against tall mountains and clouds of mist should have recalled for him China's long tradition of scholarly recluses and hermits, who renounced a life of courtly ambition in exchange for peace of mind. But Wang didn't want quiet and boredom. He later complained, "It was hard even to get drunk in a state of ennui."

Yan's family had lived in the same compound for eleven generations over three centuries. The mansion abutted a neighbor's pumpkin garden, which Wang looked out on from the latticed windows of his guest room. Except for the occasional chat with Yan, Wang was left to his own devices. This most often meant working and reworking his new alphabet, day and night.

Yan shared Wang's passion for education reform. He would soon open the first modern primary school in China in his own backyard as a private experiment, spearheading the education of young women. It became a model for the province's new school system. A significantly softer-looking man than Wang, Yan was neither combative nor hot-tempered. He had served in the capital for almost a decade as a member of the imperial scholarly academy. When the 1898 reform failed, he, too, was disappointed. But unlike Wang, he simply retreated to Tianjin and privately pursued his own reform as a scholar. During those years, Yan embarked on a series of proposals that slowly changed China's education system. Wang came to him just at the time Yan was wrestling with similar questions about the future of China. They no doubt had frequent and long conversations, for Yan was the only person who regularly saw Wang. The maidservants were forbidden to speak of the secret houseguest's presence to anyone on the outside.

While working on his alphabet, Wang never strayed from the beliefs he had shared with the emperor back in 1898: China was losing its power because language was failing its people. Their low literacy and divided dialects impeded China's ability to govern, negotiate with foreign powers, and keep pace with the outside world. China's success as a nation and an international power hinged on the single issue of an accessible spoken and written language.

There had been others who shared Wang's analysis of the problem, although they offered different answers to it. Lu Zhuangzhang, a Chinese Christian from Amoy (now Xiamen), developed the first phonetic system for a Chinese language by a Chinese. His 1892 Simple Script used fifty-five symbols, some of which were adapted from Roman letters to Chinese sound rules, to represent the southern dialect spoken in Amoy. Lu nearly went bankrupt in the process. Lu's children would bemoan how he squandered the family's livelihood financing his linguistic experiments.

Among those who followed in Lu's footsteps was Cai Xiyong, an attaché to a Chinese diplomatic delegation to the United States. He developed his Quick Script for the major southern topolect group of Min, using a rapid writing system—a kind of shorthand—created by David Philip Lindsley. Shorthand, pioneered by Isaac Pitman for the English language in 1837, was a transcription system that used specially simplified notations to record phonemes, words, and phrases in real time.

The real innovator, many later thought, was Shen Xue, a brilliant medical student from Shanghai whose reputedly ingenious scheme, according to eyewitnesses, was originally written in English but has survived only as a preface printed by a Chinese journal. Shen devoted his life to propagating and offering free lessons on his Universal System at a local teahouse. He died a pauper at the tender age of twenty-eight.

Wang stood out from the rest in one important way: while he believed in giving people the power of literacy and the ability to connect with speakers of other dialects, he ultimately wanted to hold them to a single standard—Beijing Mandarin. He saw the critical importance of a unified language, and he was the first to propose Beijing Mandarin as the nation's standard tongue. It would become the basis of the modern Mandarin, or Putonghua, that the Chinese speak today. For Wang, increasing literacy was only possible if one simultaneously created linguistic unity. To unite China's hundreds of tongues with a single phonetic scheme would be like deconstructing China's own Tower of Babel. Before Wang could tackle this problem, however, he had to contend with the native sound system that had been in place for centuries: a way of learning and teaching characters based on sounds called the reverse-cut method.

As part of a serious education, any learned Chinese down to Wang's time would have had to master the reverse-cut method for learning how to pronounce characters. Reverse-cut first appeared in the third century and remained in use until the early twentieth. Each Chinese character has a one-syllable sound associated with it, and all syllables have two parts: an "initial" (the consonant sound that begins a syllable) and a "final" (the rest of the syllable sound). For a guide, a novice would turn to a rhyme book, which functioned like a dictionary of pronunciation. In it, the sound of each listed character was "spelled out" by cutting together two more commonly used and familiar characters. One character's *initial* sound was added to another's *final* sound to indicate the pronunciation of the character in question. To pronounce the character for "east" 東 (*dong*), for instance, you would look up 東 in a rhyme book and it would tell you that the pronunciation is the initial of "virtue" 德 (*{d}ek*) combined with the final of "red" 紅 (*h{ong}*).

This technique used the phonetic parts of two known characters to sound out an unknown third character in the same way that $(5 - 3) \times (1 + 1)$ conveys the number 4. That's a complicated way to arrive at 4 if all you want is the number.

The old reverse-cut phonetic system solved many problems—like accommodating the translation of the exotic sounds of Sanskrit when Mahayana Buddhism's scriptures were introduced into China in the late seventh century—but now it had itself become the problem. It required years of rote memorization to learn and was no longer accurate—speech habits had drifted and evolved over time. "Virtue," for example, is no longer pronounced as "dek" but as "de" in modern-day Chinese. Pronunciation also differed wildly between dialects.

The Chinese spelling system was woefully outdated. At the same time, the Western alphabet was viewed with suspicion in a climate of hostility to foreigners. A middle path had to be found. People like Wang realized there needed to be a system that *acted* like an alphabet for Chinese without simply using Roman letters. The task before Wang during those months in Yan's guest quarters was of epic proportions, and his efforts were the first in a century-long quest to find the perfect phonetic representation for a standard Chinese language, to restore the Chinese script's past splendor by finally making it a practical, user-friendly tool.

WANG WAS SITTING in his study at Yan's house one day, going over yet again the possible combinations of initial-final spelling. It was late summer 1902. Already a hint of fall was in the air, and the sunlight shining on the plump pumpkins in the neighbor's garden must have given off a deep orange glow visible from his window. But Wang had no appetite for idleness and no time for beauty, even if the scenery afforded him both. He busily tinkered with different inflections of each character—one, then the other, then back to the first again—and pondered how best to capture them in his system of character-derived sound signs. None seemed quite right at this moment. Just then, Yan barged in.

With as much excitement as a Confucian scholar could permit himself, Yan held up a book in his hand: "You might think you've been struggling alone with this idea, but you haven't read this!" He raised his hand and showed Wang a worn copy of a 1726 rhyme book, *Subtle Explorations of Phonology.* It was an official dictionary personally commissioned by the Kangxi Emperor. The meticulous compilation had taken eleven years to complete under the toils of fourteen different Confucian scholars. Philological pursuits were something of a hobby for a number of Manchu emperors, and the Kangxi Emperor was no exception. Instead of imposing Manchu as the language of conquest on the vast Chinese population, the Kangxi Emperor and other Manchu rulers realized that it was better to assimilate themselves into the majority context—to Sinicize. An American missionary reported in 1892, quite accurately, that in matters of language, "the conquered race, the Chinese, have vanquished their conquerors." The Kangxi Emperor also ordered the compilation of the *Kangxi Dictionary*—the Chinese equivalent of the *Oxford English Dictionary*—which coined the Chinese term for "dictionary," or "canon of characters." *Subtle Explorations*, in contrast, was of a whole other genre and purpose. The handbook was intended to correct the age-old system of reverse-cut, updating it with Manchu phonetics to reflect modern speech sounds, the type of northern vernacular Mandarin that was spoken in the capital. The key point was that Manchu used a kind of alphabet. Unlike Western alphabets, which are classified mainly as vowels and consonants, Manchu is phonetically divided into consonant-vowel syllables as the phonetic base (pa, pe, pi, po, pu, for instance, as opposed to a, e, i, o, u). Manchu possessed the ability to notate the sounds of Chinese characters in a non-Western style.

Upon reading *Subtle Explorations*, Wang was ecstatic: "I couldn't help myself and started dancing around the room! Ah, such a thing does indeed exist! From this point on, I can build on this good work and not worry about other people accusing me of pulling it out of thin air."

Essentially, what Manchu offered Mandarin was a scheme indicating a Chinese pronunciation using a combined-tone approach, by sounding out two component characters as a single syllable. The approach was so compelling that Wang put it in the title of his own *Mandarin Combined Tone Alphabet*. Unlike reverse-cut, there is no reconstruction necessary, no extra step of slicing and recombining. Combined-tone represented Chinese sounds alphabetically, using a contemporary spoken northern vernacular. It is no wonder Wang found a strong echo between this marvelous text and what he was trying to do.

Jolted by this discovery, Wang went back to his Mandarin Alphabet with revamped tools and refreshed understanding, unveiling a new version in 1903. His Mandarin Alphabet was composed of fifty symbols for sound initials and twelve other symbols for sound finals, making for sixty-two symbols in total. Remember: All Chinese syllables are made up of the opening consonant sound (an initial) and the sound that completes the consonant (the final). The fifty initials were borrowed, with further simplifications, from the Japanese derivations of Chinese characters, *kana*, a syllabic script developed in the eighth century. Wang's twelve finals were modeled directly on the Manchu script's twelve classes of letters and syllables. *The Mandarin Combined Tone Alphabet* made the transcription of Chinese fast and accurate to real-time speech. It used Chinese-derived symbols but essentially functioned phonetically like an alphabetic language, where the way a word sounds is generally evident in the way it is spelled. Using Wang's Mandarin Alphabet, if you wanted to indicate the pronunciation of the character for "east" 東 (*dong*), you would use one of his character-derived phonetic notations from his fifty initials and one of his twelve Manchu-based finals: simply add the initial *do* and the final *ng*. That was it.

The refined Mandarin Alphabet was recognized immediately as a landmark achievement. It helped that Yan wasn't just a generous friend; he was also a member of the Imperial Academy, a major instigator in provincial education reforms, and soon stepped into the big leagues at the newly established Ministry of Education. By 1906, Wang's Mandarin Alphabet was used to teach schoolchildren Chinese in textbooks on a variety of subjects, from botany to foreign relations, and appeared in more than half of China's provinces.

Beijing alone had about twenty schools that taught this alphabet exclusively. They focused on not only children and the illiterate but also on soldiers in military camps, who were often recruits from the peasant population. A rare extant copy of *Talking to the Troops*, which was published in 1904 and is now held in the Vatican Library in Rome, shows that the accessible alphabet was used as a vehicle for patriotic messages as well, urging soldiers to abide by the moral lessons of the chain of command through the practice of discipline and frugality. Yet despite its growing fame, the authorship of *The Mandarin Combined Tone Alphabet* had to remain a secret: Wang was still a fugitive in the eyes of the law. Anything explicitly associated with him could easily be tainted. So closely guarded was the author's identity that some thought Yan was the real inventor.

HAVING RISKED CAPTURE to come back and complete his Mandarin Alphabet, Wang was now held captive by its enormous success. He grew restless in Yan's compound; he was ready to move back to the capital. He found a space in a quiet alley in Beijing to establish a school to teach his alphabet. Wang personally carved each character, example, and illustration in his manual into woodblocks for printing the text-books. Still using a false name, he grew out his hair and trimmed away his beard. Known as Mr. Zhao, he kept his public exposure to a minimum. He delegated all of the face-to-face teaching to a trusted former student. He himself remained out of sight, keeping a watchful eye on the classroom from behind a screen.

Wang's friends warned him to be careful, but Wang thought he was safe in his out-of-the-way alley, working behind the scenes. Then a former associate from the 1898 movement was betrayed by an informant and turned over to the authorities. The man was promptly sentenced and beaten to death. Now Wang was concerned. He realized that many people would like to see him behind bars—or worse.

Something else was bothering him. Wang complained bitterly about charlatans who stole from his Mandarin Alphabet with impunity. One copycat published his own version under Wang's pen name, while another replicated his alphabet wholesale. In his memoir, he wrote of a man from the Gaoyang Prefecture who smeared his good name by falsely attributing the principle of the Mandarin Alphabet to a different rhyme book. When Wang confronted him, the perpetrator expressed no shame and accused him in turn of piracy.

He had been willing to live in exile in Japan and labor in obscurity, but he would not tolerate hack copycats or blackmail. That was where he drew the line. "I suddenly realized," Wang wrote, "that I was being terribly exploited by other people because they knew I was a wanted outlaw." He decided that he needed to claim ownership of the Mandarin Alphabet to ensure that it was properly adopted and taught, even if he had to risk his life to do so.

In early March 1904, Wang voluntarily went to see the governor-in-chief commander of the infantry and Five Police Battalions at his imposing security headquarters. Chief Natong oversaw the security of all nine city gates. No one could slip through without his knowledge.

Once Wang was in his headquarters, there was no telling whether he would come out again—dead or alive. When Wang didn't make it home that night, his friends probably suspected that he was being tortured and forced into a confession for crimes against the Empress Dowager and the empire.

The preliminary process could have taken weeks, and torture was a regular part of extracting and verifying a confession. The Five Police Battalions station would have followed the protocols and reviewed Wang's case to see if further adjudication was necessary. If the anticipated decision involved temporary banishment, it would then be sent to the Board of Punishments for further review and sentencing. Day turned into night; night turned into day; one day became two. While Wang's supporters on the outside waited nervously to learn his fate, they feared the worst.

After he walked in, Wang was led to the hall residence in the west courtyard behind the main station and assigned an attendant to look after him. Rather than an interrogation, he enjoyed a lavish meal in a room replete with books, tea, and even chess sets. If anyone seemed nervous, it was Chief Natong. Natong's journal entries record how frantically he tried to figure out what to do and whom to consult about Wang. This was too important a case to be handled by normal procedures. Natong left early both mornings to seek counsel from his contacts at the Imperial Summer Palace, and he appealed directly to the prime minister of the imperial cabinet, a Manchu nobleman with access to the Empress Dowager. She was away from the capital, which gave Natong a window to negotiate terms. Whether to incarcerate Wang or let him go was the subject of much debate. The prime minister finally offered to guarantee Wang's safety from death but could not promise full immunity. They must make a show of the law. After three days, Wang was officially arrested. The sentence was promptly handed down: life imprisonment.

Word of Wang's reappearance and incarceration, meanwhile, became a major topic of conversation. Newspapers dug into his past and dramatized it for popular consumption. Opinions were divided but on the whole sympathetic. Wasn't he a mere lackey in the failed 1898 reform and hadn't he played second string—even third—to Kang and Liang? Could the imperial family weather another public outcry, after having just executed one of Wang's former associates from 1898? Had Wang not already paid for his sins—seven years of exile—and did he really deserve to be in a dark cell alongside murderers and bandits?

Despite the outpouring of sympathy and support, Wang was imprisoned as a high-risk criminal and labeled as Kang's associate. The newspapers tried to monitor his condition and keep the public informed, but the imperial prison system was a labyrinth for tortured souls. Bribery was the only way to make life tolerable, but Wang had already used the paltry sum he had brought with him to the station. Without greasing the palms of the jailers, a prisoner had little chance of surviving a month—let alone a lifetime. Gone were the chess sets, the good food. Wang was denied bedding the first night in the moldy cell, and the conditions worsened after that: he survived on food so rotten that it was unfit for livestock. Concerned friends and supporters tried to send him money, but even silver ingots could not penetrate the forbidding walls of the imperial dungeon.

Wang was put in the same prison cell where his former associate had been held and beaten to death. "There were dark traces of blood splatter as high as four, five feet on the painted walls. This is where his blood was spilled," Wang wrote as he sat on the damp earth, strewn with wisps of hay and pungent with urine. Even for a man of Wang's mental strength, it must have been incredibly difficult not to despair in that dark cell, still fresh with the sights and smells of death and agony. He had fought various battles in his day, but now he was defenseless and alone. But he remained stoic. Through intermediaries, he warned his Western friends not to intervene: "It would only quicken my death." While confined mostly to his cell, Wang was occasionally allowed to visit a traditional temple on the prison grounds, where the condemned could seek some redemption before the temple's idol. Wang wrote in a poem:

> The morning breeze grazes feebly over the prison temple,
> With their cries the young doves pass by, bearing warmth.
> Contemplating the cause and effect of things my thoughts
>   are ever changing.
> At the crossing of light and darkness I briefly forget my
>   circumstance,
> As I watch the guards wielding their power with abuse.
> The prisoner across the way grows thin, mirroring my own
>   body.

Perhaps Wang's "ever changing" thoughts, if only for brief moments, carried him outside his walled-in existence and back to his beloved Mandarin Alphabet. If he languished in jail, his life's work would not reach its full achievement: national adoption. He still needed to ensure that his country would move toward linguistic unity. If he made it out alive, he would not spend the rest of his life simply enjoying aged ale with friends in the comforts of the evening sunlight; he would keep fighting his single-minded battle.

Two months later, Wang was released, to everyone's shock. He received an imperial pardon from the Empress Dowager. On the eve of her seventieth birthday, she granted amnesty to all the 1898 perpetrators—all except for Kang and Liang, who remained outlaws. Whether it was the sway of public opinion, an act of mercy, or the fact that the prime minister had a little scandal of his own (embezzlement) from which he was happy to distract the public eye—no matter. Wang's supporters greeted the dramatic turnaround with cheers and relief. But Wang was constrained, even unmoved. As he later recounted, "They told me that the prime minister went to great lengths to secure my release and urged me to show my gratitude to him in person. I said, resolutely, 'From this point on, I wish only to live the life of the commoner, therefore I vow to never again come face-to-face with anyone from the imperial ranks.'" A simple thank-you would have bent that resolve a bit too far for his taste. Wang was now free to do what he had wanted to do for so many years. Though they offered to reinstate him to his former position, he declined. He devoted himself instead full-time to the propagation of the Mandarin Alphabet, and its success reached an apex in the following years.

Recent research shows that Wang did a lot more behind the scenes to establish his innocence than he admitted. He sent a grateful letter to Natong, feeding him all the things the official wanted to hear, which was then passed on to the court verbatim. Wang explained that "due to a moment's foolishness" he fell in with the company of Kang and Liang and didn't learn the true extent of their seditious intent until he had already reached Japan. By then it was too late, and he looked guilty by going into what appeared to be voluntary exile, which then became real as the court dispatched warrants for his and others' arrests. Wang also did not miss the opportunity to cleverly recall the loyalty of his family to the empire, the grandfather who bravely battled against the British in the First Opium War, and a brother who, carrying on the family tradition, fought the Boxers and died while on duty. He brilliantly positioned himself as one in a long line of loyal Chinese servants to the throne, who had fought the encroachment of the West for the sake of the empire. Wasn't Wang carrying on their legacy of fighting to keep China alive? He played the pity card, cast himself as the victim in order to free himself and redouble his efforts to perfect his language system. He and his country were the same—underdogs. If he could push through his language reform, extending literacy to the masses by simplifying the script and creating a common tongue, then perhaps he could finally earn back the respect that the Chinese Empire deserved.

AS THE MANDARIN ALPHABET spread in the years following Wang's pardon, China's long-standing political rifts widened to a breaking point. Revolutionary ideas had penetrated deep into people's hearts and minds, and the doctrines of Kang and Liang began to seem conservative in retrospect. All eyes turned to the young Sun Zhongshan (Sun Yat-sen), who for years had been staging grassroots revolts and uprisings with the help of secret societies across the country. Now, it seemed, he was emerging as the only man capable of leading China into a new future. A charismatic leader with a peasant background who was educated in British and American schools in Honolulu, he had the credibility of the everyday commoner and the formidability of a great man. Sun would soon become the founding father of the Chinese nation.

Desperate attempts were made to salvage an imperial order on the brink of collapse. The Empress Dowager implemented some reforms, but people were hungry for more than a token tweak of the status quo; they wanted Manchu blood. Sun campaigned and rallied his troops on a racial platform: he called for ousting the Manchus, while others wanted to stage a wide-scale massacre to extinguish the foreign rulers once and for all. While ethnic hatred provided the rhetoric, it was the urgency to reclaim China's own budding capitalism and industrialization from foreign ownership that made the revolution the cause of every man, woman, and child. China's railroads were built with foreign loans, and land rights were not equal. Fanning public passions, members of Sun's clique expounded on these issues, fist to podium, on street corners and factory floors. One of them cut off his own finger while giving his rallying speech so that he could write out an oath in blood; another extremist threw himself into the ocean to strengthen the resolve of his fellow Chinese with his self-inflicted martyrdom. Assassination of Qing officials, secret poisonings, and bombings emerged as new methods of protest. The atmosphere was dizzying with slogans and overt and covert violence, a headlong rush to bring everything to a finale, the end of China as it had been known for thousands of years.

The watershed moment came after a mutiny in Hubei Province in October 1911. There had already been mass arrests and protests over efforts to take back and nationalize China's railway system. Amid the tense atmosphere, the revolutionaries bided their time—until a bomb accidentally went off in the city of Hankou, forcing them to launch their attack prematurely. It was quickly suppressed, followed by arrests and prompt executions, but no matter—the long fuse had been lit once and for all, and it would lead to a final, massive explosion.

Revolts rippled across the south; by late November, fifteen of twenty-three provinces and regions had declared themselves completely independent from the Qing dynasty. The monarchy in China finally came to an end after two millennia, and a republic took its place. The Revolution of 1911 was China's first real political revolution, one of many upheavals to come, beginning a new century of bloodshed and violence.

Sun's fellow revolutionaries who pushed China into democracy had little idea of what it would look like or what changes it would bring about, but they were committed to embracing an uncertain future. In retrospect, many saw the revolution as a failure, because they had swept away the old but had few constructive plans for what would replace it. The revolution gave the country a new face, a new international persona, but it also opened a chaotic phase of power struggles among warlords and revolutionary leaders. Modern China's birth pangs were only beginning.

The same was true for its script. Wang was ready to push for the Beijing-based Mandarin Alphabet to become the standard that could unify the nation. It would have to overcome competing schemes that privileged southern dialects or went back to using ancient tones. When Wang developed his Mandarin Alphabet, his contemporaries were still debating whether the written script should be superseded by a phonetic system—like Romanization. By 1913, it was clear that China's new nationhood required that it have its own national language and standard tongue. After the founding of the republic, it was evident there would be no more open talk of abolishing the Chinese script. The importance of Wang's proposal, just as this change took place, was that it turned the Beijing-based vernacular behind the Mandarin Alphabet into a candidate for the national model. There would be one final push to immortalize his life's work.

In December 1912, just a year after the end of the imperial dynasty, the Ministry of Education created the Commission on the Unification of Pronunciation to settle the issue of the national tone. Eighty specialists were summoned from all the provinces—Wang among them. Most of the ministry's delegates, though, were from the Jiangsu region, which was considered more in the south than the north. Wang did not like the look of things.

The attendees congregated in the solemn halls of the Ministry of Education, formerly a royal palace, in mid-February 1913. The buildings still carried the ghostly presence of an old education system that prized civil exams and compositions in high literary Chinese. Its multiple courtyards connected one hall to the next, rich with vermilion pillars and ornate architectural design that recalled an elite past where the brush pen was held by only the chosen few. The delegates came to exorcise the last traces of that faded past. Together, they would free the Chinese language from the pages of bookish knowledge and return it to the life of everyday speech.

As for the best model of this everyday speech, each delegate could only see the merits of his own spoken version. They all had a stake in promoting the dialectal or topolectal variant from their home provinces. The Guangdong delegates wanted Cantonese, while those from Sichuan fought hard for Sichuanese. The odds were stacked in favor of the southern speakers. Proportionally speaking, they had more representatives across similar dialect groups.

After the careful inspection of more than 6,500 samples collected from all over the country, factions emerged as the members moved to the more sensitive question of which geographical area would lead the standard pronunciation. Attendance dwindled as the deadlock persisted. It was not a contest for the fainthearted. Those with slightly weaker constitutions or who suffered from tuberculosis—a common affliction at the time—endured a few weeks of contentious lobbying before their health gave out. Some delegates fell ill from exhaustion and had to withdraw from the congress. Others spat up blood during the heated debates, unable to carry on after being cornered and humiliated by their opponents. Wang barely grunted through a violent flare-up of hemorrhoids from sitting for days on end. Blood, he later recalled proudly, soaked through his pants and trickled down to his ankles. Eventually, only the diehards remained.

One of the southern representatives made the appeal that no southerner could go about his business for a single day without using a particular inflection. To be a truly national pronunciation, then, his southern colleague argued, the standard had to bend toward the south. To prove his point, the man broke into an operatic demonstration. Wang had little patience for such theatrics. There was no way that the north, the seat of the nation's capital, would cede to the south on the national tone question. Wang called a separate meeting less than half a mile away at the oldest Anglican church in Beijing. Inside those thick walls, under the famous three-tiered traditional pagoda bell tower sitting atop the sparse lines of Anglo-Saxon architecture, he carried out his mutiny. He instituted a new rule that carefully rearranged how the votes were counted. Each province would now cast only one vote, regardless of the number of delegates it sent. This maneuver didn't just level the numerical advantage of the south, it transferred the advantage to the northern vernacular Mandarin-speaking provinces, which were greater in number. The other delegates protested when they found out what Wang had done on the sly, but it was too late.

His brute maneuvering came to a symbolic and literal climax when he rolled up his sleeves and physically chased a southern delegate out of the room. What set him off, ironically enough, was a dialectal inflection. The delegate had said the word "rickshaw" to a neighbor in his thick southern Wu dialect. To Wang's Mandarin ear, just a few seats over, it sounded awfully like he was calling Wang a son of a bitch. It was precisely to resolve this kind of verbal misunderstanding that had brought them together in the first place. Wang jumped out of his seat, tried to grab the delegate by his collar, and ran the poor man out of the hall. That episode was subsequently remembered as the most raucous exchange witnessed in the solemnly decorated halls of the ministry—the echo of the escapee's scuttling footsteps, drowned out by Wang's obscenities bouncing down the long corridors.

The battered delegate was too intimidated to return, and Mandarin ultimately emerged as the truly viable sound pattern for the national phonetic alphabet. To this day, when asked, a southerner in Hong Kong or Guangdong will say, were it not for this fateful crossfire, Cantonese would have been chosen over Mandarin. The world would now be striving to master the varied intonations of southern China instead of crisp Beijing-speak.

Having lived through a dynastic change and a half-dozen sizable uprisings, Wang remained steadfast in his central goal: Mandarinization. And he saw the project through to the end, even if his own alphabet was destined not to last. An indigenous phonetic alphabet that was first devised in 1908 was gaining traction. Created by the venerable scholar

Zhang Taiyan and derived from an ancient calligraphic style called small seal script, the original notations of thirty-six initials and twenty-two finals were designed to preserve elements of the Chinese script in the writing of the new phonetic alphabet. That insistence on maintaining the integrity of the Chinese script went against the loud clamoring for Esperanto and even simplified, Japanese *kana*-inspired scripts like Wang Zhao's phonetic alphabet. Zhang's phonetic symbols, revised, came to be commonly known as Bopomofo—a portmanteau phrase made from the first four phonetic symbols of the alphabet's set of eventually thirty-nine phonetic letters (bo, po, mo, fo). Like the old reverse-cut system, Bopomofo mainly divided characters into two parts (initials and finals). It overtook Wang's Mandarin Alphabet—but kept Wang's more important conceptualization of a phonetic script—and was passed as the National Phonetic Alphabet at the 1913 conference. As for Wang, he gradually waned like his script, after having blazed the trail for phoneticizing Chinese. Aged and slightly more penitent, he took stock of the battles he had waged in one of his poems from the late 1920s:

> I've hurried through tens of thousands of miles,
> And rumbled for twenty years.
> Most of my acquaintances have turned to ghosts,
> While the sound of cavalry drums still soars into the
>   heavens.
> In the mirror I see a head of overflowing white hair,
> Even though there is not an acre of land under my name.
> Could I have wished this for myself?
> I can only brace up and say that I chose to let go of my
>   ambitions.

Wang spent the rest of his late years out of the limelight. He built a small house on the edge of the Lake of Pure Deeds in the northwestern corner of Beijing. The lake was once a famous retreat where literati frolicked and made up verses in their wine boats beneath fireworks on summer nights and at lunar festivals. The fertile soil still gave bloom to the lotus flowers that perched on the mirrorlike water, though there were fewer visitors. It was nonetheless a sight that Wang took pleasure in, as he looked on from his study and strolled—with ever greater difficulty—along the willow-dotted shores. Perhaps he saw in the lake's faded past a shadow of the bustling harbor of Yantai, the place where his monumental effort began.

Wang's legend would be recalled in discussions and anecdotes about China's tumultuous shift from empire to nation for decades to come. Some sung his deeds, but he eventually dimmed in the public view. People who remembered his feisty years would always express admiration, though they also recalled the difficulty of dealing with him. No testimony perhaps captures it better than Wang's own, summed up in a letter to a fellow script reformer just two years before he died of lung complications at the age of seventy-four. Reflecting further on his own past, he said, with his trademark frankness:

> Most people suffer a lack of self-knowledge—me most of all. From what I can reflect on now, I can only say that, from my youth to middle age and now sunset years, my greatest flaw has been that I did not learn to be tolerant or forgiving toward others. From beginning to end, I've made things difficult by isolating myself more and more in a narrowing circle, until I'm finally powerless. . . . That I will regret to the end.

But Wang left his mark on history because he was prepared to do anything for the success of his mission. He had seen clearly that if China did not take this first step in reforming the way it communicated within its own borders, it was destined to trail behind the modern world. Wang knew that his effort marked only the beginning in the longer revolution of the Chinese script. It would take many more ingenious, remarkable, and determined fighters to carry the process forward. With Mandarinization, the Chinese language was in principle nationally united in sound. It was a start, but China was still far behind. The next battle would be to determine how the Chinese script would make its way in the world. As Wang brawled at the 1913 conference, a few Chinese students in America began to feel the stirring of the next skirmish. Writing was becoming mechanized, and the global race for Chinese typewriting was about to begin.

TWO

CHINESE TYPEWRITERS
AND AMERICA
(1912)

MAPPING OUT THE
IDEOGRAPHIC KEYBOARD

On an early spring day in Boston in 1912, Zhou Houkun took his usual brisk walk from his apartment to Huntington Avenue. The lingering wintry air began to warm in the sunlight, though the twenty-three-year-old engineering student was too preoccupied to notice. His mind was swimming with thoughts of what to see that day at the annual mechanics trade show. Maybe the latest design in aircraft propulsion and road machinery. Or perhaps something that could help him figure out how to make bamboo as durable as concrete—the topic of his upcoming senior thesis. Lately, local newspapers had been filled with sensational ads for specialty automobile and motor vehicle shows. A six-cylinder Silent Knight motor by Stoddard-Dayton that had made headlines in New York and Chicago was going to be on display in an open case so visitors could touch and feel the cast-iron engine for themselves. The exhibition was also expected to attract industry celebrities. Rumor had it that the "spark-plug king," Albert Champion, planned to make a cameo. It was the public event of the season—an occasion not to be missed.

To get to the exhibition, Zhou would have had to cross St. Botolph Street, cut across Garrison Street in the opposite direction he normally took on his walk to school at the Massachusetts Institute of Technology, and then wait for the Pullman trolleys to pass. On the other side of the street sat the impressive redbrick Mechanics Hall. It was the landmark building of the Back Bay until it was razed in 1959 to make way for the Prudential Center. Stretched out on a triangular plot of land, the warehouse covered 110,000 square feet like a slumbering beast, its head a tower peeking out on the north side of Huntington Avenue.

Inside the hall, a young woman seated in the room caught Zhou's eye. Other visitors to Mechanics Hall would recall the bevies of young women in fitted dresses who were often hired during special events to circulate between the bunting-covered walls in the main hall, accompanied by cordial men with greeting signs. Yet the young woman Zhou noticed was not among them—and serendipitous romance was not on his mind. He had spotted a truer love—right there, spitting out a long reel of paper with cut-out holes, solicitously tended by the young woman's nimble fingers.

He asked a bystander for the name of this gurgling beauty. It was a Monotype machine, he was told, one where the typist "sat in front of a keyboard, touched the keys, punched multitudes of little holes in a long reel of paper, and, when finished, placed the latter in a machine which produced fresh, clean, clear types of lead all lined up and ready for the printing press." Free of fumes and grime, the type-minting process took only minutes to complete. The sight of this marvel sent Zhou into despair. He thought of the typical scene in a Chinese pressroom using traditional movable type. There, typesetters toiled in stale air reeking of oil, toting trays back and forth like ants carrying grains of rice, picking out one type cast at a time from a maze of thousands of characters, which then had to be rearranged by hand on a tray before a single impression could be made. The process was slow, tedious, and inefficient—Zhou was overcome with shame to realize that China's reliance on such an archaic technology was the greatest obstacle to the country's aspiration to modernize. He decided this was a problem he wanted to solve.

Wang Zhao had tackled the cacophony of spoken Chinese dialects with the political goal of establishing one common language. That was a crucial step—to nationalize, people needed to unify—but only the first. Exchanging printed information with the outside world was another matter. The Roman alphabet enabled the West to dominate modern communications tools like typewriting and telegraphy, and the Chinese would need to find their place in that existing infrastructure. Zhou, thirty years Wang's junior, knew that the answer lay in technology rather than philology.

The Monotype's keyboard was what caught Zhou's eye: it gave the commands and controlled the machine with relentless exactitude. The young woman in Mechanics Hall just had to tap on the keyboard and then let the heavy machine do the rest—from casting to print. While the Monotype machine was man-size, the keyboard was compact and elegant, displaying the twenty-six letters of the alphabet in the already-standard QWERTY format. A similar keyboard for the Chinese language, accommodating its thousands of characters, yet small enough to fit on a table, would require a conceptual and technological leap. Zhou's course became clear: He would do for the Chinese language what famous office typewriters like the Remington had done to transform America's workplace. He would give it the speed, precision, and efficiency of mechanical reproduction. It was just the kind of challenge the young engineer was itching for.

IN THE 1910S, there was no better place for a young Chinese to witness the power of the modern age than the United States. America was the shining example of industrialization, bursting with entrepreneurism and creative energy after undergoing tremendous technological change in the latter half of the nineteenth century. The early twentieth century marked a transition to big businesses, corporate power, and production efficiency, and the increase in patents during this period reflected the abundance of new inventions. Efficiency and organization were key to maximizing the margin of returns, from building a car every two and a half minutes on the Ford assembly line to expanding bulk and mass production. Maximizing labor per unit of time according to principles of scientific management helped to power factory floors worldwide. From typing at the keyboard to laying a brick, a worker's motions could be analyzed in increments of one-thousandth of a second. By the second decade of the twentieth century, America's industrial production accounted for one-third of the world's total output.

For any Chinese watching, the contrast was inescapable. America, about the same geographical size as China but with a smaller population, built around 340,000 miles of railways to move people and goods across the country, whereas China had only 6,000 miles (most of which were foreign operated and owned). America also produced 30 million tons of iron a year, while China's output was less than 0.5 percent of that. There was no lack of figures to indicate the United States' clear industrial superiority. Yet nothing was more compelling than seeing it with one's own eyes. The United States organized more world's fairs than any other country, drawing close to 100 million spectators to witness its industrialization miracle between 1876 and 1916.

For a long time, China had distrusted participating on the international world stage. It did not care to look beyond its borders, let alone shores, and its court emissaries had only just begun to travel abroad. The idea of crossing the "western ocean" (*xiyang*) to the land of the barbarians—or needing to learn from them—was nearly unthinkable until the last quarter of the nineteenth century. China had consistently refused to participate in the West's expanding network of commerce, and while the First Opium War forced open its gates, it did not open its people's hearts. The first world's fair, launched by the then-powerful industrial leader Great Britain and staged in the Crystal Palace in London in 1851, invited China to participate. Fearing more of the devilish tricks and wicked crafts of the red-haired barbarians, China was the only country to decline.

That did not stop the British from staging a China Court display—mixed in with Japanese and Burmese objects. Or from fabricating a firsthand report called *An Authentic Account of the Chinese Commission, Which Was Sent to Report on the Great Exhibition, Wherein the Opinion of China Is Shown as Not Corresponding at All with Our Own*, which served up a scathing portrayal in long verse, penned by a fictitious Chinese mandarin who was disappointed not to have a good old-fashioned beheading as part of the spectacle.

Other opportunists took further liberties. A junk boat owner pulled off a stunt by dressing up as a mandarin and making his entrance into the opening procession. He shook hands with the Duke of Wellington and bowed before the queen, scamming his way in under the guise of a fake Chinese. The image of the mandarin was made into a joke, a perfect foil to the grand splendor of the British Empire that the exhibition was meant to flaunt. China was being painted into the world picture, regardless of its wishes.

By the time America held its world's fair in Philadelphia in 1876, China had come around, thinking it best to manage its own international image. Also, Chinese reformers had tried their hand at building

THE OPENING, IN SHORT, WAS AS DULL AS COULD BE;
THERE WAS NO EXECUTION WHATEVER TO SEE.

Fictionalized caricature of Chinese attendance at the Great Exhibition in London.
China chose not to participate and did not actually send an official delegation.
From *An Authentic Account of the Chinese Commission, Wherein the Opinion of
China Is Shown as Not Corresponding at All with Our Own*, 1851.

their own shipyards and arsenals in the 1860s, but progress was slow and the results mixed. They realized they could benefit from studying the West's industrial success.

At President Grant's invitation, an official Chinese observer was sent to the Philadelphia exhibition. The fair was timed to celebrate the one hundredth anniversary of America's independence and to display the full spectrum of the country's economic success. The young official meandered through thirty thousand exhibitions in the towering glass-paneled wood-and-iron buildings. He stood in awe of Krupp's large steel breech-loading cannon and the humming Corliss Centennial Engine that powered the entire exhibition. He paused to study fine handicrafts and firearms, which included double-barreled rifles and Gatling guns. Though he had difficulty grasping the changing scale of modern warfare, he did appreciate the everyday utility of sewing machines.

Other official Chinese visitors to the United States from the 1870s through the 1920s saw how technology was transforming society at large. The hydropower plants at Niagara Falls and the open trolleys whizzing down the steep, winding streets of San Francisco impressed upon them the importance of providing public services and transportation. Electric cables, hanging from pole to pole, routed power to every household, while cable cars connected the neighborhoods to city centers, delivering men and women to their workplaces every day like clockwork. The quality of life seemed incomparably better: the Americans had entertainment halls and cinemas, even superior dental hygiene. Their standard of living set the bar for prospering modern nations, and Chinese consumers preferred that life to the one they had at home. China's total imports of U.S. goods rose dramatically after 1900, from 2.65 percent of its total global trade in the last thirty-five years of the nineteenth century to 22.05 percent in the first four decades of the twentieth century. In 1911, in contrast, China's investment in manufacturing and mining

machinery was still only 6 percent of what it spent on agriculture—
and that after half a century of aggressive development.

China's exports seemed unimpressive next to the American marvels
brought into their harbors by the barge load, one after the other in the
early decades of the twentieth century—from new machinery to nylon.
The Chinese mainly shipped abroad soft and artisanal goods like tea
and silk and ceramic wares. These were the same items the country had
been trading for centuries—small handicrafts made in traditional ways.
China did not have factories that could build industrial-grade machinery or equipment to rival those of the Western nations. At the 1873
Vienna World's Fair, the same goods were on display at China's booth,
along with other cultural heritage art forms like calligraphy and embroidery and household items like scissors and knives. Granted, the
variety of scissors was dazzling—custom tools for cutting paper, silver,
copper, leather, melon, women's eyebrows, and even men's nose hairs.
But the cultural ingenuity of small goods seemed paltry next to industrial hardware like engines and farm tractors.

These exhibitions showed off the world's strongest and wealthiest
countries; they also made public the embarrassment of those that had
fallen behind. Deep assumptions about culture and race stood behind the
extravagant spectacles, imbued with the darker prejudices of their times.
Chinese supporters of westernization were well aware of the contradic-
tions in what they admired. They saw how America's prosperity was
extracted more from the blood and sweat of immigrant groups like the
Chinese than from its own native working class. Drawn by pamphlets
and flyers that mythologized the rich bounties of the golden hills of California, Chinese immigrants poured into San Francisco to work in the
gold mines during the 1849 gold rush. Hundreds of thousands of Chinese coolies worked on the transcontinental railway from 1865 to 1869.

By the 1870s, Chinese laborers accounted for one-fourth of the workers in California. They made up 90 percent of the labor force that built the transcontinental railway that connected Sacramento, California, and Promontory, Utah. It was backbreaking work that few American laborers wanted to do: shoveling twenty pounds of rocks about four hundred times every day. Fears of Chinese stealing American jobs made them a target of racial discrimination, and at the world exhibitions they were denigrated as cheap entertainment like animals in a zoo. The carnivalesque Joy Zone at the Panama-Pacific International Exposition of 1915, for instance, erected an Underground Chinatown installation. Through a small peephole, visitors could steal a voyeuristic glance at the wax figures of yellow-faced opium-smoking addicts, prostitutes, and coolie laborers lurking in the shadows of urban enclaves. China protested several times to little avail.

Zhou Houkun grew up as these unsavory images of China were being propagated abroad. He wanted to prove them wrong, like so many other young Chinese who were starry-eyed about Western-style modernity but bound to their own sense of national pride. He was part of the early Chinese student immigration to America that would begin to leave a positive image of studious, talented, and hardworking Chinese. As China tried to find its way into the world system, there was much for the Chinese to learn from a country whose revolutionary past and devastating civil war did not prevent it from embarking on one of the greatest industrial and economic miracles of the twentieth century. But getting there was no easy task. Students like Zhou would learn America's ways from the inside, and though some of them would find the freedom alluring, and even be tempted by the bright lights of America, Zhou would be a notable exception. His heart was tethered to home; he harbored a personal loyalty that would never allow him to fully Americanize. The Confucian son in him was always more sentimental than the modern scientist he was trained to be.

. . .

ZHOU'S PATH TO STARDOM began with an opportunity that most young Chinese could only dream of. Born to farmers in a small, quiet village near Wuxi, a city less than ninety miles northwest of Shanghai, he was raised to read the classics and pursue the wisdom of the ancients. His grandfather built wealth for the family by introducing silkworm farming into the region, which gave Zhou an easier start in life than many. But his grandfather's success could not cushion the blow when Zhou's mother died at a young age. His father never quite recovered, and Zhou grew up watching his father's grief. Zhou senior turned his focus and energy to raising his son properly and sent Zhou to the progressive Nanyang Public School in Shanghai, where the young boy was first exposed to Western learning and even Wang Zhao's Mandarin Alphabet.

The Zhou family—made up of generations of farmers and small traders—had little appreciation for any occupation that did not yield food or profit. Zhou senior was the first to defy the trend by studying to become a Confucian scholar. He pored over the style and philosophy of the Tang poet and essayist Han Yu and steeped himself in the writings of the sages. At a late age, he managed to become the first licentiate (equivalent to earning a bachelor of arts) in his family through civil exams. But the timing was never right for him to advance further. He grew old as an amateur scholar and lived with the regret of unfilled ambition. Yet he always had his son as a loyal follower.

Within a single generation, the path to distinction in China changed dramatically. The last dynasty's ruin—which Wang Zhao had tried to prevent two decades earlier—gave Zhou's generation a precious opportunity. In 1908, Theodore Roosevelt put forth a plan for the United States to return its share of the reparation payments—about $10.8 million—that China had been paying to the eight occupying foreign powers in the aftermath of the Boxer Rebellion. One condition was that part of the refund should go into China's education reform, including an exchange program with the United States. For the United States, the point was to help China with practical training as well as to cultivate the next generation of Chinese who would become America's friends. Along with establishing a school in Beijing that later became the renowned Tsinghua University, the money was used to support students like Zhou, who was selected to join the second class of Indemnity Scholars, named after the Boxer indemnity reparations.

The opportunity came just in time for Zhou. The traditional exam system that had nurtured China's civil elites for centuries was abolished in 1905, after decades of failed efforts to revamp its old curriculum. The civil exams provided the customary social ladder for possibly landing a job in the imperial bureaucracy, where the mastery of a difficult written language—along with the ability to cite any classic text from memory—was considered a main qualification for rule and governance. To be part of the scholar-run machinery that guided society's political and institutional values was the country's most esteemed honor. With the system gone, learned literati suddenly found themselves out of jobs and prospects. Managers, entrepreneurs, and factory workers would soon gain greater importance than the surplus of unemployable scholars like Zhou's father.

His father's overqualified tutelage gave Zhou the basis to excel in the old system while it still lasted and the chance to be chosen as one of the elites to be sent abroad. But unlike his father, Zhou was much more comfortable with practical equations and problem-solving. A career in science and technology—where China desperately needed talent—beckoned him.

Zhou and the rest of his fellow Indemnity Scholars set sail on August 16, 1910. After a twenty-six-day journey to San Francisco via Nagasaki and Honolulu, the young students fanned out to universities across the country. To the Chinese officials who oversaw the program, it was much more than just an educational exchange. The Foreign Ministry, not the Ministry of Education, was in charge of the program to make sure that the students were a diplomatic success. American advocates harbored an ulterior motive as well. They invited the students to ensure America's future influence in China by winning over its most impressionable minds.

On the ship across the Pacific, the Chinese students were given a crash course in America. They read about the customs and geography of the United States, learned the structure of its government, and memorized the names of the original thirteen colonies. They received further tutorials about how to use knives and forks instead of chopsticks and read traffic light signals when walking about in a city and were warned not to spit in public. Though the schoolmasters were too dull to render the lessons interesting, in the students' young minds America meant nothing short of utopia. It was a place "where want and pain were unknown, and contentment and happiness reigned supreme." "At last," one student recalled, he was going to America "to witness every modern wonder which Aladdin's lamp could not produce, and of which the fairy storyteller of Arabian Nights could not conceive." They were the chosen ones.

Not all of them would live up to their own promise. Only a portion of those sent abroad over the next several years would return with pride and glory. Some reveled a bit too much in their newfound freedom—taking up smoking and drinking—and were ordered to return home in shame. Those who stayed and excelled, like Zhou, had notable discipline and self-restraint. Zhou was first sent to the University of Illinois at Urbana-Champaign to study engineering, and his excellent grades enabled him to transfer to the elite university MIT the following year. Others from Zhou's class of Indemnity Scholars stood out as well. Among them were future scientists, diplomats, writers, administrators, engineers, and politicians; in just a few years, soon-to-be household names in the circle of westernized modern intellectuals like Hu Shi and Zhao Yuanren would return home with the skills and ideas to lead China through a period of cultural renaissance, exerting great influence with their progressive views. They would help introduce Western ideas of science and democracy, bring back blueprints for education and infrastructural reforms, and negotiate for China's sovereignty on the international stage.

For his part, Zhou got to participate in the making of the country's next technological frontier. At MIT, he helped the aeronautical instructor Jerome C. Hunsaker build a wind tunnel for studying aircraft design before anyone knew what aviation engineering was. And he would also return to China with a typewriting machine.

WHILE HIS ACADEMIC CENTER was MIT and its surroundings, Zhou's most important social and political outlet was his fellow Chinese students. After arriving in Boston, he found an apartment on St. Botolph Street in the Back Bay. It was a short ten-minute walk to MIT's original campus on Boylston and Clarendon Streets near Copley Square. Within these blocks, his social life blossomed. The Cosmopolitan Club gave him access to an international community, and the Rifle Club introduced him to America's deep passion for guns. Yet it was the Chinese Students' Alliance, a home for the Chinese away from home, that helped him navigate everyday life. It offered the most important and extensive social network for young Chinese student expats in America, two-thirds of whom were members when Zhou joined. They came from distant villages, cities, and provinces in China and probably would never have crossed paths back home. Here, in America, they relied on one another as reminders of their motherland and families. They debated policies and monitored the relationship between the United States and

China; they traded tips on Western dining etiquette, good tailors for the appropriate Western suit to wear to evening socials, and late-night Chinese noodle shops for study breaks and gossip.

The group's affiliated journal, *The Chinese Students' Monthly,* provided an important platform for defending and honing their views. Nationalism was constantly on their minds. The students were among the first, after all, to wrestle with China's uncertain future while opening their eyes to the alternatives abroad. In the previous decades, not even officials at the imperial court really understood foreign affairs and international law. Even the idea of traveling thousands of miles from home was unthinkable. Now, having traversed an ocean and two continents, Zhou and his peers had a more informed perspective on China's future.

The political situation back in China, meanwhile, was nowhere near stabilizing. In the six years Zhou was abroad, China experienced a national revolution, a presidency, dissolution of the parliament, and two attempts to restore the monarchy and emperorship. To the east, it faced the growing threat of Japan, which had just colonized Korea in 1910 after defeating China and Russia in succession. At the same time, Europe's Great War showed the fissures and deep-seated conflicts in Western political systems. Europe began to recede as a model of progress, while Japan's intentions in China grew more menacing. Accusations of internal collusions with the Japanese and betrayals and corruption made regular headlines in Chinese cities.

The political turmoil incited Chinese students abroad to new levels of nationalistic outrage. Those who studied in Tokyo and Paris, spurred by their exposure to anarchist ideas, demanded change, sometimes with hotheaded rhetoric. Their counterparts in America tried to stay cool and focus on their studies—they understood the rarity of the opportunity afforded them. Some felt that China had to find its own way, not through rash action but by acquiring more knowledge and changing slowly. "For a country to lack a navy or an army is not cause for shame,"

Zhou's fellow student Hu Shi wrote in his diary from the dorms of Cornell, but "a country without a university, a national library, museum, or art gallery should be ashamed."

Zhou's fellow Chinese students were more politically minded than he was. He was planning to help his country in his own way. After his fateful encounter with the Monotype in the Mechanics Hall, he began his research in earnest. He read whatever literature he could find on the Monotype and typewriting machines. He combed through manuals and popular magazines and scoured the patent records in the bowels of the Boston Public Library. He trekked to Jersey City to visit the American Type Foundry and to Philadelphia to inspect prototypes at the Monotype Company. Then he examined other similar machines—the Remington, the Underwood, the Noiseless—trying to figure out how they could be modified for Chinese.

It would be the summer of 1914 before Zhou could return his full attention to his obsession. He graduated that spring with a double B.S. in mechanical engineering and naval architecture; his thesis on bamboo as the new steel was a success, grounded in experiments with half a ton of material he had imported from China. He had fulfilled the mission of his scholarship, and it was time to do something more for his country, though Zhou now saw the technical difficulties of manufacturing a Chinese typewriter more clearly than before.

Any typewriting machine depended on four basic features: a striking mechanism to put an impression on paper, a carriage that correctly positioned the paper, a spacing mechanism to control the incremental motion of the carriage, and a keyboard. Like the Monotype, the entire operation of a typewriting machine hinged on instructions given by the keyboard, the master control that set everything in motion.

Yet a usable keyboard for the Chinese typewriter seemed unachievable. A Western alphabetic keyboard worked because it easily manipulated a fixed number of letters into endless permutations. Simple links connected each key to an individual piece of letter type. The Chinese language, with characters numbering in the thousands, required a mechanical connection that could "serve momentarily one character, but could be shifted to serve all other characters," as Zhou described it. But that requirement would change the makeup of the machine's mechanisms significantly. New links would have to be forged to deliver motions to more than one character type. More complex connections would have to be made so the machine could be directed to select the right character. The question was how to turn a typewriting machine originally designed to manipulate twenty-six alphabetic letters into one that could serve thousands of characters.

Whether it was a Royal No. 5 or No. 10—hailed as "A Machine for the Brain Worker"—or the award-winning Remington typewriter that had garnered every major award at recent world exhibitions, every Western typewriter Zhou saw had the feature of one-to-one correspondence: one key, one letter. Yet for Chinese, he reflected, putting a "forest of such keys on a machine" contradicted the very purpose of a typewriter; its core design principle was to be "compact, light and simple." In fact, Zhou noted, "Any such idea as providing one key for each character was little short of absurdity." That is why, he resolved, "the design of a Chinese typewriter must be fundamentally and radically different from any of the existing American typewriters." The very idea of a keyboard itself, as Zhou saw it, had to be reimagined.

By Zhou's time, the QWERTY keyboard was standardized and universal. But it must have stimulated his imagination to learn that earlier Western typewriters did not always have the keyboard we recognize today—or even look like modern typewriters at all. A Sholes & Glidden Type Writer at the 1876 Philadelphia fair was encased in a wooden box with a crank and wheel attached to one side of the carriage. Also known as the Remington Typographic Machine, it was beautifully inlaid with an ornate floral design and typed only capital letters. Taking inspiration from musical instruments and sewing machines, early type-writers could be operated with pedals and revolving drums. Some of the machines literally had piano keys—black and white—instead of a keyboard, while others sported a bulbous mechanism on top like a pin-cushion, with the keys sticking out like needles. An early 1856 John H. Cooper Writing Machine model had a dial pad like a rotary telephone with the letters spread out in a semi-moon pattern on a metal base rather than in four straight rows.

There were more ways than one to define a keyboard. The pincush-ion design might have baffled the Chinese typesetter, who was accus-tomed to grids and trays with thousands of whole character blocks rather than a finite set of letters that could fit on a small mound. But there was no reason why a round design could not work at least for a trial. The first attempt at a Chinese-language typewriter, in fact, took the challenge of size quite literally. An American Presbyterian mission-ary named Devello Zelotes Sheffield built the first Chinese-language typewriter in 1897, with the help of Carlos Holly, an engineer from a renowned family that invented fire hydrants.

Before deciding to spread God's word in China, Sheffield had fought in the U.S. Civil War. He was fearless and determined. Even after sur-viving an apparently random attack from a mad Chinese carpenter that left Sheffield with more than thirty wounds, he was undeterred. In the early 1880s, Sheffield began contemplating the use of stamped Chin-ese characters. Most Western missionaries at the time relied heavily on Chinese scribes for written Chinese. They spoke in whatever Chinese they could manage, and the native ghostwriters would then render it into literate Chinese. It was a laborious process that Sheffield thought put his brethren too much at the mercy of their Chinese assistants. He suspected that parts of the divine gospel may not have made it across the language barrier. Chinese who worked with Westerners had been known to change a word here and there, tweaking the meaning of passages enough to alter the intended message. The collaboration did not always end well.

On a trip to New York, Sheffield found an equally entrepreneurial spirit in Thomas Hall, inventor of the Hall index typewriter. Hall had also tried to build a Chinese typewriter, but without success. His failures, though, gave him plenty of ideas about how to break down Chinese characters into a set of standard elements that could be represented in keys and then grouped together to reproduce whole characters. But, as he now told Sheffield, Hall had found that the sizing, proportion, and relation between the different strokes that made up a character were the real problem. The internal structures of characters varied too much for this method to work across the keyboard.

Sheffield turned Hall's conclusion into his starting premise. When building his own typewriter, he did not try to index Chinese characters by parts or strokes. He took it for granted that each character had to stay "an irresolvable individual."

He designed a large flat disk that could accommodate more than

TYPE WHEEL FOR 4000-CHARACTER TYPEWRITER.

A TYPEWRITER FOR WRITING 4,000 CHINESE CHARACTERS.

Develло Zelotes Sheffield's Chinese typewriter. From "A Chinese Typewriter," *Scientific American*, June 3, 1899, p. 359.

four thousand commonly used Chinese characters. They were arranged in concentric rings on the disk's surface. Each character displayed on the upper surface of the disk corresponded with a metal cast of the character on the opposite side. The machine looked like a small table, with the disk housing the character keys on top and a carriage for the paper below.

The wheel was organized alphabetically according to the then-popular Wade-Giles transcription rather than a more traditional Chinese way of organizing characters, since Sheffield designed it for foreigners like himself. Phonetic spellings in Roman letters after every sixth ring represented the pronunciation of the characters in that segment of the wheel. To type, an operator would use their left hand to rotate the disk and select the desired character with a long, thin pointer. Then, using their right, they would precisely position the carriage holding the paper underneath by turning a small winch. In the final step, a lever and cam lifted the paper into position, where a small hammer forced the paper against the inked type, leaving a printed impression. The process was painstaking, since the ink roller had to be carefully applied to one character at a time or else risk printing parts of neighboring characters. The carriage also had to be restored to its original position after each character was printed before the entire process could be repeated for the next one.

Operating the machine was a full-body exercise. Uncommon characters required the longest reach—because they were not often used and could be stored farther away on the disk from the operator, while a nimble operator could retrieve common ones quickly. Sheffield hoped that the demanding bodily motions would develop muscle memory and lead to more proficient use over time. Lest any Westerner get lazy by relying on the machine rather than actually learning characters, Sheffield insisted that with each physical reach the user would be forced to visually go over the characters' contours and be given a chance to commit their shapes as well as their Romanization to memory. It was

similar to the way Chinese schoolchildren learned characters by drawing and redrawing patterns by hand. By using the machine, a missionary would rise to be, Sheffield hoped, a "master of his own thoughts,"
instead of staying dependent on a native informant—who might not be
a faithful scribe of God's word.

While doing the research for his typewriter, Zhou came across
Sheffield's invention and learned from its inefficiencies. Squeezing thousands of characters into a machine intended for twenty-six letters requires economizing space. Zhou knew that the typewriter had to fit
on the top of a desk so it could be operated comfortably by someone
like the young woman he saw that day at the exhibition; he knew it
should be as close in size as possible to a Western-language typewriter.
Anything much bigger would be unattractive and unwieldy, but still it
was too much to expect the machine to be the same size as a Western
typewriter. A standard Remington model at the time was advertised as
15.75 by 11 by 12 inches and weighed about forty-two pounds. Zhou's
prototype would end up with an area size of 24 by 36 inches but a
slightly lighter forty pounds.

Size also determined the amount of working space inside the machine. A single alphabetic letter only took one stroke to commit ink to
paper, but to type one Chinese character required several points of
mechanical coordination. A series of extra movements between rotating
gears, pawls, and ratchets would be needed to interpret the complexity
of the script. Zhou saw only one answer. To optimize the typewriter's
internal mechanisms, the keyboard could not be a command board on
the outside. It had to be integrated into the process of selecting and
retrieving characters, perhaps working in a manner closer to the movable
type tray—literally, a board of keys—the way the Chinese typesetters
were accustomed to seeing and organizing their characters.

Zhou studied Sheffield's manual and instructions, along with a
contemporary Japanese model that printed three thousand characters.

Japanese typewriters were helpful references, but the Japanese in general used far fewer characters. Chinese characters, or *kanji*, made up only one of three of their available writing systems, and their designs did not easily scale up to meet China's needs. Following Sheffield's lead, Zhou did not attempt to take characters apart, but he was better at economizing the operation of whole-character typewriting.

Zhou laid out a map of the characters on a flat grid so that any character could be located along an x- and a y-axis. Each character, in other words, now had its own coordinates. (This was a significant improvement on Sheffield's design, where the operator had to search by eye on a moving wheel while doing different things with each hand.) Zhou affixed metal casts of the characters to the curved surfaces of four cylinders attached to a cross-shaped frame. Each cylinder, three inches in diameter and ten inches long, featured up to 1,500 characters, with a possible range of 6,000. Each coordinate on the indicator map corresponded to a specific position on one of the cylinders.

To type, an operator moved a selector needle over the desired character on the map. Pressing the selector down would release a striking mechanism, driving the character block into the paper. Zhou's machine simplified the search task but still arranged characters according to the traditional groupings by 214 Kangxi radicals—standardized by the *Kangxi Dictionary*—leaving the issues of classification and indexing untouched. In Zhou's approach, the primary linguistic challenge was to determine which characters to include; the primary engineering challenge was to design a mechanism that connected a point on a flat surface to a point on a cylindrical surface.

To solve the first problem, Zhou consulted the imperial *Kangxi Dictionary* itself, which contained 50,000 characters, many of which were archaic and no longer in common usage. A more contemporary abridged dictionary seemed sufficient, but this still contained 9,700 characters. He needed to whittle the character set down further. After consulting with friends and acquaintances in New York, he learned that the average movable lead type printing press used by Presbyterian missionaries in Shanghai made do with 5,000 commonly used characters.

What exactly counted as a commonly used character was more obvious in some cases than others—and that remains true even today. "*De*" 的, for instance, a possessive modifier that indicates a relationship of possession like "mine," "yours," and "its," tops the list in modern Chinese, but an archaic function character like "*hu*" 乎, which is a sentence-ending character that marks a question, would be much more common in classical texts with no punctuation marks. The bar for Zhou was average literacy. Given that the everyday reader's vocabulary at the time was only two-thirds that of a sophisticated reader, he decided on 4,000 core Chinese characters for the machine he wanted to build.

For two grueling, sleepless months, Zhou worked on the prototype. He unveiled it to his fellow Chinese students at the Eastern Section Chinese Students Conference in Amherst, Massachusetts, in 1915. Awestruck by the forty-pound typewriting machine, they invited Zhou to introduce the invention in *The Chinese Students' Monthly*. After years of planning and months of hard work, he was going to be the first Chinese to invent a Chinese-language typewriter for the Chinese people. Finally, the story was about to go public.

Zhou's breakthrough was figuring out how to correlate the physical act of selecting and retrieving a character in a tray with the mechanical motion of preparing a character, etched onto a cylinder, to be inked and printed. The result was a single coordination of mechanical motions, optimally economized and completed by a human operator. In his article for *The Chinese Students' Monthly*, Zhou documented the details of his typewriter and the technical challenges he had to overcome. He had known, of course, that he was not the first. There was Sheffield's machine and an earlier Japanese prototype, both of which he acknowledged as having arrived at similar ideas independent of his endeavor. It was a respectful nod to those who came before him.

Just as he was preparing to publish his article, though, an unexpected challenger nearly derailed Zhou's debut. Qi Xuan was a fellow Chinese student studying engineering at New York University. Unbeknownst to Zhou, Qi had been on a parallel track. Relying on a different set of principles for building his own Chinese typewriting machine, he figured out how to do what Zhou, Sheffield, and others thought was impossible: arrange the characters by parts.

Compared to Zhou, Qi was a relative outsider to the Chinese students' circle. A native of the city of Fuzhou in southern China, he was almost nine years Zhou's senior. He was not a member of the Chinese Students' Alliance, and while he was funded by the government, he was not part of the same elite coterie as Zhou. He left China shortly before the 1911 Revolution and studied at the University of London for nine months, then traveled to the United States in February 1914.

His timing for leaving China was not coincidental. None of his fellow Chinese students in America seemed to have known this, but Qi had been a student radical back in China. A graduate of the Anglo-Chinese College, he was a member of a secret society that was part of Sun Zhongshan's underground resistance movement that sought to overthrow the Manchu government. Qi cut off his queue—the single long braid that was required of men under the Qing rule—to protest imperial rule and joined plots to set off bombs to aid the revolution. One such effort was foiled. Qi likely escaped and decided to study abroad as a safe alternative—like so many Chinese students during times of political trouble. The story of his invention appeared in U.S. newspapers just days before Zhou's article appeared in *The Chinese Students' Monthly*. (A report on Qi's invention was also announced in the very same issue.)

In place of Zhou's character grid, the keyboard of Qi's machine had only three keys—a back spacer, a forward spacer, and one that selected the character. But Qi's machine also relied on cylinders of type (two cylinders instead of Zhou's four). The upper cylinder, with characters inscribed on paper, served as a guide. The lower cylinder, with corresponding characters engraved on a copper surface, made the actual impression. An operator would use a hand wheel to rotate the machine's upper cylinder until the correct row appeared in a viewfinder on the front of the machine. Then three keys would be used to select the correct character from the row and lock the cylinders in position, aligning the corresponding character cast on the lower cylinder and stamping it on the page.

Though they looked very different, the underlying design and mechanisms of Zhou's and Qi's machines were very similar. And Qi's handled 4,200 actual Chinese characters, just 200 more than Zhou's core lexicon. Qi's machine, however, was different in one very important respect: he had broken with the prevailing commitment to reproduce whole, complete characters. Of his 4,200 individual Chinese characters, 1,720 were in the form of character components, radicals, and their possible variant positions in a square space, which allowed his machine to generate, in theory, more versions out of the same parts. In three steps, using these keys, the operator could purportedly produce 50,000 combinations.

Operating his machine, Qi explained, was closer to spelling an English word than producing a Chinese character. If you treat radicals like groups of letters, you can play with different combinations the way you would in a word game. Let's say you have three English words—"exist," "expect," and "submit." You can generate more words by mixing and matching their parts to form new words like "sum," "suspect," "subsist," "bit," "mist," "its," and "sex." Unlike modern English words, which have equal spacing for each letter and line up in a neat row, components and radicals can move around from character to character. In print they can occupy different quadrants of the square space that each character fills, which means their position, and consequently their size, can change. For example, the character for "fire," 火, fills an entire square space when standing alone, but it becomes thinner when it is a radical put on the left of the character "braise," *shao* 燒. In turn, it changes form altogether—into four flames—when placed at the bottom of the character for "hot," *re* 熱. Qi accounted for possible variant positions like these by giving them separate engravings on the cylinders. Consequently, there are at least three options for "fire" to be combined with other components and thereby form a greater number of characters.

Qi challenged the idea that characters had to be individual, stand-alone units. He thought of them as more modular, like alphabet-based words, things that could be recycled to compose different characters. And once he started tinkering, some of the Kangxi radicals did not sit well with him. He took more liberties and slipped in a few radicals he had devised that he thought worked better. A bigger shift than Zhou's was creeping in. Others would also start to ask whether exclusively using radicals for character classification still made sense.

Zhou had not expected someone to be so close on his heels. Soon he and Qi were each proclaimed the breakthrough inventor in different news reports in the English and Chinese media, from *The Washington Post* and *The New York Times* to China's own *Eastern Miscellany* and *The Chinese Students' Monthly*.

When Zhou learned about Qi, he must have had a moment of hesitation: Should he acknowledge his peer graciously and take the high road, or sideline Qi to claim his own preeminence as an inventor? Why draw the limelight away from his own machine by tipping his hat to Qi? After all, the two announcements were close enough together that he wouldn't be obliged to acknowledge Qi's machine as a precedent, the way he had referenced Sheffield's. He could have feigned ignorance and claimed the spotlight for himself. No one in his circle of Chinese students would have minded. In fact, when Hu Shi learned of Zhou's and Qi's inventions, he was partial to Zhou and cast doubt on whether Qi had truly resolved the issue of positioning inside a given character, because he only demonstrated it for a minority of characters. The issue was whether all character parts could be put back together in the right way, with the correct spacing between them and in the right proportions. In the end, the character had to look natural. How to do that would become a bigger problem for others after Zhou and Qi. For now, though, Zhou had the backing of his network of Indemnity Scholars; he could have done what he wanted and no one would have thought him unjustified.

But ultimately, he couldn't have lived with that. His father had taught him that diligence and persistence yielded honest work and that advancing one's own interest was different from sabotaging someone else's. He also clearly felt confident that he could come out ahead on the strength of his own machine. In his article in *The Chinese Students' Monthly,* he was willing to give credit where credit was due, beginning with those most distant from him in time. "It must be clearly understood," he acknowledged in a footnote, "that I was not the only one who was interested in the problem and who attempted its solution. There have been others who have devoted a great deal of time and energy to the possible solution of the problem."

While he dutifully paid homage to Sheffield's pioneering efforts, politely pointing out their flaws, he chose a different tactic with Qi. He discussed the principle behind Qi's invention but avoided mentioning him by name in the article. Only the editor's footnote on the first page flashed Qi's name: "This article is especially timely in that immediately after this had gone to press, H. Chi [Qi Xuan] of New York University announced the completion of his Chinese typewriter. The principle of Mr. Chi's [Qi's] invention is discussed in this article." Zhou refrained from openly recognizing him as an equal competitor. Instead, he started picking apart the concept behind Qi's invention to show that it was fundamentally misconceived.

Zhou himself had looked into breaking up characters early on but abandoned the idea. He dutifully followed the standard radical system in the *Kangxi Dictionary* and, like most people, accepted it at face value. It is unclear how much philological examination he conducted, though he did say he spent a summer studying the construction of characters. That was enough for him to learn the rules but perhaps not enough to venture beyond them. In the same workmanlike manner as Sheffield, he concluded that characters could not be treated as anything but individual wholes.

For different reasons, Sheffield and Zhou both concluded that characters were the way they were for good reasons and preserving them was of the utmost importance. Qi's scheme "looked well on the face of it," Zhou cautioned, "but they forgot, that the same 'radical' in different characters differ [*sic*] not only in size but also in shape, and, furthermore, they occupy different positions in a character." He named one example, the square-shaped radical meaning "mouth" 口, which shows up in the characters for "ancient" 古 and "cry" 哭 but in each its size and location are quite different. Consequently, one cannot use the same square for "mouth" in both cases, as they were designed to fit into different configurations. If the different sizes of 口 were forced together, they would create absurd-looking characters with overlapping strokes in all the wrong places.

Ultimately, arbitrarily dismembering characters flew in the face of tradition and convention. For Zhou, you did not just start cutting up and rearranging character parts at will in the formal writing system. Writing had always been equated with authority, a symbol of reverence for the past and a talisman of legitimacy. Hence, the line between authorized and unauthorized writing was always clear. One of the jobs of the imperial scribes was to distinguish correct characters from their variants and thereby maintain the proper form of writing. Qi's idea of combining radicals into 4,200 characters might have gotten the characters on paper, Zhou conceded, but he doubted it could have put characters back together exactly the way they were intended.

Zhou's calm condescension enraged Qi. He immediately wrote a letter to the editor of *The Chinese Students' Monthly*, generously doused in gasoline. Thank you for pointing out the obvious, Mr. Zhou, he basically said, but "as I have already succeeded in devising and building a model of Chinese typewriter, I think that I know what I am talking about." His cylinders, Qi reiterated, contained all possible positions and sizes of the chosen number of radicals—altogether 393 positional variants—which meant his design had already preempted Zhou's objections.

Zhou may be forgiven for his failure to grasp the concept, Qi continued in cool insult, because "of course, such ingenious and original devise [*sic*] requires profound mechanical knowledge together with years of intelligent study of the Chinese dictionary and etymology." Qi implied that Zhou, a scientist and not a language scholar, had only an inkling of that deep knowledge. In fact, Zhou seemed "either to lack sufficient mechanical knowledge or intelligent study of the 'radical system,' although he [wrote] as if he were a great authority."

Finally, to drive his point home, Qi sneered at the whole lot of full-character typewriter inventors for being an unimaginative, mediocre bunch: "I cannot help thinking that their inventions are merely 'imperfect printing press machine [*sic*],' which has little mechanical advantage and commercial value." Zhou, to Qi, was one of the many who prided themselves for doing things the long and hard way, constrained by their own imaginations.

Upon hearing this insult, Zhou might have wished he had put more time into lexicography when he had the chance. Knowing the origin of characters and their textual allusions was an essential element of the traditional scholar's toolkit. What Zhou learned from his father was enough for him to excel in the old system but not sufficient to reinvent it. He memorized what standard references to consult, like the *Kangxi Dictionary*, and was not about to question received knowledge. That was how he had succeeded in the traditional education system; it was the kind of learning that was encouraged and revered.

The greater truth, perhaps, was that Zhou was never quite a humanist at heart. Instead of becoming a calligrapher, he invented a special ink-grinding machine; instead of taking long contemplative walks in the fields, as his father had in his dreamy youth, he spent time building a pair of mechanical wooden clogs. He was never an eloquent writer the way his father was and left very little beyond the descriptions of his own typewriter. He was raised on the cusp of two worlds—the traditional one, where he was the good Confucian son, and the modern one, where he needed to be the daring scientist and engineer.

Though Qi rightly identified Zhou's vulnerability, his retort, in the end, did not do much damage or elicit more support for himself. He was much less known to the readers of *The Chinese Students' Monthly*, which was run by an elite circle of the young, handpicked future leaders of China like Zhou. Moreover, his own contribution of breaking characters apart, while important, was a one-off experiment. Component-based analysis was still in the early stages, as most people—like Zhou—still observed the age-old practice of radicals.

Qi's typewriter did receive due recognition elsewhere. It qualified as one of China's official national entries into the Panama-Pacific International Exposition in San Francisco that year, garnering interest from a Chinese merchants' association curious about commercializing it for mass consumption. He also had the personal support of the Chinese consul general in New York, Yang Yuying, who financed a large portion of Qi's research early on and publicly endorsed the invention when it

was unveiled in March 1915 by typing a letter on it to send to his office
in Washington, D.C. That same month, Qi gave his own demonstration to a group of reporters in his small apartment on the Upper West
Side near Columbia University. *The New York Times* ran a favorable review two days later. He passed along the details and sketches of his
typewriter to the Ministry of Education back in China through the
local office for Chinese student affairs. The Ministry of Agriculture and
Commerce then issued him a five-year patent in September. Two and a
half years later he also secured a U.S. patent for it.

Still, in the end, Qi's invention was never as prominent in China as
it was in the United States and his typewriter never received the investment it needed to be mass-produced. Important people like Hu Shi
were more predisposed to Zhou, who was already known and respected.
Zhou was also being wooed with multiple job offers from back home
while he was building a solid career as an engineer at an American
airplane company. He was poised to become a leading scientist in aviation technology, at the time a new field. He could have stayed in America, perhaps even taught at MIT someday, like many of its illustrious
alums. He also could have patented his typewriting invention in the
United States, like Qi did, and concluded his venture that way. It would
have been the secure path.

But he chose not to stay. Back home, Zhou's father was growing
older and frailer. While there was no aviation engineering in China, a
Chinese typewriter might do more for the country than state-of-the-art
airplanes. Besides, he had an enticing offer from the Commercial Press
in Shanghai, which was working to become the most important publishing house in the country. It wanted to develop Zhou's typewriter
into a commercial product and was willing to give him the money and
time he needed. So Zhou decided to go home, put aside his aeronautics
career in America, and bring back the one invention that might make
all the difference.

. . .

ZHOU RETURNED TO SHANGHAI in the summer of 1916 and immediately received invitations to speak about his typewriter, aeronautics, and his experience abroad. He was treated like a minor celebrity. The city was very different from his time there as a schoolchild. It had grown into a vibrant center of commerce and consumerism—banks, tobacco companies, theaters, competing foreign and domestic goods, and billboards. The country was also far from politically stable, with the nascent rise of military cliques who would carve out their own fiefdoms. At the same time, it was an unprecedented period of cultural awakening for China's youth. They were eager to part with the old and embrace all that modernity had to offer. Many of them went to hear Zhou speak for the first time.

It was July 22, a sweltering Saturday night. Zhou stepped up to the podium and set down his bag. People were slow to find their seats, queuing up in the aisles for the next open bench. Zhou took a head count and steadied his breathing. In the back, a few stragglers gulped down free ice cream, already melting in the heat. Rustling between the rows and aisles, entrepreneurs greeted cultural progressives, while students waved their friends to the last empty seats. Their teachers were too busy looking around the room to keep watch over their charges.

Those already settled had a chance to gaze at the young speaker— by then a twenty-seven-year-old freshly returned from America—there to unveil the industrial innovation of the decade, his Chinese-language typewriter. He had an angular face and stood straight as a board yet was not quite tall enough to be imposing. The small, round silver-rimmed glasses that framed his cool, distant eyes did not flatter his clenched jaw. The oiled black hair, though, coiffed short to look Western, was convincingly modern. The clock struck eight and the crowd fell silent. The air was thick with anticipation.

Instead of beginning to speak, Zhou did an odd thing: Pulling a worker's uniform and gear from his bag, he began to put it on over his tailored suit, one piece at a time. Helping one hand into the glove as though preparing a difficult task, he spoke softly but firmly: "I have one phrase to impart you with today—'Don't be afraid to get your hands dirty.'"

The audience puzzled over this mysterious message. Perhaps he meant it as a piece of earnest advice, or maybe there was something deeper to decipher—but what was one to make of the workman's overalls? They were not sure, but they were hooked. After all, they were promised an evening of surprises. For weeks now, flyers and newspaper announcements had been drumming up interest in the special event, hosted by the progressive Jiangsu Province Education Association's summer session near the city's bustling old western gate. The venue sat on the dusty thoroughfare between the faint line of the old city's former walls and the privileged Westerner-occupied zone, the International Settlement. There, between the landmarks of past glory and foreign domination, industrial proponents mingled with influential cultural progressives, getting the latest updates and insiders' gossip. Zhou was the main attraction. His presentation was to be followed by other entertainment that would stretch the evening toward midnight—a magic lantern slide show, a musical interlude with a zither performance, and an ample supply of ice cream to cool off the restless sitting bodies.

Good honest work, Zhou began to explain, the kind you do with your hands, had always been looked down upon in Chinese society. Tradition favored the survival of physically feeble literati, who spent their lives buried in old books and shaking their brush pens furiously over paper. Prizing learnedness over craft, they sneered at workmanship and practical labor. So much so, Zhou warned, that they could not wrestle down a chicken with their bare hands if their lives depended on it.

He paused to let the image sink in; the audience felt the fowl's feathery neck slip from under their weak grips. Then Zhou delivered his central point: the post-1911 republic had turned against tradition and all that it prized, but it also faced the enormous challenges of reconstruction. The next generation was left to build a future that was promised but never concretely outlined, and nothing was more urgent than rebuilding and modernizing the country's infrastructure. Yet new upheavals already seized the young nation. Power grabbing among the old guard and young liberals split the fragile republic, and even the de facto leader Sun Zhongshan had not been able to stop it from falling into the hands of the military cliques of dozens of warlords. They fought one another and colluded with foreigners to gain the greatest advantage over the chaos that was China's political situation. The most powerful of them, Yuan Shikai, who had the loyalty of the strongest army at his disposal, even made himself emperor for almost three months, while another tried to reinstall the last Manchu emperor on the throne—an attempt that lasted twelve days.

Political turmoil notwithstanding, enormous work had to be done to reclaim and develop the basic industries of China—mines, railroads, telegraphs—that were largely run and owned by foreigners. China had plentiful natural resources but not the technical know-how or modern machinery required to convert them into capital. There was also the age-old prejudice against manual labor. Awakening people to the challenge of the future was never more critical. Zhou was privileged enough to have experienced an example worthy of emulation: America. Its spirit of democracy and industriousness contrasted sharply with the Chinese way of doing things, which fed a useless army of scholars and blocked true progress. He hoped his audience would be persuaded by the comparison. He continued:

> The Chinese people loathe getting their hands dirty . . . they
> shun all activities concerning industry and artisanship, which

has made the learned inept at anything practical, and the peasants ignorant of real knowledge. President Roosevelt is the revered head of state of the United States, yet his relatives were woodworkers. The customs of the East and the West may be different, but the wealth and power of nations will always tie the rich together with the poor. The gravest problem that confronts the world today is livelihood. If our people needn't worry about making a living, I would have no more to say. But if we want to improve our livelihood, then we must start by promoting industry. The clothes I have on are from my days as a student abroad in America, from the time I interned in a factory. Shabby and filthy these clothes may be, I don't abandon them, because they bear the marks of a worker. They are the ones whose work generates profit, and those who make profit avoid becoming parasites. China is full of parasites—and the majority of them are scholars.

Zhou's indictment was harsh, but not without justification. After the façade of the empire fell away, the extent of China's backwardness became even more obvious, and many Chinese—not just Zhou—thought America offered an appealing model. Others, for the same reason, feared it. But Zhou reached a different conclusion. He had been trained to think with a cool head and approach problems with reason, and the proof was in his forty-pound typewriting machine. That July night was the promise of a future to come. The arena for science and democracy—soon to be the twin slogans of China's era of enlightenment—was no place for timid souls. Who better than an engineer, after all, to answer the call to action? It was the homecoming of a lifetime. That night, people called him an "industrial star," and the world seemed his for the taking. He had delivered the results of his hard work studying abroad. Now the question was what China was going do with the message he embodied. The thought must have been on everyone's mind that night. But World War I had already engulfed Europe and was about to throw China into more turmoil. It would compound the difficulty of what Zhou was trying to bring home.

WHILE ZHOU WAS TOILING away in America, China was drawn deeper into Europe's problems. In August 1914, Europe entered one of its deadliest conflicts of the twentieth century—and China made an early calculation. At the time, the Germans occupied the port city of Qingdao in Shandong, their one and only prize colony in East Asia since 1898. The British and the French occupied concessions in both Shanghai and Tianjin, and Japan had been a growing threat ever since it annexed Taiwan in 1895. Every major player in the world war exerted a sphere of influence in China, and the risk of the war breaching its borders was a real and present danger. China declared neutrality from the start, yet segments of the Chinese political elite did not think impartiality was the smart strategy. There was no better way to turn China into a respected member of the family of nations, they argued, than to contribute diligently to the war effort. Even better would be if China could use the occasion to kick out the Germans and take back Shandong, the birthplace of Confucius and Mencius. Yuan Shikai, then president, offered the Allies fifty thousand troops, but the British declined. China's help was not needed—and perhaps not substantial enough.

The Japanese, meanwhile, also spotted a window of opportunity. They had entered an alliance with the British in 1902 to repel the Russians and now sought to use that alliance as a possible wedge to widen the opening to the continent, starting with China. Japan declared war on Germany just days after Britain officially entered the war. They delivered an ultimatum to the Germans to relinquish their possessions and appointed themselves as the official brokers of the process of returning them to China. In late August, the Japanese naval fleet landed at Longkou, a port city about 130 miles to the north of Qingdao. By November, the Germans had surrendered.

The Europeans suspected that Japan had bet on getting into China all along, as the Japanese never showed any interest in sending troops to continental Europe. The Chinese remained hopeful that, if they earnestly engaged in the war effort, the international community would hold Japan to its word. Chinese minister Liang Shiyi came up with a plan. Both the British and French suffered tremendous casualties: 1.3 million for the French, 750,000 for the British. They could not spare able-bodied men to tend to the war infrastructure—digging trenches, stocking and transferring munitions, and burying the dead. Liang offered what they needed: manpower.

Soon, China began to export what came to be known as the Chinese Labour Corps. By the end of the war, about 140,000 Chinese men had been transported to western Europe. It was the largest state-sponsored exportation of labor by the Chinese state, preceded by only a much smaller Qing experiment from 1904 to 1910 that sent 60,000 northern Chinese laborers to work in the gold mines in South Africa. Unlike most of their nineteenth-century brethren, who were often kidnapped and forced into indentured servitude in places like California, Peru, and Cuba, the Chinese laborers who were recruited by the state enlisted of their own free will. They were carefully screened for selection as part of Liang's so-called laborer-as-soldier diplomacy. Unfortunately, the effort did not counteract the threat from Japan.

In January 1915, Japan presented Yuan with a set of twenty-one conditions. Far from returning Shandong to China as promised, Japan pushed for more. It demanded, among other things, that China transfer all rights and concessions formerly granted to Germany to Japan and hand over all mining and railroad rights in the province, along with granting Japan treaty ports and residency for its citizens. In addition, China was to consult with Japanese advisors on all military matters in the province and send the appropriate representatives to Japan regularly for such consultations. By then Japan held all of Germany's previous colonies, not only Qingdao but also the islands of Micronesia—Palau, Chuuk, Pohpei, Yap, Korsrae, Marshall Islands—in the western Pacific. Japan was establishing a new foothold in Asia and the Pacific and had no intention of withdrawing. Seeing no viable options, Yuan agreed to all of the terms. The agreement was not made public until six months later.

News of the Twenty-One Demands appalled international observers and threw China into crisis. Yuan had sold out his own country, people cried, and Japan must be stopped. The outrage reverberated overseas. The young Chinese students living in and aspiring to emulate the very Western countries that were siding against China felt deep disillusionment and betrayal. In America, France, and elsewhere, they vowed to act. Members of the Chinese Students' Alliance wrote to politicians, published articles and opinion pieces, and called emergency meetings across campuses all over the United States. The students tried to reason with and appeal to the international community, especially the United States, to condemn Japan's actions.

May 9, the day the Chinese government signed the Twenty-One Demands, was promptly declared National Humiliation Day by civic organizations. It was the first of twenty-six dates to be given this name during the Republican period. Year-round (except for the month of December, which had none), National Humiliation Days were there to remind the Chinese of the imminent danger of national extinction and the so-called Hundred Years of Humiliation, a series of defeats and exploitations at the hands of the Westerners, starting with the First Opium War. Mass boycotts of Japanese goods followed, rallying tens of thousands of protesters including merchants and industrialists, while four thousand Chinese students in Japan returned home en masse in protest.

After the war, China did not get the justice it had hoped for. Its pleas were ignored at Versailles—in fact, the Chinese were not even officially invited—and the Western powers did not contest Japan's actions in Shandong. The words of world peace and equality in President Woodrow Wilson's speech to end the war rang hollow. The students reached a shared conclusion, as one of them wrote: "We at once awoke to the fact that foreign nations were still selfish and militaristic and they were all great liars." The U.S. minister to China at the time agreed: "It sickened and disheartened me to think how the Chinese people would receive this blow which meant the blasting of their hopes and the destruction of their confidence in the equity of nations."

The year 1919 was a turning point. China's first student-led demonstration took place on May 4. It came to be etched in the national memory as the famous May Fourth Movement for anti-imperialist nationalism, and the first of the country's modern tradition of student-led protests. The event began with more than three thousand students taking to the streets in a peaceful march. The movement grew in the following months as workers, merchants, and teachers joined them. For the students in particular, these protests weren't just about the Shandong betrayal or the Treaty of Versailles. Four years earlier, they had already sensed the need for China's own cultural rejuvenation. They felt the time had come for China to dethrone its elites and tend to the salvation of the masses—the workers, coolie laborers, and illiterate peasants whom a number of them had encountered firsthand as part of the labor corps in France. The students had helped them write letters home and taught them how to read, and the experience made an indelible impression on their budding sense of international and social justice. They saw up close the oppressed who were silenced because they were, first and foremost, illiterate.

The cultural movement beginning in 1915 took up language as its cause—to cast off the elite, high literary language of the past and to elevate the people's vernacular tongues as the blueprint for a new written language. Zhou's fellow Indemnity Scholar, Hu Shi, who returned to China the same year he did, was the leading advocate of the New Culture Movement. Hu called on the writers and intellectuals to write in plain everyday language. Mass literacy became a critical platform in wide-scale social and education reform.

Zhou's fellow Chinese students in America anticipated a civilizational showdown, reflected in the fitness of language. As with world affairs, the alphabetic writing systems of the West, they passionately argued, were at a much greater advantage compared to Chinese. In the global struggle for survival, the Chinese language—along with the nation's fate—was facing Darwinism at its most ruthless. Anxious doubts set in. Was the Chinese language worthy of preservation? Had it been responsible all along for the Chinese people's ignorance? And if that were the case, then the Chinese language must also be culpable for putting China behind the West.

Such was the deep skepticism that Zhou had returned home to reverse. He carried in his arms a prototype to show all of China that its script was not responsible for its political problems and that technology could open a path forward. He believed in the Chinese language's future as surely as he believed in himself. Unfortunately, that future would not come to pass the way he hoped.

A FEW MONTHS AFTER RESETTLING, Zhou was dismayed by the reality on the ground. Factory and industrial conditions at home were nothing like what they were in the United States. Though he had prepared himself for a challenge, he had not expected having to overcome quite this much.

Labor was cheaper in China—one dollar for a day's labor, compared to eighty cents per hour in the United States—and it showed. Chinese technicians did not have the tools or the training to manufacture to the specifications of his typewriter design. The gears cut in a Chinese workshop, Zhou was appalled to see, were "like the ragged teeth of an old Chinese lady past sixty." Dimensions and widths were eyeballed at best, and anything less than a thousandth of an inch couldn't be measured accurately. Reliable mechanical experts and draftsmen, like those in the United States who could carry out any engineer's instructions from a blueprint, were nonexistent. Speaking before a Chinese audience at the YMCA in Shanghai after his return, Zhou lamented, "I could and should have had the first machine built in the U.S.A."

He came to realize that his return to China might have been a mistake. It was a struggle, and not entirely due to the poor conditions. Though he came back as China's "industrial star," after the flurry of lecture invitations and media hype he had to face down mismatched expectations. The Commercial Press had hired a prizewinning engineer, but Zhou was unable to deliver. After two months, whispers began when the executives at the press heard of another, more "superior" typewriter— namely, Qi's—that had made better inroads in America. Zhang Yuanji, the director of the press, still wanted to manufacture a successful Chinese typewriter but clearly had doubts about whether he had hired the right person.

Meanwhile, Zhou stuck stubbornly to his vision, unwilling to settle for inferior workmanship. He tried ten different factories and met with ten disappointments. Shanghai was at the forefront of China's industry, but still couldn't produce anywhere near the quality Zhou required. None of the workers were able to help him make the fixed fonts on the cylinders adjustable. It was a simple alteration but crucial to improving his machine, as the modification would allow swapping characters in or out according to the frequency and context of use. A historian was more likely to repeat the word "ancient," for instance, while a novelist would use "cry," and both would expect the same typewriter to have the characters available. Zhou eventually gave up. He decided that the only place to build his machine was back in the United States, with his familiar contacts and network. He was going to request permission to move production abroad, even though his contract was for domestic employment.

It was a big ask—Zhou knew that and was anxious as he went to see his boss. Others were becoming interested in the idea of inventing a typewriting machine for the Chinese language. There would be another Qi Xuan before long.

Zhou went to the main office of the Commercial Press at 453 Honan Road. Director Zhang was already in his office, reading as usual through the English- and Chinese-language newspapers piled up on his worktable. He was an affable man, except when it came to business. Having been trained under the old civil exams system, Zhang had qualified for the distinguished imperial scholar ranking (the equivalent of a doctorate). He possessed a traditional scholar's demeanor and was a seasoned businessman as well. He never divulged more than was necessary. A progressive thinker and a beloved former teacher at Zhou's alma mater, Nanyang Public School, he turned to publishing solely because he believed in its mission—to educate the young with new knowledge and modern textbooks. While he shared in the higher cause of saving the nation through education, he was also fastidious when it came to running a publishing house. There was never a penny short in his account books and he always made good on his royalty payouts.

Matching his meticulousness was his sharp eye for young talent. So when someone mentioned to Zhang that there was a young man who had excelled in engineering at MIT and won a prize for his brilliant master's thesis, he was keen to have him on board. That day, though, sitting in his spartan office, his face must have looked rather humorless.

It had been ten months since Zhang had hired Zhou, and still no machine other than the prototype had materialized. When Zhou showed up, he probably knew not to expect a positive report. The young man walked in with the look of someone who had a favor to ask, not good news to deliver.

Zhou wanted the press to pay for the whole production process in the United States, but—he was quick to add—he would pay for his own travel expenses to and from America. It was clear to Zhang that Zhou was too much of a perfectionist to adhere to cost limits and deadlines. And it was bad business to move production offshore and put money back into America's coffers. Zhang explained that it would be difficult to justify such a large expense, given the uncertainty of the profitability of the machine. "Why don't we do this," Zhang offered slyly, as though doling out a favor. "Let's annul the old contract so you can freely go about pursuing this."

It was not the response Zhou had hoped for, and he was undoubtedly disappointed. Reading between the lines, he knew what the publisher meant. Zhang was cutting him loose, and this was all business. Zhou had to decide. Though the typewriter was his personal passion, other career paths were still open to him. Soon after that meeting, Zhou left the Commercial Press. Eventually he became the director of technology at China's most important state coal and iron company, Hanyeping. As for his typewriter, it was now the property of the press.

Zhang found someone hungrier and more eager to take over Zhou's project. Shu Zhendong was a proud graduate of Shanghai's very own Tongji University and did not have the prestige of a fancy American college degree. He had tried to intern in Germany, but the war disrupted that prospect. The Commercial Press offered him the best opportunity he could find, and he was not going to squander it.

He improved upon Zhou's prototype by eliminating the cylinders altogether, leaving all characters in plain view on an external tray instead, extractable by moving a needle forward and back and sideways. On the third try, he brought out a version that was fit for marketing. The Commercial Press put everything behind the final product. For the launch, they commissioned a short silent film—the first animation ever made in China—as an advertisement. The machine, with subsequent improvements, did what the press hoped it would do. It garnered interest from a wide range of companies and brought glory to the publishing house, which grew hungry for influence and power. A number of typewriting machines were built and sold, but mass production and distribution were still a distant goal. In another few years, Shu would enjoy an even bigger success. At the Philadelphia Sesquicentennial International Exhibition in 1926, his typewriter won the Commercial Press a medal of honor for its "ingenuity and adaptability."

Exactly fifty years after the first official Chinese observer wrote home about the Western typewriter at the Philadelphia fair, China was

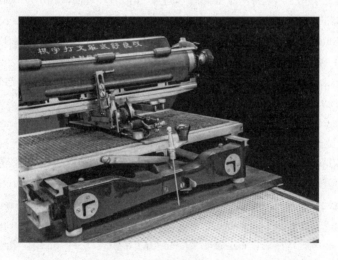

A later improved model of Zhou Houkun's original typewriter
by Shu Zhendong at the Commercial Press, ca. 1935. Hong
Family Papers, The Huntington Library, San Marino, CA.

able to shine a spotlight on its own machine. No longer was China the sick man of Asia on display, but instead it was the emerging master of its own fate in the mechanical age. Shu's model is now the only surviving version of Zhou's original invention. One of its later improved models ended up where Zhou would have wanted it—back in America. By way of a Chinese businessman who brought it with him from China and donated it along with his papers, it now rests as part of the permanent collection at the Huntington Library in San Marino, California, with a librarian looking after it. Though the contours of the engraved slugs are now worn smooth and the pointer too fragile to be sharp, it still bears the residual sheen of a once revolutionary machine.

WITH HIS TYPEWRITER, Zhou had reached the pinnacle of his scientific career, yet his brief star faded as quickly as it had risen. The idea of a Chinese typewriter would outlast him, but he would no longer have a hand in its evolution. It was ultimately not his engineering skills or commitment to the project that failed him, however. If anything held him back, it was likely something deeply personal. Few could have known at the time that, ten days after his victorious return to Shanghai, Zhou's father had died from a sudden illness. Zhou had dedicated his prototype typewriting machine to him. The loss was irreparable, the shock profound. His reunion with his father was too brief.

Zhou held on to his father's scattered texts for nineteen years until he himself was middle-aged. He spent his time editing and finally publishing his father's work. In the postscript he confessed his regret for having gone to the other side, abandoning his father's path in preference for Western learning. Glued to the very back of the thread-bound pages is a map he had personally drawn, carefully marked with the exact location of his father's birthplace. As far as we know, he never married; he eventually retired in the United States.

It's not hard to imagine that Zhou had seen his career path in much the same way he viewed the characters—with inviolable principles. He was an orderly man who set out to restore order. Qi, however, had more freedom or perhaps the ingenuity to think more flexibly, and he thereby imagined a different alternative. The Chinese script revolution faced two paths: it could keep its writing system intact and develop technology to keep it viable, or it could seek a deeper transformation within the structure of the character itself. To preserve tradition at all costs meant respecting the way the Chinese had always known their own written language, while taking chances meant remodeling the language on the structure of the alphabet, to see it anew from the perspective of outsiders and nonnative users. Certainly, some felt that the time had come to find out once and for all the alphabetic powers of the Chinese script, if any were hidden in its folds. There were rumors about a clever genius named Lin Yutang, who was neither an engineer nor an iconoclast but a literary master with words. He had apparently figured out a way to tap into those powers.

But a different, more public and official battle was also heating up. For at least as long as the late Qing script reformers clamored to phoneticize Chinese, attempts to use Chinese in international telegraphy had been a diplomatic nightmare. Instead of clever young inventors, this battle involved adroit negotiators from China's official ranks. As with the typewriter and world's fairs, China's interest in telegraphy was a matter of sovereignty. This time, however, there was no actual character form to puzzle out; it was all about numbers and codes. China had no native advantage and would have to claw its way to claim one that was entirely its own.

THREE

TIPPING THE SCALE
OF TELEGRAPHY
(1925)

WRITING IN CODES

When the first International Telegraph Conference convened in 1865, there were only twenty countries in attendance—nineteen European states plus Turkey. In the intervening six decades, telegraphy had grown at a breakneck pace. By the time China's Ministry of Transportation sent its first official delegation to the seventh conference in Paris, in 1925, they were joined by representatives from sixty-five other countries. China needed to make an important appeal before the international community. Under the existing rules of international telegraphy, users of the Chinese language were at a considerable disadvantage. The Chinese delegation had to explain why that was so, why it was a problem, and, most of all, why other countries should care.

At the time, the shortcomings of telegraphy in Chinese were exclusively China's concern. Telegraphy had been designed first and foremost for Western alphabetic languages—English above all. Its original inventors, Samuel Morse and Alfred Vail, did not expect it to spread around the world to countries where ideographic writing prevailed.

The first successful transatlantic telegraphic cable was laid across the Atlantic Ocean in 1866. Copper wires wrapped in gutta-percha rubber and surrounded by layers of iron wire encased in jute or hemp (for protection from fish bites and ocean tides) spanned 1,852 miles of the ocean floor, connecting Ireland to Newfoundland. It was heralded in *Scientific American* as an "instantaneous highway of thought between the Old and New Worlds." Breaking news, stock prices, business transactions, military directives, contract negotiations, and other time-sensitive communications could henceforth travel from Europe to America in what seemed like an instant—seventeen hours, compared to ten days by steamer. Telegraphy was the internet of its era. Anyone who couldn't use telegraphy did not just lose time; they were also disconnected from the progress that the technology enabled.

The original promoters of telegraphy promised that it would allow countries to leave strife and wars behind, ushering in an era of open exchange and collaboration; it was the beginning of a new age. Europe's great powers had restrained themselves from waging major wars against one another for most of the nineteenth century, and now they saw greater benefits in cultivating mutual respect and striking a balance of powers. One of the first test messages sent across the ocean floor brimmed with optimism: "Glory to God in the highest, and on earth, peace, good will to men." Telegraphy was seen as the harbinger of peace and prosperity.

At least, it was seen that way by Europe and the United States. The problem for the rest of the nations was planted at the beginning. In Morse code, the basic symbols were dots and dashes. The system's

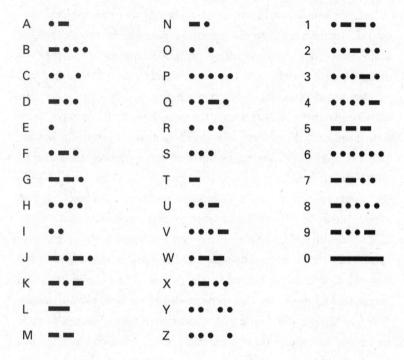

Morse code.

twenty-six combinations of dots and dashes, ranging from one to four symbols, were meant to accommodate the twenty-six letters of the alphabet, with another ten combinations of five symbols each for numbers zero to nine.

To send a message, a telegraph operator pressed an electric switch, in the form of a key: a short tap for a dot and a long one for a dash. The message was converted into an electric current that traveled along the wires and was reverse translated into letters and numbers on the receiving end. The sound of clicking patterns could become so familiar that an experienced telegrapher could tell what word was being coded from its distinct rhythm.

Telegraph costs were determined by how long they took to transmit—each dot or space was a single unit, and a dash—three times as long as a dot—was three units. As Morse explained early on, his system was designed to be cost-efficient. The most frequently used letter in English, "e," was also the least expensive: It was represented by a single dot. The high frequency of "e" holds true for most European languages, from Italian to Dutch. But Morse code clearly favored the American English alphabet. An English letter takes up somewhere between one and thirteen units. To add even a single diacritical mark to the letter "a"—as when making the French "à"—required ten more units. So there was already plenty to disagree about among Roman alphabet users.

The inequities of Morse code were on a different scale for the Chinese. International telegraphy recognized only the Roman alphabet letters and Arabic numerals used by the majority of its members, which meant that Chinese, too, had to be mediated via letters and numbers. Whereas English could be English, and Italian mostly Italian, Chinese had to be something other than itself. Every Chinese character was transmitted as a string of four to six numbers, each of which cost more than a letter. The assigned code for a Chinese character first had to be looked up in a codebook before being converted to the dots and dashes of Morse code. Coding and converting Chinese characters into an ordinary telegram of twenty-five words required at least half an hour, whereas a comparable message in English took only about two minutes. Untold opportunity costs accrued with every telegraph that was delayed when the operator had to pause to check a character against its assigned number in a codebook or had to take extra time to correct an error. Imagine the time and lives sacrificed when a military command cannot be relayed quickly to a general on the battlefield. Or the profits lost when competitors have the means to make bids more quickly. That was China's situation relative to all foreigners who were conducting business on its soil. The Chinese also paid more for the same message.

A telegraph in Chinese sent to England in the 1880s was twice as expensive as one sent in English. The costs weren't just due to the extra length of Chinese messages. Most telegraphic lines in China were built and run by foreign companies and governments who were free to set their own tariffs and standards. China did not own its own physical infrastructure until eleven years after the first cable was laid on its territory in 1870 and had to pay foreign operators to send telegrams on its own soil.

China suffered for being a latecomer to international telegraphy at the end of the nineteenth century, and its disadvantages grew with time. The country's repeated complaints went unheeded by the major national stakeholders and members of the telegraphic union in Europe. They were too busy fighting among themselves and defending their own interests to deal with the grievances of non–Western alphabet users.

China could not afford to lose at the negotiation table in Paris. With mounting debt and the majority of its railways and mining rights still under foreign ownership or co-ownership in the 1920s, Chinese leaders saw the urgency in not missing any more opportunities to assert the nation's rights. For decades China had been on the receiving end of imposed treaties. But the May Fourth Movement of 1919 awakened the national consciousness and brought it to a turning point. Anti-imperialist sentiments gripped the nation, and popular indignation focused on China's concessions to Western nations, past and present. The people were demanding that the country reclaim its sovereignty. Let China regain what was rightfully its own, angry editorials in magazines and newspapers insisted. It was time for China to repossess its abundant natural resources and develop them into raw materials and industrial products. Put an end to the foreigners' pillage, and China would have more than enough resources to power its own much-needed industrial revolution. But when the young nation fragmented into fiefdoms under the Chinese military warlords, each with their own interest to look after, that disunity within made it even more difficult to deal with the different European stakeholders.

There were a few ways for the Chinese language to bridge the technology divide, but none were without problems. One option was to send Chinese telegrams in Romanized spelling by using the transliterations that missionaries had left behind. But those transliterations were legion, each tied to the native language of the missionary and the local dialects they encountered in their treks to the most remote corners of the empire. Their idea of Chinese was whatever dialect they heard on the ground. The question of how to represent the tones of a standard Chinese pronunciation in a single Romanized system would not be resolved until the 1950s by the Chinese Communist Party. For the time being, Romanization remained an ongoing experiment.

Another option was to develop telegraphic codes and machines specifically for the Chinese themselves. The earliest known Chinese telegraphic machine was devised by the American Baptist missionary Daniel MacGowan in 1851. But the machine was more of a one-off curiosity than a technology the Chinese themselves would have found easy to use. The next known attempt to create a machine was by a Chinese businessman named Wang Chengrong, who lived in Paris in the 1860s and knew both French and English. He apparently invented a prototype Chinese-language telegraphic machine that managed around a thousand characters, arranged into sixteen categories and ten subsidiary groupings. He sent a letter to China's foreign-affairs bureau soliciting funds to develop it for mass production. But the court was not interested in Western technology, having already rebuffed preliminary telegraphy proposals from the French and Russians. Wang Chengrong's proposal was shelved and the machine never saw the light of day.

The only viable route for making telegraphy more equitable for the Chinese language was diplomacy. The ruling Nationalist government needed someone at the Paris proceedings who could be not only an observer but also an effective advocate. Leverage was necessary, and as China had none, the government searched for someone to perform no less than a miracle. Someone diplomatically adroit who also spoke English like a gentleman and knew how Westerners thought.

AT FIRST GLANCE, Wang Jingchun did not seem fit for that role. The managing director of the Beijing-Hankou Railway and head of China's delegation, he was not a terribly robust-looking man by any account. He had a long oval face that rested delicately on a slender neck and a smile too faint to make out behind his dense mustache. His coworkers in the government bureaucracy made fun of his introverted demeanor, which was seen as a sign of timidity. If you didn't see Wang sticking his neck out for anything, they offered, it was because he was nursing his frail constitution in a remote sanatorium. What they missed was the steeliness of his quiet persistence. Wang had an even-temperedness that made him personable, even disarming. His hooded eyes could lull people into divulging too much when he fixed his gaze on them. He was a patient, inconspicuous strategist.

He had been at this game for a long time, attending international congresses since he was twenty-two, and his sense of calm came from a deep well of experience. He first represented a Chinese merchants group at the Louisiana Purchase Exposition in St. Louis in 1904, then stayed on to study science at Ohio Wesleyan University before pursuing a degree in civil engineering at Yale, followed by an M.A. in railway administration, and finally a Ph.D. in economics and political science at the University of Illinois. He edited *The Chinese Students' Monthly* for a year and was the president of the Chinese Students' Alliance, where he garnered wide respect from his peers.

As a technical expert to the Versailles Conference in 1919, Wang witnessed China's deeply felt betrayal when the German concession of the Shandong Peninsula was not returned to China but was instead given to Japan as part of the victor's spoils. Though he was patriotic, he did not let his anger boil over. If anything, the event convinced him of the importance of trying to understand the West from inside its institutions—their histories, structures, and methods of operation. China's position in the international arena would remain precarious for some time to come, and its future depended on advocates as much as on engineers.

During his years in the United States, he made the best of his opportunities. He learned English, French, and German and the nitty-gritty details of managing national infrastructures. He traced the financial history of Britain's railway system and mulled over its strengths and weaknesses. Wang's skills and fortitude were well recognized by leaders of the republic. He was later put in charge of unifying the accounts of China's own railway system, which was still under different spheres of foreign influence. It was a swamp—all the different foreign powers used their own accounting and standardization systems, in their own languages. Even the track gauges varied, meaning trains couldn't run on tracks built by different operators. All the while, Wang maintained his role as an informal ambassador. He was good at drawing comparisons to make it easier for the Americans to grasp the Chinese point of view. In one article, he explained to the Americans why railway loans were such a complex issue for China. A loan in the United States, he pointed out, is understood to be a commercial transaction between two parties. Both sides enter into a pact willingly. But in China, such loans are considered treaties between the Chinese government and other governments, often forced by one side. Colonial asymmetry, he conveyed, colored every aspect of China's present need for industrialization. China could not begin to develop or modernize because of this skewed balance of power.

His calm rhetoric, at the same time, tamped down any impulse toward resentment. Wang always stressed that solutions could not be found in blame, and he stuck to that advice before Western, as well as Chinese, audiences. "With us," he once advised the minister of communications in Beijing, "the question is not to regret or complain over the past but to endeavor to make the best out of the future." That was his mission.

In 1911, like many others of his generation, Wang returned from America to a sobering state of affairs in revolutionary China. The streets were stained with blood and the country was gripped by the pathos of national survival. Indemnity payments and foreign loans had been taking up half of the government's budget, while the foreign control over tariffs meant that China had no means to save itself from bankruptcy. On top of that, fledgling industrial and banking systems rested on a still largely agrarian society with a low literacy rate. Once the overthrow of the dynasty was complete, he assessed, China would find itself in a crippled state. The country had no real means for reconstruction, let alone modernization.

Wang was eager to offer his institutional know-how, diplomatic skills, and industrial knowledge to the government. Sun Zhongshan soon appointed him to the post of foreign affairs secretary in the new provisional Republican regime in Nanjing. As the young republic plummeted into fractious warlordism, Wang's diligence and honesty boosted morale among his colleagues and subordinates. Despite the chaos, he managed to put the railway system on sound footing during his appointment by streamlining the different accounting systems. It was no small achievement, as every contract had to be individually negotiated with the different foreign-owned telegraphic companies and railway operators, which were often intertwined in proprietorship. It was like dealing with different state entities behind every set rate for transmission or share of dividends. Contracts worked like treaties, and every clause and agreement came with political stakes.

Wang's success meant he was soon entrusted with more international roles. He was sent as an official delegate to the Fifth International Congress of Chambers of Commerce in Boston in 1912. During his student years at Yale and the University of Illinois, he had learned the mannerisms that made Americans feel at ease—he was friendly and jocular, polished yet approachable. He knew just what to say. "The new China will be a new United States," he pledged to the American public. Half a page of *The New York Times* was taken up with a report of his address at the Congress of Chambers of Commerce, where he promised: "What we want now is to do business with the United States and other foreign nations—real business, not business hopelessly mixed with international politics." To show that China was entirely onboard, he advocated for the use of the Gregorian calendar instead of China's own lunar calendar to facilitate trade and commerce with the outside world.

As the associate director of the Beijing-Mukden (now Shenyang) Railway, Wang was clearly determined to show America and the world that China was no longer weak, sleepy, and begrudging. He graciously shrugged off the Western invasions and unequal treaties of the past. They belonged to old-style imperialism, whereas now China was ready to engage in commerce. Many of its aspiring future leaders had graduated from American colleges, like he had. They were Americans through and through, he counseled, and could talk football like anyone in the Midwest: "Our Government is American; our Constitution is American; many of us feel like Americans." A black-and-white photograph taken at his speech that day showed him with a rare broad smile. To his left side, a shiny American-built steam locomotive was poised to charge toward the reader as though it were barreling off the printed page.

To his right was the scene of a crowded train station in China that awaited better technology. Wang stands between the two worlds, a mes-

Wang Jingchun addressing Americans on China's desire to do business.
The New York Times, November 10, 1912.

senger of hope ready to connect America's industrial power with China's hunger for progress.

Everywhere he went, Wang repeated the same message: You can do business with China, and China wants to do business with you. He made a cameo at the Panama-Pacific International Exposition of 1915 and helped plant China's new five-striped national flag on the exhibition grounds to a twenty-one-gun salute. Three years later, he was dispatched to Europe as an official representative of the Ministry of Transportation to negotiate China's industrialization and railway rights. Wang was a near contemporary of Zhou Houkun. But unlike the young MIT engineer, poised to be an inventor, Wang was rising through the government ranks. From clerkship to directorship, he proved himself time and time again to be one of China's most able bureaucrats.

His long list of credentials earned him a ticket to Paris in 1925 as the managing director of the Beijing-Hankou Railway and the head of China's delegation at the International Telegraph Conference. Outside the cavernous hall of the Romanesque chapel at the Sorbonne where the International Telegraph Conference was taking place, the French capital donned the yellow and rust colors of fall, and the shade in the parks drew lovers to benches. Street cafés spilled over with laughter and clatter. But Wang expected little love at the Sorbonne. Telegraphy was a cutthroat business, with the industry growing more profitable by the day, sharpening the rivalry among the Europeans and raising the stakes for China.

During the next two months, Wang and his team would have to marshal every international statute and every means of persuasion to regain China's sovereignty. From the West's own evolving international legal framework, Wang knew that all nations enjoyed the right to act in accordance with and to protect their sovereign interests—at least in theory. That much he had to work with. He would appeal to the very terms that the Westerners themselves held dear. Although prepared to fight, Wang harbored little animosity toward the West. He was as clear-eyed about the shortcomings of his beloved country as he was about the numbers in an accounting ledger. The truth was that the West had not put China in its present beleaguered state; China was responsible for what China had become. The country could have been part of telegraphy at the very beginning; it could have claimed its sovereignty. But it gave it all away—and didn't realize it had done so until it was too late.

IN THE 1870s, the outlook for telegraphy was upbeat, even euphoric. Before the decade's end, it was predicted that 90 percent of the human race would be enmeshed in its communication network. Yet China seemed bent on defying that prophecy. As the Danes, the British, the French, and the Russians rushed to build more cables to connect telegraphy networks beyond their territories and into East Asia, China demurred.

The Chinese still recalled vividly how the British had made China sign away its right of tariff autonomy at the end of the First Opium War. Under the term of the Treaty of Nanjing, apart from paying reparations, China had to open five treaty ports to foreign trade, and the tariffs were to be determined solely by the British. A year later, the Americans followed suit and extracted similar terms. Then the French—and the Swedes and the Norwegians—elbowed their way into the country using the American model. Working in concert, the Western powers piggybacked on one another's extractions and closed in. They had cleverly written the "most favored nation" clause into the Treaty of Tianjin during the Second Opium War. It stipulated that if China granted any privilege to one power, it was legally bound to grant the same privilege to all. By the end of the nineteenth century more than eighty treaty ports were opened to foreign trade.

So as telegraphy took off, Chinese court officials feared it was just another pretext for foreigners to extend their reach. Some officials warned that telegraphy embodied Western imperialism's latest method of infiltration, this time in the name of communications and technology. If the foreigners were given the permission to lay cables on their soil, they would surely not stop there. And should there be a scratch on a single cable, the foreigners could be expected to blame the Chinese and demand reparations.

When Russia came knocking in 1865, proposing to connect a Siberian line to Beijing, China declined. The empire had no need of such technology, said Prince Gong, who dealt with the barbarians on behalf of the court. It was the same answer he had given to the French minister five years earlier, when he tried to solicit interest with the gift of telegraphic manuals. The kingdom had its own extensive imperial courier service in place, Prince Gong explained, with good men on horseback. Telegraphy, he sniffed, would be useless at best.

The Europeans paid little heed to Prince Gong's refusal. Instead they took a more aggressive approach, going behind China's back. The Danes were the first to act. On a cloudless moonlit night in November 1870, they ran a stealth operation, unloading cables from a Danish frigate via a French marine base and laying them in the ground along the western bank of the Wusong River. The job was completed before dawn and went undetected.

While taking a lion's share of the Chinese market for themselves, the Europeans were also locked in a competition with one another. Denmark, which owned the telegraphic monopoly the Great Northern Telegraph Company, had its eye on dominating the East Asian market and was trying to stay one step ahead of Britain's Eastern Telegraphy Company. Each used different excuses to get the Chinese to make allowances: the lines would ease communication between their own citizens in China; telegraphy would facilitate the rescues from shipwrecks off the coast.

Resentment brewed in the countryside against the intrusion of cable lines. They cut across swaths of the hinterland, and it was believed that they disturbed the spirits of ancestors in the burial grounds and strangled the fengshui on property, damning crops and harvests. That brought ill luck, it was reported, as well as sudden death and calamity. An 1875 report to the throne explained why: "The foreigners know of God and Jesus, but not ancestors. Upon entering their religion one must first destroy the idols in one's home. In China, the life after death is treated the same as life in this world. This has been so for thousands of years, and great importance is attached to where the body and spirit are stored. The foreigners bury their telegraphic wires in the ground, burrowing through and forcing their way across in all four directions until the earth's veins are all but severed, making the burial sites vulnerable to wind and flood. How can this sit well on our conscience?"

Popular reactions to Western telegraphy were also duly exploited. During their uprising in 1900, the Boxers tore up cables and knocked down lines from Zhili to Shandong. The Empress Dowager was not the only one who knew how to direct resentment against the foreigners. Local officials also learned how to play up popular grievances and superstitions. They encouraged peasants to vandalize or steal segments of cable. At times, the telegraphic poles and lines were simply stolen for their high-quality metal. The authorities were purposefully slow to make arrests, dragging their feet while registering the foreigners' complaints.

In 1881, influential ministers at court like Li Hongzhang—who recognized that westernization was unstoppable—saw that the country needed to start taking back control and finally established its own telegraph bureau. A line connecting Tianjin to Shanghai was built with a lot of public fanfare. But by then, the technology bore the irreversible stamp of Europe's first-mover advantage. The Danes had designed a telegraphic code system to use for the Chinese script. It was the first ever, and it moved the advantage further into the Europeans' court. China had a lot of catching up to do.

CRACKING THE CHINESE CODE for telegraphy was the culmination of a long process of Westerners grappling with the Chinese language. The Chinese script had fascinated European admirers since the time of sixteenth-century Jesuit missionary Matteo Ricci, yet few foreigners had been able to learn the language well enough to earn the respect of the Chinese. Ricci's quick memorization of thousands of characters was legendary, but his curiosity and stamina were rare. Many others would falsely claim to have grasped the language's hidden key.

Europeans often took fancy for fact. The Sinologist Athanasius Kircher's famous illustration of strange-looking Chinese characters in *Oedipus Aegyptiacus* (1652–54) was the first publication to show to Europeans how the Chinese script actually looked. Its funky script was lifted from a Chinese folk almanac that no learned Chinese at the time treated as a legitimate source. Nonetheless its illustrations fueled the imagination of European missionaries and scholars who obsessed over the Chinese script for the next several centuries.

The age of telegraphy steered that long fascination in a different direction. The Chinese script was no longer just a distant fanciful object; it was a technical puzzle to be worked out like a geometric equation. That was when a French adventurer joined the quest of devout missionaries and pedantic scholars. Count Pierre Henri Stanislas d'Escayrac de Lauture was a pioneer in developing Chinese telegraphy. In 1860, he volunteered to be attached to the joint British and French expedition to Beijing. The purpose of the mission was to refresh the terms of ongoing treaties and China's understanding of Western superiority. D'Escayrac was captured by the Chinese on a morning scouting mission and was tortured and mutilated while in prison. During that time, the joint forces overran and burned down the emperor's Summer Palace as punishment for not honoring the First Opium War treaty. After several weeks in a mud cell padded with excrement, d'Escayrac was rescued.

Any lesser man would have been irreversibly traumatized by the experience—d'Escayrac had trouble using his hands to write after his imprisonment—but the encounter did not turn him against China or its culture. Instead, d'Escayrac set out to devise a telegraphic code for the Chinese language, using a typographic engraver's logic of dividing up the characters into two halves, much as Qi Xuan would later do with his Chinese typewriter in the 1920s. But he lacked the knowledge of modern linguistics and engineering, and he ended up designing a rather abstract "tekachotomic" table—made up of semantic grids—with little practical use. It was a specimen of ingenious but perhaps isolated imagination and remained nothing more than that.

It took a pragmatic, unsentimental Danish financier to bring the long pursuit of the Chinese telegraphy to a decisive turn in the last quarter of the nineteenth century. C. F. Tietgen, an industrial magnate and bank mogul, was also the head of the Great Northern Telegraph Company. A ruthless capitalist who looked as stern as Martin Luther, Tietgen had been hoping to make a foray into the untapped Chinese market. In 1868, a visit from a Chinese diplomatic mission prompted him to reassess the country's potential. China had embarked on a quest for "self-strengthening" in the early 1860s, an attempt after the two humiliating Opium Wars to build up military and industrial capacity by constructing shipyards and arsenals with the help of foreign advisors and instructors. Tietgen spotted an opportunity.

He saw that what stood between his ambitions and China's enormous market was language. Tietgen's first objective was to make it as easy as possible for the Chinese to use telegraphy, going straight for the preference of the consumer. He began looking for someone to develop a telegraphic code for the Chinese script, but Denmark was a small place. The best expert he could find in the tiny southern Scandinavian kingdom was a professor of astronomy at the Østervold Observatory, Hans Schjellerup. The professor had learned Chinese after a long study of Arabic, which he acquired in order to compare the records of lunar eclipses in the Middle East and Europe.

At Tietgen's request, the professor began to work on compiling a list of characters, making paper-thin flashcards by hand. By April 1870, he had made good progress. He sent along the first two pages containing the initial 260 characters of the proposed Chinese telegraphic dictionary in a letter to Tietgen. He ordered them in the way a Chinese dictionary would—by the 214 radicals of the *Kangxi Dictionary*—so that any Chinese user would find it familiar. The characters were sequenced according to their radicals and stroke counts. He also called the radicals "keys," harkening back to the term used by Sinologists before him who believed there was a deep secret to unlock within the Chinese script.

That preliminary draft of a telegraphic code for Chinese was all the professor managed to complete before he had to return to his research at the observatory. But it was enough to get things off the ground. The draft was passed to the next overseer, Edouard Suenson, Great Northern's first regional managing director of the Far East, who then took it to the port city of Shanghai. There, foreigners bustled on the Bund, and information traveled fast in the expat network. If anyone needed a license to import a shipment of goods or to find out which way the political wind blew at the foreign affairs office, they could find the right contacts there. The director hoped he might just as easily find someone who could finish the professor's work for the company. And he did: a dashing, thirty-three-year-old French harbor captain named Septime Auguste Viguier.

VIGUIER POSSESSED THE CONFIDENCE and skill set that Great Northern was looking for. He had already worked on developing a code for Chinese telegraphy years earlier for the French government in support of their failed efforts to interest the Chinese Empire in their telegraph cables. He was well versed in early word-copying machines like the Caselli pantelegraph, a precursor to the modern-day fax machine. When the French project was shelved, Viguier ended up in Shanghai—ripe for the Danes' recruitment.

He was the best candidate but not well-liked. Colleagues immediately noted his preening and boastfulness—the French way, they sneered. Viguier later also had a nasty exchange with the managing director Suenson, and his relationship with the company soured over questions of compensation and credit. Nonetheless, Viguier was able to

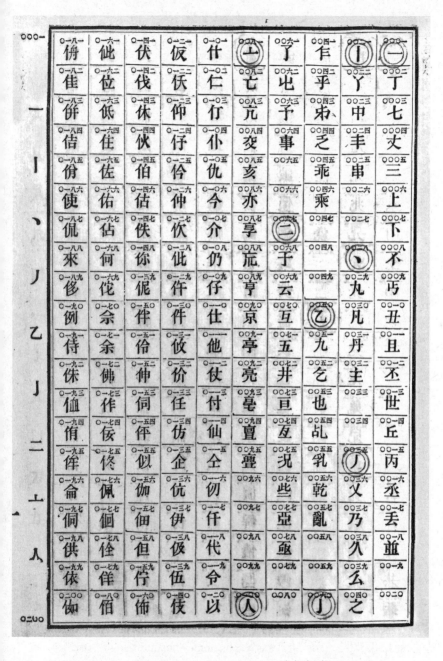

From Septime Auguste Viguier, *Dianbao xinshu* 电报新书. Shanghai:
American Presbyterian Mission Press, 1872. Danish National Archives.

work quickly enough to build out the Danish professor's incomplete scheme. By June 1870, he had the first version. In 1872, he delivered the final, standardized telegraphic code table for 6,899 characters in *The New Book for the Telegraph* (*Dianbao xinshu*).

The professor's idea was that the scheme could include 5,454 characters, but he himself did not get far. He recommended using numbers to represent each character so it could be sent and decoded back into Chinese at the receiving end. It was up to Viguier to flesh out the system according to that concept, assign the actual numbers, and figure out how best to organize and delimit the number of characters in the final codebook.

Viguier came up with a tabular form of twenty rows and ten columns per page. He assigned an arbitrary four-digit code from 0001 to 9999 to each character, with empty spaces left for potentially 3,000 more codes to accommodate customized vocabulary for individual business purposes. Each page contained 200 square spaces for listing 200 characters and their numerical codes. The code only included a relatively small number of characters out of the 45,000 or so that were extant. The mass scaling of telegraphy meant that it was geared toward the common person and the common tongue, so restricting the number of characters was not only efficient but also practical.

Beneath the manipulation of numbers, though, was a more important conceptual reorientation. The arbitrary numeralization of characters meant that there was no longer any meaningful correlation between characters and their codes. No longer an enigma or possessing a "key," there was little romance about the Chinese script in the eyes of the telegraphers. It mattered little what characters looked like or how they had gained their shape through centuries of use. The last vestiges of the radical, in dictating any shape or form of the telegraphic code, disappeared. What remained was a consistent—but indifferent—application of four numbers. The Arabic numerals indicated nothing of a character's shape, meaning, or sound. Western telegraphic codes turned the Chinese script into a technology in the true sense—a practical instrument shaped to solve a practical problem.

In Viguier's system, a Chinese sender would essentially have to grapple with his or her native language as a foreign code. Viguier left only a couple of aids for the native speaker. The sender would still be able look up a character by its radical by referring to the "dispatch table," which was arranged by Kangxi radicals, but that would be it. The sender then took the four-digit code written above the character and entered it as Morse dots and dashes. On the receiving end, the process would be reversed. The operator would use a mirror version of the codebook, the "reception table," which contained the exact same characters except this time arranged by number rather than radical, and restore the character from the four-digit code. To make it slightly more palatable, Viguier *chinoisai*—"Sinicized"—the system by using Chinese numerals: 一, 二, 三 instead of 1, 2, 3, etc. But that did not change the fact that the nature of the character had been drastically altered.

Viguier seemed confident that once the Chinese could easily use their own language for sending telegrams, all the other problems—the mistrust of Western technology, the destruction of the cables, the hesitations of the court—would vanish. Instead of requiring translation into European languages for transmission, the Chinese script could directly participate via numbers. That took at least one extra step out of the equation.

It made perfect sense to a Frenchman who was thinking of the Western alphabet in the only way he knew how—from his own perspective. He assumed that if the alphabetization of Chinese was offensive or gave the Chinese pause, then using the neutral representation of numbers would solve the problem. No forced assimilation, no antiforeign hostility. But, in fact, he merely made Chinese a second-class citizen in the alphabetic system because of the original provisions made in the Morse code: numbers were priced higher than letters. Sending a telegram composed wholly of numbers was in fact the most expensive way of communicating in Morse, as every digit took up more dots and dashes than any letter in the alphabet. Viguier, in short, dealt with a problem but not the premise that created it. But neither Viguier nor the Great Northern was going to concern themselves with that. They had achieved their immediate goal; they got what they wanted out of the Chinese script.

With the company's powerful backing, Viguier's four-digit model spread. He also recommended the installation of three major telegraphic lines to consolidate Great Northern's influence. The lines would criss-cross China from north to south and east to west and extend smaller capillaries deep into its distant provinces. Now that the Chinese script could be transmitted through the electric pulses of telegrams, Great Northern saw no reason to hold back. One year after the Danes installed a cable by stealth at night, they were now emboldened to make a concerted, open push.

Thus the Chinese telegraphic code was born. What a handful of Danish company men—who did not know much Chinese—had dreamt up to sell a product was now something China would be stuck with for more than half a century. Viguier's codebook became the model for all subsequent Chinese telegraphic codebooks, right down to Wang Jing-chun's time.

But Viguier's telegraphic code did not go unchallenged. Almost immediately, the Chinese tried to outdo and improve upon it. A quiet young Chinese translator who had been part of that diplomatic mission to Europe in 1868, Zhang Deyi, became the first Chinese to do so. Zhang noted the pain of having to send Chinese messages back to the Chinese office in China in "foreign letters" whenever more urgent service was required. He also saw how Western telegrams were more secure, as secret messages were sent in numbers. That inspired Zhang to construct his own Chinese telegraphic codebook by following a similar format.

While the published version of Viguier's work was an important landmark, Zhang zeroed in on its sloppiness. Viguier's numbering of characters did not make them terribly easy to use for the Chinese. The continuous numbers did not separate out characters into groups, which was how the Chinese were accustomed to searching for characters in a dictionary. He decided to trim down the format of Viguier's system and do some reorganization to make its content clearer. Zhang's own *New Method of Telegraphy* (*Dianxin xinfa*) was published two years after Viguier came up with a draft of his telegraphic code in 1873. It reordered the characters so that the numbers were less arbitrary. Zhang used the same 214 radicals, but reselected about 7,000 characters from the *Kangxi Dictionary* and assigned them numbers from 0001 to 8000.

The main difference between Zhang's and Viguier's codebooks was their visual arrangement, which mattered all the more if you were a telegraph operator under pressure to be fast and exact, with little time to linger over any entry for confirmation. Zhang provided a better organizing index and included more characters. The rows and cells were rearranged in a ten-by-ten grid. All 214 radicals were labeled with red ink, reasserting the organizing principle of traditional Chinese lexicons, leaving lots of blank squares for other characters. Zhang also left space for keying simple encryptions. This was done in Western telegrams by shifting the code a few letters down the alphabet. For instance, if one were to set the encryption key to go back three letters in the alphabet, SECRET would be instead spelled as PBZOBQ. A multiple of ten in cell structure made that easier to do with Chinese characters, giving each character a specific coordinate on the grid. To make a character easier to look up for positional encryption, Zhang had each

From Zhang Deyi, *Dianxin xinfa* 电信新法, 1873.
Danish National Archives.

page contain the same size grid of characters. That meant they could be located more conveniently than if they were simply listed, line by line, as in a typical Western telegraphic codebook.

Sending a secret telegram in Chinese had turned out to be a huge ordeal. There was no easy way to encrypt the characters other than a briefly popular domestic trick of using certain pairs of Chinese characters to stand in for dates. China's own encryption methods, using Chinese characters, did not amount to much. Later attempts to compose or encrypt Chinese telegraphic codes were disorganized, and secret codebooks, color coded, also fell victim to the general lack of bureaucratic efficiency or security. Top-secret codebooks were often copied or circulated without authorization, in short supply or unavailable, duplicated with the wrong color labels, or simply leaked. By the conclusion of the First Sino-Japanese War in 1895, which ended in China's defeat and the ceding of Taiwan to Japan, it was revealed that China's telegrams had been intercepted and decoded by the Japanese for more than twenty years. The political and diplomatic costs were incalculable.

Zhang's most important change to Viguier's scheme, however, was to essentially offer a new Morse code, the Chinese way. He did not just keep it limited as a scheme for the Chinese language but also went through the trouble of adding a four-digit code for each of the twenty-six alphabet letters and ten Arabic numerals. His idea was to make this system accessible to all, not just the Chinese, thereby signaling that his improved version was as good as any existing, universal telegraphic coding standard. He was already thinking of reclaiming the code from the perspective of the Chinese script, even as it was being made subject to the rules of foreign standards. While Viguier made a local gesture by writing the numbers in Chinese—so the Chinese operators could easily recognize them in the codebook—Zhang was decidedly more global and took the long view by changing them to Arabic numerals. While the alphabet mediated the Chinese language's access to telegraphy, Zhang turned the tables by coming up with China's own way of representing and accommodating the Western alphabet and all its possible script systems.

Yet for all the contributions Zhang and others made to advance telegraphy for the Chinese script, their efforts were relegated to the background. It was Viguier who enjoyed the fame, while Zhang's invention remained little known and incorrectly recorded. Two generations of Western scholars and experts did not realize that Zhang Deyi went by the aliases of Zhang Deming and Zhang Zaichu (it was a common practice for Chinese to have a given name and one or more studio names as an artist or a literary persona) and that he signed his telegraphic codebook with his two aliases—Deming Zaichu. Historians mistook it as someone utterly different named De Mingzai, lobbing off "chu" from "Zaichu," thereby wrongly identifying the family name as "De." It is just as if they, too, had encrypted his name by shifting it one character over, thereby failing to bring this important historical link to light. A crucial connection, direct from Tietgen to Zhang Deyi, had been buried for most of the last century.

At long last, in the 1920s, the time came for a reckoning. The task was given to Wang Jingchun, who, despite the entangled history of Chinese and Western telegraphy, knew that harping on a long list of grievances could backfire. It was unlikely that China could shame the Westerners, for whom shame was not a central cultural value, into voluntarily correcting the situation. If neither complaint nor guilt would work, a different tactic had to be found.

BACK AT THE SORBONNE, the telegraph conference had ground on for two weeks. The sessions were held from nine a.m. to five p.m. every day, with four simultaneous sessions running on topics such as rules and regulations, pricing, and editorial work. Wang's team put in extra hours in the mornings and nights to review the proceedings, making sure they understood what had been said in order to plot their strategies and responses for the next day. None of them spoke fluent French, so they hired a native French speaker to help. The proceedings, though, continued to be centered on Europeans' issues, and so Wang had yet to speak.

The European delegates aired their complaints, one by one. Wang sat through the conversation and no doubt tried to figure out how he could steer the conversation without seeming partisan to China's own national interests, so as to gain the trust and respect of his international counterparts. Except for China and Japan, every delegate was from a country or locale that used some form of alphabet—Latin, Cyrillic, or Arabic. Even Japan had a syllabic writing system and was not solely dependent on ideographic writing the way the Chinese were. China's case was unique.

The country had by then built tens of thousands of miles of telegraphic lines, enough to link it to global communications and trade. It bothered Wang that while the four-digit code got the Chinese language into telegraphy, it did so at a steep premium and didn't get the characters themselves recognized as a telegraphic language. They were entirely absent, proxied by numbers. Most of the meetings at international telegraphic conferences were spent debating the rules and setting the regulations for how many letters ought to be used to convey a message, and at what price. The goal of an international body like the International Telegraphic Union that sponsored the Paris conference was to make sure that no one gamed the system unfairly, but the truth was that cheating was rampant.

Given that telegrams were priced by the letter, senders tried to be brief. A telegram, recorded in 1854 from a mother to her son, was as succinct as it was to the point: "Come home. A rolling stone gathers no moss." To which the son responded with equal force in persuasion: "Come here. A setting hen never grows fat." The shortest Twitter-like communication was between an American merchant seeking news from his London agent: "?" The reply was "0."

More often, people skirted the rules a little. They came up with shorter spellings—like "immidiatly" for "immediately," "nuf sed," for "enough said"—or used foreign-language words when the pricing was by letters rather than words. After pricing by word count was introduced in the late 1860s, users began to combine words—"smorning" for "this morning," "frinstance" for "for instance." They also caught on quickly to the idea that they could pay less by packing more content into each message, this time by manipulating words into representing something that had nothing at all to do with their original meaning. There were even how-to books about cutting corners. An 1884 manual on how to cheapen the rate of telegraphy recommended "CELESTIFY" for "I think it will be no cheaper" and "DANDELION" for "if it is damaged." "GULLIBLE," according to the 1896 *Atlas Universal Travelers' and Business Telegraphic Cipher Code*, meant "baggage seized by custom," while "REVERE," appropriated by a mining stock brokerage firm in 1910, was diverted to stand in for a whopping thirty-one-word phrase that was no doubt useful for dealing with customers' complaints: "Wires being down, your telegram did not reach us in time to transact any business today, and as your orders are good for the week, we will try to execute tomorrow." Telegraphic companies grew weary of unauthorized orthography, and the persistent rule bending pushed them to define several times what a word was. Over time, stricter rules and definitions about what was permissible, and more important, whether the word used was in accordance with its meaning in a dictionary, had to be made explicit. A foundational distinction between plain text and secret text gradually emerged.

Plain language, reaffirms Article 8 of the International Service Regulations of 1925, is "that which presents an intelligible meaning in one or more of the languages authorised for international telegraph correspondence," while code language is "composed of words not combined in intelligible phrases in one or more of the languages authorized." To many members, that was still oblique. What is intelligibility even among alphabetic languages, an American observer asked, when a secret code is perfectly plain to the person for whom it is intended, and a plain text in one language might as well be encrypted to someone who does not know the language?

There were blistering debates about word manipulation in the Paris conference hall, as the representatives from not only nations but also telegraphic companies jumped in to lobby for their interests. Meanwhile, no one was talking about numbers. From the beginning, the Europeans took it as a given that numbers, zero to nine, would be treated as secret language. Numbers are abstract and symbolic to begin with. Whenever used for purposes other than counting, it was clear that they stood in for something else—as secret text. Code manuals used that to their advantage as well. Consider the incomparable economy in using 1 to say, "I send you by mail a book, a duplicate of which I have with me, whereby I shall be enabled to let you hear from me often with very little trouble." Or the wistful 214: "Composed and entirely resigned to the will of God." Or perhaps the vengeful 7571—"You will *rue* the day if you do."

There was a dizzying array of clever schemes to circumvent pricing rules used by just about every country. Yet China stood out as a lone exception—and not by choice. Western ways of outsmarting the pricing system in alphabetic and numerical transmissions did not work for the Chinese, because their language was represented entirely in numbers. A single Chinese character could take up a total of forty-four to sixty-eight units. That is almost four times more than a single English word, and therefore more costly. China had no way to cheat. If you were participating in a system where everyone else was allowed to cheat—and did so regularly—not cheating yourself did not signal virtue. It was a penalty by default.

Wang knew that telegraphic rules grew out of a context that was utterly indifferent to the needs or habits of the Chinese. The Chinese were not trying to dodge pricing inside the system; they were trying to gain the chance to participate in it. The real trouble started in 1912, when a technical special class of service was made widely available. In response to the growing range of senders and what they were willing to pay, telegrams that did not have to be sent right away by rush or normal service—and could wait up to forty-eight hours for transmission—could be carried under the new service as deferred telegrams, offered with a generous discount at half price.

The catch, though, was that the message had to be sent in plain text. This was meant to guard against users who might double dip by manipulating message length or content, using acronyms, trademarks, punctuation marks, or random groups of letters. There was also a limit on the numbers of syllables a word could have and the rule that the word must be pronounceable. The new service barred the use of encrypted or secret text—which of course included numbers. What had been a gap between Chinese and alphabetic scripts now widened into an unbridgeable gulf.

Wang's role in Paris was to explain this situation as gently and firmly as possible and to show the bind it created for the Chinese. He realized that while they could talk pricing and tariffs, his Western counterparts had no inkling of how Chinese characters worked or how that would pose a problem in telegraphy. His diplomatic skills were put to better use by explaining language instead of statecraft. This meant offering basic lessons in how Chinese characters were composed, why their structures rendered them difficult to systematize, and why a representation by numbers was a necessary but flawed solution.

The after-hours sessions at the conference were when his real work began. Wang and his delegation put on short demonstrations of the Chinese language at evening salons and parties. Knowing that the Westerners would be quick to exoticize or disparage the Chinese language, they made sure that wine flowed to soften their reactions. They tried every imaginable way of going over the basics—radicals, strokes, characters, etc. They engaged their audience in a manner that was instructive but not condescending. Wang plied them with anecdotes about the origin of the ideographic script. Once they were primed, he moved on to the more technical matter of the frequent occurrence of phonetic likenesses, or homophones, in the Chinese language. He tried to impart the lesson that Romanization, otherwise a simple solution, was challenged by homophones. Same-sounding words made Chinese much harder to distinguish in alphabetic form, because letters cannot indicate the tones or details that a good visual of the character script itself makes plain instantly. However you Romanize it, Chinese inevitably loses its essential, physical cues for identification—unless a different method can be found to represent it. It was another way of saying the obvious: while China wished to internationalize, it could only do so in a way that was in keeping with its historical, cultural, and linguistic particulars.

By mid-September, the International Telegraphic Conference was holding its seventh session. The delegates were once more back on the topic of pricing and rules that day. They needed to close the loopholes in plain and secret text transmissions. When there was a call among the Europeans to form a subcommittee to study code language and the existing rules regulating its use, Wang volunteered his delegation. But, he added, it was not for China's sake, because the problem was distinct to Europe. He gently pointed out that any taxation on telegraphic transmission based on the existing distinction between plain and coded texts would be of no help to China because of its reliance on numbers, but in the spirit of cooperation China was willing to make the sacrifice and put an equitable solution for others before itself. He made sure that his counterparts were reminded that Chinese characters were unique in their representation by four digits. As with the evening salons, he made his point with polite insistence and humility.

Wang never demanded it, but over the course of several weeks he managed to make a convincing case for the other countries to give China special consideration. It worked. On October 9, more than five weeks into the conference, the proceedings were opened to presentations from individual nations. Wang made it clear that something had to be done to stop the penalty on China for its dependency on numbers. If a core definition of plain text was that it must be in the sender's mother tongue at the origin of transmission, then China's four-digit code system must count as a way of representing its native language.

Through sheer diligence—sitting in the same room, actively participating, and showing China's ability to be a civilized team player—Wang provided the final assurance the Western delegates were looking for: China's willingness not only to enter into the complicated web of international relations but also to play by its rules and live with its exceptions. Finally, he was able to make them see that what was good for China was good for them, too.

The European delegates came to understand how resolving the pricing disadvantage for China would benefit all parties. If they wanted to extend their business ventures into the new nation with the least resistance, it was best to grant a special exception. Here was Wang's official ask, simply and dispassionately delivered:

> Whereas the foreign public has been granted, since the intro-
> duction of the "deferred" service in China, by the Admin-

istration of this country in 1912, the benefit of a reduction of
50 percent of the tax for its telegrams of lesser importance,
the Chinese people did not, however, benefit from this advantage because of the restriction on the use of figures. The fact
is that, because of its peculiarities, written Chinese cannot be
rendered in telegrams by any other or better means than groups
of four digits, each representing a word. As the figures, with
the exception of those which have their ordinary meaning, are
not admitted in the deferred telegrams, the Chinese abroad,
as well as those residing in their own country, were prevented
from speaking in their own language, in this correspondence;
in other words, they were excluded from benefiting from the
half-price service. . . . In these circumstances, the Chinese
Administration proposes that figures in groups of four units
having their own meaning in the Chinese language be admitted in the deferred telegrams exchanged with China.

The International Telegraphic Union was persuaded and offered a
solution—also within its constraints. It was not possible, or desirable,
to change the alphabetic premise of Morse code in order to accommodate one nonalphabetic script system. But an allowance could be made
for China and the Chinese script alone. Where taxation or pricing of
word length was concerned, then, they agreed to insert a special clause—
"*exceptionellement*"—which specified China and its use of four digits as
plain text.

It seemed the battle had been won. Wang emphasized that the proposal was not cheating but rather recognizing that the rules for cheating had been misapplied in China's case. Let the Europeans continue
their squabble, if they wished, but let China play fair and square.
Wang's painstaking efforts had paid off.

Back home, his colleagues were ready to give Wang a hero's welcome. What Wang had done would have lasting significance. At last, China had taken a stance in the international arena of telegraphy—and the country would only become more vocal and determined in winning back its stature in the world. But before boarding the ship to return home, Wang was already discontented that he had not achieved the ultimate goal of wrestling back the Chinese script's full sovereignty. All those weeks of negotiations and diplomacy had gone as well as could be expected, but the fundamental problem was still unresolved. Why should the Chinese language, after all, have to be represented by numbers for the world to accept it? Getting the international organization to grant the exception was a quick fix to close an urgent gap, but the root of the problem was still unresolved. As long as China was merely tolerated as an exception, it was still denied full admittance into global communications' inner circle. Receiving special treatment did not put China on a course to fully claim its sovereignty. At a time when political outcomes could be shaped in minutes or seconds by telegraphy, China was not yet part of the world system on its own terms.

DURING THE NEXT SEVERAL YEARS, Wang stayed very busy. He was even more in demand after his success in Paris, but he wasn't ready to give up entirely on making the Western alphabet work for the Chinese script. The more international conferences he attended where Western industrial and political values reigned, the more he became convinced of the necessity of firming up China's position. Two years after the Paris conference, he went to the International Radiotelegraph Conference in Washington, D.C. There, he tried out a more assertive stance, letting it be known that no foreign firms would build or set up telegraphic or wireless stations on Chinese territory without China's consent.

These small victories still felt like short-term reprieves, however, not lasting guarantees. There ought to be some kind of telegraphic code that could utilize the phonetic advantage of the Western alphabet and at the same time remain true to the Chinese script's nature. Wang summoned a group of more than fifty linguists, officials, teachers, and telegraphers in China to help him study the matter. Under the sway of recent Romanization campaigns at home, they tried a new, modified use of the alphabet system. It would not be modeled on the English or other European spellings. Instead, it would be adapted to account for the Chinese script's three most dominant features: sound, shape, and syntax.

Before, Westerners like Viguier had mapped Chinese onto numbers. Then the Chinese themselves had tried to use numbers to remap the alphabet. They kept bending the stick back and forth. Wang was increasingly of the mind that one could put the Western alphabet in service of Chinese Romanization more permanently. He turned to Bopomofo, the Chinese phonetic alphabet approved at the 1913 National Language Unification Conference in Beijing, and its idea of an auxiliary phonetic alphabet formed from different styles and parts of Chinese characters. Working from this basis, Wang designed a use for Roman letters that was Latin in name but readapted to signal the three linguistic properties of Chinese characters: the phonetic representation of sound, tone, and the radical.

To indicate sound in his New Phonetic System, Wang mapped the sounds of Bopomofo—represented by symbols ㄅ, ㄆ, ㄇ, ㄈ, etc.— onto alphabet letters that shared similar starting consonant sounds. So ㄅ, ㄆ, ㄇ, ㄈ would match the letters "b," "p," "m," and "f." To show tone, Wang picked five letters to represent the five tones used in traditional and medieval phonology: "B" stands for the level or even tone; "P" marks the second or rising tone; "X" represents the third tone, which falls first then rises; "C" is fourth or falling tone; and "R" denotes the fifth or neutral tone. The last property, the radical, takes up two letters—a consonant and a vowel. Wang used two letters to spell the pronunciation of the radical part of the character only; e.g., *tu* for 土, *li* for 力, *ko* for 口, etc., in a way that was not dissimilar to what Wang Zhao had done with the Mandarin Alphabet.

With one letter for sound, another letter for tone, and two more for phoneticizing the radical's spelling, this system yielded a four-letter code for every character. The Chinese character could then be transmitted via telegraphy without using numbers at all. Wang's idea took after other Romanization systems of the time, which were developed not for telegraphy per se, but to address the broader question of literacy. He borrowed from that conversation, run by linguists and ethnographers, to design a solution for what he had seen in the diplomatic arena.

His scheme got attention, and his authority meant it was considered seriously. He created a dictionary that recompiled all the characters from the public telegraph code according to his phonetic system. His dictionary was reprinted in three editions. The system was approved and promulgated by the Ministry of Communications and took effect on January 1, 1929. It was a personal victory, but there were already others who had begun to conduct bolder experiments with the Chinese script itself. By the mid-1950s, Morse code would be largely replaced by a binary code, devised by Émile Baudot in 1870, that uniformly represented every letter with five basic units of equal lengths, using a base-two numeral system. But Viguier's four-digit format, which spawned other systems for parsing characters, remained in use internationally and within China well into the 1980s.

Wang's contribution to Chinese public welfare and governmental policy was incontrovertible. After the Washington conference, he left his post in railway and transport administration. He spent three years heading the Chinese Education Mission in the United States, where he fostered young Chinese talent, and transitioned to being a consultant for the government's telegraphy department. He spent eighteen years in London, his longest stint abroad, as a purchasing agent of raw materials and industrial equipment for China. Eventually, he was more comfortable living abroad than in China.

Still, Romanization was something he never let go, and he continued to revise his ideas. He called his last system Gueeyin. It became a hobby in his sunset years, when he made his final move to Claremont, California, after the Communist takeover. He remained there until his death in 1956. In his lifetime, he had done what he could to help China along—to win back its sovereignty by taking charge of its own telegraphic infrastructure. It was just as he had always said: China could only move forward by not dwelling on its past sufferings. Wang remained a Nationalist and a Chinese Republican to the end. It is perhaps a small solace that he did not live to see the start of the Great Leap Forward, just two years after his death. America was where he had made his debut as one of China's top negotiators, and perhaps he returned there because of a personal conviction that was rooted in more than diplomacy and rhetoric. He truly believed in America as a model for China's future, just as he had said to its people in 1912.

Yet it was not unambiguously clear to many in China that Romanization was the only solution to an old problem. By the time Wang worked out his Romanization schemes in the 1930s and 1940s, a more expansive discussion about revamping the Chinese characters in a fundamental manner was under way. It explored a different path, outside of the alphabet and letters, by analyzing Chinese characters themselves. This conversation generated wide-scale interest across the nation. Wang joined it late in life and was not able to push it forward as he had with telegraphy. The leadership had to come from elsewhere. A large number and variety of people—not bureaucrats or officials, but intellectuals, publishers, and factory workers—were at the forefront of this effort. They were imagining an alternative future: Why try to redefine the alphabet for Chinese use when an alphabetic capacity could possibly be developed from the Chinese script itself? Unlike telegraphy, this new phase would start in a quiet corner, far from the political limelight: a group of old-fashioned librarians would lead the so-called character retrieval index race. They would have to soldier through another politically tumultuous period, as the country's survival hung in the balance. Some would rise and others fall during this trial. Everyone would be tested.

FOUR

THE LIBRARIAN'S CARD CATALOG

(1938)

BREAKING DOWN THE CHARACTER INTO ITS ABCS

The Chinese answers to the problems of typewriting and telegraphy were both rushed patches, ad hoc efforts to retrofit Chinese characters to technologies designed for alphabetic languages. In both instances, Chinese inventors and linguists were trying to overcome the disadvantages that accompanied being late entrants in systems intended for a different kind of written language. But many wondered if the Chinese script itself was the problem.

In the West, the Chinese script had been accused of not being fast, simple, or efficient enough—in a word, not sufficiently modern. The script's most vociferous critics at home did not come to its defense either. They blamed the character system for endangering China's chances for survival in the future. Many echoed the lament often attributed to writer and intellectual reformer Lu Xun: "If the Chinese script is not abolished, China will certainly perish!" The sense of urgency was already palpable in the late nineteenth century among Wang Zhao's cohort, but it grew prominent as China moved deeper into the Republican period of 1912 to 1949. After the twelve-year period of warlordism ended in 1928, China barely had a chance to catch its breath before the 1930s opened with the Japanese invasion of Manchuria, the Pacific War, and then a bloody civil war between the Nationalists and Communists. For at least two decades, China was embroiled in major life-and-death struggles within and outside its borders, battles that were decisive for the rest of the twentieth century. There was no more time for speculative ideas or philosophical theories. Pragmatism and national survival were paramount.

Despite a deeply ingrained sense of national emergency, there were those in the country who did not believe that abandoning the Chinese script—along with jettisoning the nation's past—would ensure China's path into the future. Was the script really that hopeless, the more moderate intellectuals asked, so worthless that people should, as some advocated, abolish it along with China's classical learning?

For the moderates, the challenge of the language was the characters themselves. It was not just that the language had too many tones and homophones, was too difficult to write, and took too long to learn. All these problems could be alleviated if there were predictability and ways of regulating the system. The real question was how to organize a language without a clear structure. The Chinese character inventory was almost infinite, and without delimiting a finite set, there was no way to organize or incorporate them smoothly into machine design and technology. It was like trying to come up with a solution without a clear sense of the dimensions of the problem to be solved.

The Chinese writing system needed a thorough examination, conducted by native Chinese speakers. The true nature of the task would be difficult for users of the Western alphabet to grasp, accustomed as they were to a fixed, neatly organized set of twenty-six units. To get a sense of the challenge, try a simple exercise: Choose a word, look it up in an English dictionary, and then consider how easy it was to locate. The letter "b" will never come before "a," "g" is invariably between "f" and "h," and "s" will always be followed by "t." Based on this predictability, one can find the right letter section and the right word within it by the same logic, moving from left to right. If a word shares the same initial letters as another word, as "address" does with "adrenaline," simply look right to find the first distinguishing letter. Letter by letter, the process of location by elimination is pretty much automatic— one letter, one step. One can build, store, and find all the words one could ever possibly want with twenty-six letters. The one cornerstone of the system is to learn the alphabet by heart, which you most likely did in kindergarten.

The linear organization of the alphabet is inviolable. We start with "a" and end with "z," and even reference it as such by calling it the ABCs, not the CBAs or the UVWs. This rule can be used to sort anything, from a bullet-point presentation to a shopping list. The alphabetic sequence, in short, is essential to the way information is organized, recognized, and prioritized. This is true not only of dictionaries but also of telephone books, directories, indexing systems, encyclopedias, computer files—anything that needs sequence and order.

Now, open a Chinese dictionary. Step one: Go to a table, usually inserted in the front or the back, where the radicals are listed, and then locate the radical of the character, which can be any of the 214 (once 540) organized according to the ascending order of strokes. Step two: Assigned to that radical is a number. Follow that number to another table (you are not yet in the body of the dictionary proper). There, under the radical are listed all the characters that contain it, which can be as few as one and as many as sixty-four. Those characters, too, are all arranged by ascending stroke count. Step three: Once you find the character you want in the radical list, go to the indicated page in the dictionary. Unless you can tell right away how many strokes a given character has just by looking at it, you'll likely have to scan through all the characters on the page until you recognize the one you want. A search can spill across several pages. With patience and some luck, you may find a match on the first try.

A number of things can go wrong, of course. You may be unsure about what part of the character is the actual radical because even to a native speaker, that is not always obvious. This could send you down the wrong path, deep into step three before you have realized it. Sometimes a whole character constitutes a radical in itself, so you can be duped by that, too.

Suppose, however, that you are stumped by none of these difficulties because you know the correct radical and how to find it in the dictionary. You can still forget how the rest of the character looks and thus not know the correct number of strokes. Then there's the risk of the same radical appearing in different guises and sizes, depending on what character it occurs in—another pesky feature of written Chinese. Different radicals that have nothing to do with one another can also, conversely, look very similar. Try explaining to a novice that "grass" 艸 is really the same as "grass" 艹; "moon" 月 can be another way to write "meat" 肉, or that "mouth" 口 is not at all related to "enclosure" 囗, even if the former appears to be simply a smaller version of the latter. All these potential quagmires are inherent in the Chinese script because each character is composed of clusters of parts that vary in size and shape, stacked in different proportions to fill a square space.

Consider a reverse exercise: What would happen to the alphabet if it did not have a sequential order? How to organize the twenty-six letters and by what criteria would be an open question: Do you go by the frequency of use, complexity of shape, or the number of ascenders or descenders in a letter? Suddenly, the situation gets considerably messier—and also closer to what users of Chinese have lived with all along.

If grouped by the way they looked, the capital letters "C," "G," "O," and "Q" surely deserve to be next to one another for sharing a similar circular outline. What of "P" and "F," which are both top-heavy, or "P" and "B," because "P" is just one semicircle away from "B"? Seen in this way, "K" and "R" should also be closer neighbors in the alphabet because of the same leg that kicks out at an angle from under them. If someone objects—and it would be reasonable to do so—that shape and looks are too subjective and dependent on the eye of the beholder, then one might go deeper into the structure of the letters' composition, breaking them down to their components—the sticks and lines—for better indicators of physical consistency. To do that, a real mind shift might be required.

We do not readily think of an alphabet as amenable to being deconstructed into strokes because the letter is held to be the basic unit. Deconstructing "A" into two diagonal lines and one short horizontal, or "B" into a vertical line and two curves, is a futile exercise because alphabet letters are valued for the sounds they represent, not the shapes. Yet letters, too, are physically composed of strokes. One can say this has been the much-neglected property of the alphabet. A stroke is any continuous line—straight or curved, short or long, and sometimes even bent. Most alphabet letters are made of one to three strokes (the exception being "E," which has four strokes).

If the alphabet were organized by descending stroke count, then "E" instead of "A" would be the starting letter, followed by "F," "B," or "H," all of which have three strokes. If the alphabet looked like EFBH instead of ABCD, one would, among other things, have to expunge expressions like "A-list" or "plan B" from the English language immediately. There would also be no more A grade in school or C-class shares to own in a company. Not only does order matter in the alphabet, but that sense of order has also become deeply embedded in language, shaping our orientation in the world, the ways we express priorities, and how we organize affairs in order of importance, preference, and hierarchy.

But whether "E" comes first in the alphabet also depends on how it is written—and here orthography comes to challenge stroke count. If you write "E" as it appears in print, that requires four strokes. But if you write it by hand and draw something like a reverse image of a "3," only one stroke is necessary. If we go by the latter, then "E" has to be dethroned from the top slot and sent to the back with the other one strokers: "C," "O," "U," "V," "W," and "Z." Thus, rules of orthography—how a letter is written and in what order—matter more as the analysis of structure becomes more complex and finer grained.

If stroke count can still seem arbitrary, subjective, and unreliable—because it depends on the human hand and habits of writing—one might be tempted to split more hairs by looking at *how* strokes are made and then try to come up with rules based on a finer level of detail: Are they straight like "L," curved like "C" or "S," or a combination of straights and curves, like "D," "Q," "J," "U," and "R"? Or, as an even finer differentiation, one might ask whether the letter is not only straight but straight upright like "I," "L," or "T," or straight angled as in "A" and "Y," or straight-bent like "Z." One could be even more dogged by looking at the way the strokes interact, whether they touch or intersect at a point like "T" or pass all the way through like "X," stay open like "C" or closed like "O." You can mix and match different criteria as needed, but be prepared for exceptions because no one rule covers all, including the idea that the alphabet must consist of a finite set of letters.

Strokes, stroke count, stroke order, stroke type, orthographical inconsistencies, calligraphy, delimiting a finite set of linguistic units—these are the obstacles that the Chinese have had to account for in their script system from the very beginning. Chinese typewriter inventors and telegraphers each addressed some aspect of these issues but never tackled them head-on or thoroughly. They were pragmatists, doing the minimum amount needed to get the job done. Yet simultaneously with their efforts, a thorough reexamination of the language was happening among people who were intensely interested in the problem—the librarians and indexers who dealt with scripts, books, and organization day in and day out. Trained to arrange, categorize, and store systems of knowledge, they could analyze the script system with a level of nuance and detail that few others could.

As the custodians of China's written tradition, librarians certainly did not want to abandon the Chinese script or its native knowledge system. They recognized that a way had to be found for Chinese to interact with the modern technological environment. If they wished to preserve the past instead of jettisoning it, however, they would have to figure out how to reorganize the language for systematic use. To even out the discrepancies between the alphabetic and Chinese scripts required nothing less than bringing two distant worlds together within the space of a bookshelf. A few of these tinkerers knew early on that the key to China's peaceful coexistence with the world could hang on something as small as a stroke. A librarian would be the right person to create a successful filing system for Chinese, but someone else had to broach the subject first. A young English teacher inadvertently led the way.

TWENTY-THREE-YEAR-OLD LIN YUTANG made his publication debut in *New Youth* in 1917. Founded two years earlier in Shanghai's cosmopolitan French quarter, the journal gave a platform to China's restless and most brilliant young minds. Its parallel title, in French—*La Jeunesse*—signaled a cosmopolitan flair with a Marxist edge. Between its red-inked soft covers, novice thinkers got to air their radical views, sound out ideas from the West, and question received knowledge. The editor made the mission clear: If China had to shed the dead weight of all past tradition to compete with the outside world, so be it.

Amid the iconoclastic shots fired, Lin's article was a quieter salvo. He chose a seemingly innocuous, dry topic that would have been more fitting for a librarian: "A Chinese Index System: An Explanation." A neighboring article promised more fireworks by introducing the French philosopher Henri Bergson's conception of the inner experience of time, which at least seemed novel. Though not quite the thunderous idea on which a rebel youth might hang his subversive identity, Lin's seven-page proposal would do what no other piece in the journal could: irrevocably change the landscape of old and new knowledge alike.

His deceptively modest offering was nothing more or less than a guide for organizing characters. Lin took the characters, broke them down into strokes, and identified five different stroke types: horizontal, vertical, diagonal, point, and hook. One detects an echo here of the classic eight-stroke prototypes traditionally demonstrated for teaching calligraphy in the character "eternity," 永. But Lin defined his five stroke types much more broadly. He followed the direction of the stroke execution rather than the style of any specific stroke. For instance, a horizontal stroke included not only the obvious straight line across, as in the character for "one," 一, but also any stroke drawn with a similar motion, from left to right—and it did not have to be level.

Stroke and component order, practiced and ingrained over millennia of calligraphy, had evolved into a reliable set of rules about what comes first, second, and so on in the construction of a character. In English, it is conceivable to write the letter "A" with the short horizontal stroke first, but the convention is to start with the long slant on the left, then the right, and finally with the short stroke last, touching end to end. You can similarly write "X" by starting with either stroke, and the end

Lin Yutang's five basic strokes.

result would be the same. But Chinese characters are much stricter about which stroke and which component must come before the others when they are written by hand. Lin used the type of the first written stroke in a character as the first order of categorization but found that it wasn't granular enough. He expanded on the basic five stroke types to identify another nineteen first strokes, any one of which can appear as the initial stroke at the start of writing any character.

From that, he created a second-level taxonomy, coupling the first with a second stroke, and identified a set of twenty-eight first-plus-second-stroke patterns that accounted for almost all characters. It is as if one were to classify, first, all alphabet letters that began with a single vertical stroke—"B," "D," "F," "H," "K," "L," "M," "N," "P," "R"—then

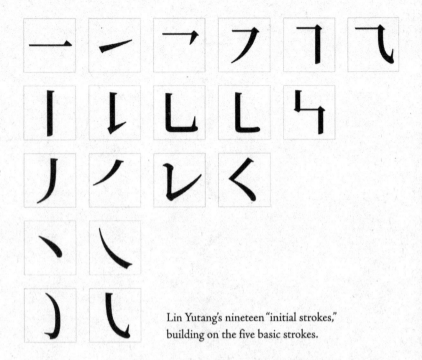

Lin Yutang's nineteen "initial strokes,"
building on the five basic strokes.

add a second stipulation that the first vertical stroke has to be followed
by a curved stroke, which brings the set down to "B," "D," "P," "R."
Identifying characters by a defined set of first and second strokes
yielded an organizational pattern with an alphabet-like logic.

With this simple and elegant scheme Lin challenged the millennia-
old tradition of how Chinese script writing was studied, understood,
and canonized. He demonstrated how characters could be classified
according to their capacity to self-organize, without having to rely on
other external principles, be it the Western alphabet or codes. The idea
of the radical had dominated how to classify and search for characters
in a dictionary. No Chinese before Lin had really offered as complete an
alternative to the radical system in this way. People like Qi Xuan had
only begun to unravel that thread.

Traditionally, principles of classification were driven by accumulated habits and cultural practice rather than abstract language theory. Philology and lexicography had been at the heart of the Chinese classical tradition, and the written script was an object of study in its own right. Scholars over the centuries strove to preserve ancient wisdom by verifying what was meant in which characters; that was key to the revered practice of textual exegesis. Before print, that was harder to do than one would think. Hand-copied manuscripts, even when composed with regulated penmanship and style, were graveyards of misaligned character strokes. A slant instead of a straight line could send generations of scholars bickering over how to identify the corpses.

Managing the total size of the Chinese lexicon was a dry and thankless task. Collating and recording characters in glossaries supported the Chinese knowledge base in critical ways. It was necessary upkeep that required custodial patience, tedious and repetitive comparisons, and hairsplitting taxonomies. All this meticulous work was carried out under a basic rule. For two millennia, only one part of a character, the radical, was used to identify it for the purpose of classification. Radicals were first identified about 1,100 to 1,500 years after the earliest evidence of Chinese writing. They were invented for housekeeping. By then, there was already a sizable number of characters.

The first compiler of radicals, Xu Shen, was a Confucian scholar and commentator on the classics during the Eastern Han dynasty, 25–220. Because no one had taken stock of the characters or studied how they were used, he identified 540 radicals to bring order to the chaotic landscape of 9,353 characters. Xu believed in the philosophical and cosmic significance of the proper naming of things, which left a deep signature on his organizing principle. The magic number 540 was allegedly derived from multiplying the symbolic numbers for the *yin* and the *yang*—6 and 9—and then by a factor of 10 to give enough categories for the classification. The system begins with the radical "one," signifying the origin of things, and ends with twelve radicals that mark cycles of time, offering a conceptual completeness to the system.

Radicals were, in a word, sacred. Throughout the centuries they were respected and observed. Every so often, though, someone came along and wondered whether there had to be so many, or what the optimal number was. Opinions differed. In the tenth century a monk trimmed it down from 540 to 242, and nearly five hundred years later a father-son team opted for 444. The final number of 214 was settled on during the Ming dynasty and collated in a dictionary compiled by a student at the Imperial College, Mei Yingzuo. The 214-radical system was then adopted by the bibliophile Manchu Kangxi Emperor in the eighteenth century, who ordered a team of lexicographers to compile an authoritative dictionary in his name that sealed the authority of the 214 radicals.

By the early twentieth century, the radical system was showing cracks. Despite centuries of revisions, patches, and adjustments to keep it viable, the system remained time-consuming and less than intuitive to learn and use. There was no easy, systematic logic for the storage and retrieval of characters, nor for the rich trove of stories, songs, and dynastic histories they recorded in scrolls and books, which had grown into an unwieldy inventory.

Long before China heard of the taxonomy of Aristotle or Melvil Dewey's decimal system, the Chinese had their own distinct way of organizing things. They did not rely on numbers and decimal points like Dewey, nor did they use alphabet letters like Charles A. Cutter, who around 1880 started using alphabet letters to indicate different subjects in a system that later became the basis for the Library of Congress catalog system. Rather, bibliographic classification in China properly began in the first century B.C.E., and it was based on a perceived moral order. A Confucian scholar devised an elaborate scheme of seven main subject divisions—with thirty-eight subdivisions—prioritizing the Confucian classics first, with science and medicine—astronomy, geomancy, pharmacology, sexology, etc.—occupying the last two categories. Two centuries later, the division of seven began to give way to a trimmer, tighter division of four, proposed by an imperial librarian. After a couple more reshufflings, the four divisions settled in their modern form: classics, history, philosophy, and poetry, in that order. There were many books and records to store and classify under these divisions. By the end of the fifteenth century, it was reported, more titles and volumes were produced in China than all other nations put together.

The four divisions were standardized in a mammoth imperial book project in the eighteenth century. Teams of scholars were assigned to each of the four divisions of the Collection of Four Treasures; it contained almost eighty thousand sections and took a decade to amass. The order in which the four divisions appeared reflected their order of importance. This Confucian-oriented bibliographic system made perfect sense in a China-centered universe, but from Lin's perspective in the 1910s, its utility in the modern age was slim when compared to the library system of the West.

In the pages of New Youth in 1917, Lin Yutang treated the problem of Chinese characters and Chinese information management as one and the same. If one could find a character easily in a dictionary, one could just as quickly locate the first character of the title of a book. So what solved one must solve the other, and the answer was there all along in the physical structure of the characters. The Chinese script, Lin demonstrated, could more than meet its modern challenges. It could advance without outside aids—no Roman letters, no numbers, no codes. Chinese required no other system of representation beyond what was already contained within the script's properties—strokes and stroke order.

Lin's ideas struck an immediate chord. They offered hope and reassurance, even confidence, at a time when China was filled with doubt and anxiety. A leader of the cultural renaissance movement, Qian Xuantong, saw that Lin was years ahead of his peers' thinking and heaped accolades on the young indexer. Others joined the chorus. Not only did Lin reconceptualize the function of strokes, the influential education reformer Cai Yuanpei noted; his system also offered a rich description of just how strokes guided and constituted a character's total contours. And how ingenious of Lin to uncover a logic in the Chinese ideographic script that rivaled the organizational power of the Western alphabet, without using a single Latin letter.

It was Hu Shi, an Indemnity Scholar freshly returned from Cornell, who had the deepest insight. He saw Lin tackling the very infrastructure that would underlie the survival of China's past into the future. Lin's achievement was recognizing the Chinese script's power to self-organize, further enabling the ability to save, search, classify, select, and call up any desired information in China's enormous and rich knowledge base. It was a power extendable to ordering systems of all kinds, perhaps even in other languages, and to restoring the cultural power of China's intellectual riches. Lin's indexing scheme was the door that opened other doors, Hu observed, just the kind of foundational work that those who were criticizing tradition had missed:

> To "order" is to find a logical thread in chaos. . . . It may be the most pedestrian but at the same time the key to anything meaningful. Though rudimentary and tedious, it is the threshold to all deep knowledge . . . the most difficult and indispensable of this kind of labor has to go to the reorganization of the Chinese scripts—that is, their categorization and arrangement.

At a time when modernity was forcing China to break with tradition, and the entire country was shaken by a sense of crisis, there were plenty of revolutionaries ready to take dramatic action and shed blood for the cause. Lin was different: his contribution to rebuilding China would be to help rescue its tradition and legacy from obsolescence. But Lin himself did not think he deserved the recognition he was receiving. Deep in his heart, he felt that he was an impostor, a misfit in the Chinese world.

RAISED IN A CHRISTIAN household in a mountain village in the southern province of Fujian, Lin Yutang grew up with psalms, English, and evening prayers, interspersed with excerpts from the Confucian classics and Chinese language lessons. His father was a local pastor, and as a teenager Lin rang bells in his father's church, which stood across the street from a Buddhist temple. He did not attend traditional Chinese schools, nor was he immersed in its curriculum like most of his peers.

While his fellow university classmates began to agitate for a Western-style cultural renaissance in the mid-1910s, Lin had been imbibing Western culture all his life. He did not approach it with their rebellious ardor; he had a free, roaming curiosity and a whimsical nature that steered clear of ideological labels or zealous slogans. Lin delighted in reading and learning the English language and carried a small English dictionary with him wherever he went.

In 1916, Lin graduated from St. John's College in Shanghai, and accepted a job teaching English at Tsinghua College in Beijing. To make ends meet, he also took a second post as a researcher for the Commercial Press. Now that he was living in the cultural capital of Beijing, Lin realized something was missing: his command of Chinese culture and tradition was rudimentary. Though he saw clearly how the Chinese script could work as an index system for stores of knowledge, he did not feel he had sufficient intellectual access to that knowledge himself. The learned allusions his university colleagues used in conversations went right past him, and he did not share their comfort or ease with the vernacular classics. He knew by heart the biblical tale of how the walls of Jericho fell after Joshua's army blew the trumpet for six days but could not recall a single detail about Lady Meng Jiang, who—legend had it—brought down the Great Wall with her tears after her husband died from the hard labor of building it for the emperor. He felt ashamed to be a stranger in his own culture. Even a laundryman, he later recalled, knew more about the heroes and legends of the Chinese tradition.

Lin began to read voraciously to catch up—not just Lady Meng, but also classic novels like *Honglou meng,* or *Dream of the Red Chamber.* Lin learned the novel's Beijing vernacular and diligently memorized the local colloquialisms. He frequented the local antique market to hunt for old books. At a time when his peers, embroiled in the New Culture Movement that began in 1915, denounced any classical text as poison and wanted to throw out tradition, Lin was just beginning to discover the treasure trove of China's five-thousand-year written tradition. He began to question his Christian faith.

Because he was a latecomer to Chinese culture educated in the Western tradition, Lin was able to see character script in a fresh, new light. Foreigners had been trying to crack the Chinese language puzzle for centuries, based on how their own Indo-European languages worked. Lin turned their frustrations to his advantage. He reconstructed how they saw Chinese, perusing the dictionaries Westerners compiled to learn Chinese, and studied how they organized it according to their own sense of alphabetic taxonomy. This comparative frame helped him develop his own ideas. Why the Chinese script could not behave the way an alphabet could was a puzzle that did not end with his character index—it was merely his first attempt at solving the problem.

Around 1915, Chinese universities became embroiled in debates over the direction of a modern cultural renaissance. Lin's peers argued for the revival of the vernacular language in modern forms of print while retiring classical, literary Chinese to the sepulcher of archives. These debates gathered force for four years before the May Fourth Movement overtook all and merged with the student movement's cause. Yet the dispute over replacing the elite, classical written language with the vernacular, and possibly Romanized, script left Lin ambivalent. He was not willing to Romanize Chinese at the cost of abandoning the Chinese script, as many of his contemporaries demanded. He found it difficult to embrace their radical call to smash tradition.

Lin decided to leave Beijing and China altogether. There was so much more that he did not know about the world beyond its borders, despite having lived as a Christian on Chinese soil. He set sail for the United States in August 1919, to study at Harvard. He continued his studies in Germany, where he received a doctorate in comparative philology from the Leipzig University. He would come to appreciate the public-mindedness in Western learning, especially its library systems. Thanks to Leipzig's Bibliotheca Albertina, he borrowed books from Berlin while he was writing his dissertation, and Harvard's Widener Library gave him free rein in the neatly organized stacks. The convenience and ease of the Western library classification system allowed anyone to locate a book and take it down from the shelf. It was not like it was in China, where only the rich and powerful had—and hoarded—books, the largest depot of which was the Imperial Library.

The pastor's son would become the most beloved Chinese Anglophone novelist of the twentieth century, eventually spending three pivotal decades engaging the American audience as a voice of China, authoring bestsellers like *The Importance of Living*, *My Country and My People*, *Moment in Peking*, and *A Leaf in the Storm*. He would also continue to contribute to the character index, but via a different route.

For the time being, it was left to others in China to propel his idea forward. Lin's index method drew attention to what China needed to do to preserve its own cultural legacy. He started the race to complete what came to be known as the character index method—a way to systematically organize the Chinese script with practical implications for managing information. It took Lin's peers a few years to catch on to the true potential of the system he outlined in his 1917 essay. But once they had, they, too, began to focus on the question of shape—of not only strokes but also other parts of the characters' internal structure. There were many who were eager to make their mark in his absence— and to take down one another in the process.

AND SO IT BEGAN. At first a trickle, then a deluge. Proposals for the newest and most improved character index appeared one after another in the 1920s, focusing mainly on three areas: shape by components; shape by numbers; and shape by some other spatially defined unit. The point for any of these approaches was to make characters quick to identify and categorize, with minimal steps to follow. Meanwhile, a wider call for not only a strictly Chinese but also broadly conceived Han script revolution launched by leading intellectual and linguist Qian Xuantong in 1925 called for a full-scale assault on the Chinese script as it had been known. "Bring your guns, grenades, and bombs," he urged, so as to toss them into the lair of the classical language. The language question lured other opportunists to take advantage of the public's attention. A secret society of mesmerism put on a séance in the streets of Shanghai, calling on spirits and sages of the past to give lessons on how to phoneticize the Chinese script. Qian, who thought himself a high-minded intellectual with a serious scholarly mission, was flabbergasted by the cheap gimmick.

The race to improve the character index looked like an obstacle course. It required more strategy than spectacle: the index scheme had to have clear, simple instructions; characters needed a logic of ordering; there could be no secondary layers of analysis, like having to first look up a radical or count the number of strokes; and the index method had to be based on objective, stable criteria.

Many rushed to enter the race in a quest for the holy grail. Some riffed on Lin's idea of basic strokes and came up with their own magic number. There was Huang Xisheng, who identified twenty possible strokes as the core elements for composing any character. Then Shen Zurong and Hu Qingsheng decided on twelve strokes in their collaborative effort. In Guangdong, Du Dingyou offered a complete Chinese character retrieval system using reorganized shape analysis, followed by Gui Zhibo of Hubei, who tossed a twenty-six-stroke scheme into the ring. Wang Yunwu of the Commercial Press in Shanghai rallied to return to the use of numbers, and still others wanted to use both shape and numbers. The list of contestants grew. People began to dissect, splice, and turn characters on their heads in a race to find any hidden, objective laws that could help regulate their organization.

This was not the first time this question had been raised. How to arrange characters had been a prime topic of study and debate among Europeans since the missionaries tried to produce bilingual Chinese dictionaries for their own use. Such dictionaries were essential for proselytization and, later, trade and exploitation. They debated intensely about whether to use the 214 Kangxi radicals, as the Chinese would have it, or their own alphabetical arrangement. The Japanese, too, used their Chinese-character-derived syllabaries to form a phonetic writing system for Japanese—called *kana*—and to arrange Japanese-Chinese dictionaries. But the priority of these foreign efforts was always oriented toward their own language and purpose. None of these examples resolved the problems of China's Chinese script.

For those working on character index schemes within China, the goals were also diverse—as were the participants. Chen Lifu, a highly placed official in the Nationalist government, was primarily interested in making complex record-keeping easier in the government's archives. He came up with a five-stroke system that aimed to leave the radical system behind. For Zhao Rongguang, an educator, character indexing was a consideration second to his textbook project for basic literacy. He was part of a small cohort that supported launching a basic vocabulary for learning Chinese, in the 1,000-to-1,300-character range. This was similar to the 850-word model of BASIC English (British American Scientific International and Commercial), a compilation of more elementary vocabulary for nonnative English speakers to pick up.

Someone took notice of the fast-rising phenomenon and counted around forty character index proposals in 1928. Another collated list of thirty-seven proposals appeared by 1933, which was still only about half of the total sum that would exist in the 1940s. As the competition expanded, new entrants had to work harder to come up with new ideas. Amid the increasing intellectual clamor and branding campaigns, it grew difficult to tell whose system was better than the others.

The scheme that ultimately prevailed was the Four-Corner Index Method, invented by Wang Yunwu. Wang was also the powerful editor in chief at the Commercial Press, a business-savvy executive with a nose for profit. He ran the press's printing floor on the principles of Frederick Winslow Taylor's scientific management and knew how to maximize an opportunity as well as how to squeeze maximum labor from someone's working hours.

Wang Yunwu used shape identification to determine a numbering system, which he made his first and last selling point. He partly revived the telegraphic coding method from the nineteenth century—with one crucial difference. Rather than assigning random numbers to characters, Wang used the fact that characters are written within an imaginary, abstract square space—characters are often referred to in Chinese as "square-shape script," or *fangkuai zi*. He used that hypothetical space to identify a character's four corners, then assigned to each corner a number between zero and nine. Each number correlated to a particular stroke type, harking back to Lin's idea.

Wang Yunwu went to great lengths to market his scheme, mobilizing every advantage at his disposal and becoming one of Republican China's first modern capitalists. He had raised the profile of the Commercial Press several times over by making profitable decisions to publish multiple series of reference works like encyclopedias and anthologies. Hundreds of thousands of young students across the country flocked to these tools for modern learning. His Four-Corner system was approved by the Ministry of Education in 1928 and promulgated as the official index system for standard reference tools, in part bowing to his position and influence.

Leveraging his position, he got the Four-Corner Index Method into every major reference work that appeared under the aegis of the Commercial Press. Its influence spread from there, to municipal telephone books, provincial and university libraries, Esperanto societies, governmental agencies, encyclopedias, dictionaries of all kinds, foreign universities, and even to rival presses; the Four-Corner Index Method was impossible to avoid. Some publications even bore his name, like the *Wang Yunwu Comprehensive English-Chinese Dictionary* and the *Wang Yunwu Pocket Dictionary*. Pretty much everyone had to learn the Four-Corner Index Method in order to learn anything else.

So legendary was Wang's success that people began to buy into his carefully crafted inspiration story. Whenever anyone asked how he came up with the method—his favorite question—he attributed it to an innate joie de vivre that made him look forward to waking up every day at three-thirty a.m. for a brisk ten-mile walk, sometimes mixing up his routine with thirteen hundred steps of stair climbing. He also told the story of how, as a teenager, he spent three years reading the *Encyclopaedia Britannica* from cover to cover. This early autodidacticism planted the idea of developing learning tools for others and led to his later monumental publishing projects. His critics turned into acolytes. Others rushed to pirate the details—and even exact wording—from his autobiographical accounts.

But Wang Yunwu wanted absolute dominance. He set out to give his Four-Corner Index Method the authority of empirical science. The Commercial Press launched summer courses and training workshops in Shanghai, where middle-school to college students from all over the country were indoctrinated in his method. They got a lot more than just classroom instruction, too. Included in the program were class competitions and visits by famous speakers who came to expound on the virtues of the Four-Corner Index Method and the future of China's cultural heritage. In a race to look up characters, a Shanghai teenager beat out a former champion by spending under eight seconds per word.

Of course, other independent evaluations of the Four-Corner system were more circumspect. Was Wang Yunwu's system really that much better than the good old radical system? An elementary school that compared both methods thought not. In fact, his system was harder to learn, because one had to memorize which number went with which component. The relationship between the number and the part of the character it represented was not intuitive, which violated the principles of being easy and accessible, immediately recognizable, and requiring no additional steps. But Wang simply shrugged off the skeptics. He was a brand name by now, and the Commercial Press moved swiftly to squelch any opposition to his leadership. They simply stopped publishing any work requiring an index that did not abide by the Four-Corner Index Method, while selling *Wang's Four Corners Numerical Code Petite Dictionary* at a discount.

It almost became a sport to watch Wang Yunwu deflate his challengers. In 1928, a hapless twenty-eight-year-old newcomer, Zhang Feng, challenged Wang to a duel of character retrieval systems. Zhang was feeling confident, having just published his eponymous *Zhang Feng Dictionary* that year. In it he proudly introduced his Plane-Line-Point Character Retrieval System, which draws on a two-dimensional geometric structural analysis of character shapes. He had clearly thought it through, using a set of three numbers to identify a character. Each number stood for the number of times that a given geometric unit—plane, line, or point—occurred in the structure. Its advantage was that it contained all the information you needed to figure out how to locate the character.

Zhang saw Wang Yunwu's treatment of shape as superficial and crude. Wang's focus on the four corners failed to give an accurate, precise analysis of character structure itself. Convinced that he deserved a greater mark in history, he made a bold pledge: "Zhang Feng may perish, but his method will live on." He challenged Wang in an open letter. But Wang knew just how to handle a young upstart, hungry with ambition. Zhang's and Wang's systems shared similar concepts, but Zhang couldn't compete with the resources and influence Wang wielded to turn his Four-Corner Index Method into a household name. Zhang could only promote his method on the cheap: he peddled his pamphlets on foot, carrying them in a bamboo basket and handing them out for free in college dormitories. Wang did not dignify Zhang's challenge with a real response and lightly brushed him off. In the decades thereafter people would remember Zhang and his attempt as foolhardy, until they could no longer remember his name at all.

It was not known at the time, but Wang had a dirty little secret. He had a decisive advantage over his competitors, having had early access to young Lin Yutang's ideas before they had been made public. Back in 1917, when Lin was teaching English at Tsinghua, Wang learned through a mutual acquaintance of the character index scheme he was working on. He offered to help by buying out Lin's teaching obligations and arranging a one-year research contract with the press, which Lin accepted. According to its terms, he had to submit monthly reports on his research, which were then forwarded to Wang. Lin was deep into his radicals and stroke analysis and no doubt related every stage of his findings in the reports.

Wang later maintained that he did not have the time to read Lin's reports in the first several months of the arrangement due to his heavy responsibilities at the press. And when he finally did, Wang found himself arriving at "quite a different opinion" on the matter. He realized that Lin's proposal only achieved part of the solution. Driven by his own will and ideas, Wang miraculously saw his own path a few weeks later: the radical system had to be replaced entirely with one based on numbers.

Over time Wang shrewdly distanced himself from his connection with Lin. He acknowledged Lin's research on top strokes in the first unveiling of the Four Corners Numerical Code in a 1926 English-language pamphlet but left Lin out entirely in the revised version, published two years after. It was not until decades later that Lin revealed that he was in fact also the one who supplied Wang with the idea of a numerical system of classification, one of the different avenues he explored while working on the index system, assigning a number to each kind of stroke from zero to nine. So not only did Wang borrow liberally from Lin's earliest ideas, but even the part he claimed to be his own had its roots in Lin's findings.

Lin, meanwhile, was charting out a path of his own, just as he had wanted. While he was busy studying and traveling abroad for several years after his opening salvo in 1917, he did not stay idle. He continued to build on his index proposal in new ways and returned to China just as the index race was heating up. Yet already his linguistic interests were branching into other areas. During this period, he wrote articles on the Chinese language question, from the broadest to the most minute aspects: dialectology and Romanization, employing numbers to tag character shapes, using the last—not just the first—stroke of a given character for retrieval, and harnessing traditional rhymes to build a library card catalog. The question had become more expansive for him, no longer limited to the arena of rivalry that had absorbed Wang, Zhang, and others.

The fact was, Lin was searching for something big. By then, he had found his true passion, despite his rising reputation as a literary writer. He wanted to build a typewriter. He was familiar with the typewriting machines of Zhou Houkun, Qi Xuan, and others. But Lin was imagining a design that would set itself apart. His would be based on deep linguistic knowledge, drawn from the East and the West, ancient and modern, literary and scientific. It would take him two more decades to build a prototype that he was willing to unveil to the world.

Meanwhile, the colorful era of individual innovators and competition under the Nationalists' reign was coming to an end. In the early 1920s, the Chinese Communist Party was becoming a greater threat to the Nationalists, even though the two parties would come together several times to fight internal and external enemies. Between those temporary alliances, the Nationalists' bloody purges of the Communists set the tone for greater political and civil discord to come. For now, people were losing their appetite for sensationalized gossip. Even a textile factory worker who had his own character index scheme to offer was noting how the pursuit was becoming a plaything for the influential elite. The Japanese invasion in 1931 began one of the country's most devastating modern wars. The War of Resistance against Japanese imperialism beginning in 1937 would soon be part of the political theater of the Second World War. With Lin abroad and the war turning people's focus to survival, it took a bona fide librarian to do what was necessary to put the character index race back where it was always meant to be—in the library.

ON OCTOBER 12, 1938, the forty-year-old librarian Du Dingyou was ordered to evacuate the city of Guangzhou. The Pacific War had advanced to a new stage. By dawn, the Japanese had invaded the nearby Bias Bay from both sea and air, pinching off the arteries to the city's heart. They would soon blockade China's southern coast and choke off the supply route at the opening of the Pearl River, while sequestering the neighboring British port of Hong Kong, close to eighty miles to the southeast. Panic rippled through the streets. It took minutes for the city's inhabitants to realize that the low droning sound they heard came from the approaching enemy planes and not the passing ships in the harbor. Confusion and rumors spilled into the shops and alleyways as people hurried home, some with baby strollers and bicycles. They had not thought the ravage of Japanese imperialism would come so near their rooftops. Once the Japanese troops breached the city, the provincial capital of Guangzhou would fall in ten days. The takeover was swift, the resistance minimal. The entire province, which was the size of Oklahoma, would come under siege two months later.

When the evacuation order came, Du was hunched over his disordered desk at the Sun Zhongshan University library, surrounded by uncataloged books and scattered notes. As director, "Bismarck Doo"—as he sometimes liked to refer to himself—had a small window in which to act. He had been expecting this day; the scent of burned concrete and wood from the first shelling of the university's grounds six weeks ago still hung in the air. Students and professors had since fled the campus in droves, their lessons left unfinished in the abandoned classrooms. The classical revivalist Chinese buildings now lay empty and mute. Above, thin white contrails from the bombers flattened out across the sky as though drawn by a child's hand.

While the sirens screeched through the air, it was not thoughts of imminent destruction or his own mortality that churned in Du's mind. His pressing thought was for all those dusty books on the shelves, in storage, and in the stacks. They were still under his stewardship. He felt no greater responsibility than to save China's precious written records from destruction. The Japanese imperialists might brutalize China's people, rob them of their sovereignty, and massacre their women and children, but they would not cut off its cultural bloodline, too. By the time the sirens had become a low howl, Du had made up his mind—he would personally shepherd the books to safety.

For the next seventy-two hours, he packed up about three hundred thousand volumes from the library's collection. The few staff members who stayed behind worked frenetically under his direction. They hacked apart the reading tables and removed the blackboards in chunks to cobble them into boxes. Amid the flying dust and debris, he later recounted, they did not pause to rest. Du ordered whatever would not fit in a box to be taken to the basement room and sealed in with concrete.

Someone objected. The city would soon be flooded with refugees seeking bomb shelters—should not the extra space be saved for them? He disagreed. Surely, others pleaded, people's lives mattered more at this perilous hour! Not so, he grunted back. Human beings will always be clever enough to find other solutions, but not books. They were vulnerable and helpless. Books did not have legs and could not very well move themselves, could they? Hushing the dissenters, Du put people back to work, noting down the names of the faithless who were walking out the door. He expected a full reckoning of words and deeds after the war.

But no one really knew when the war was going to end. As the nation teetered on the brink of disaster, a train of librarians clandestinely escorting carts of books across five provinces might not have been the heroism one expected. The 2 million Chinese soldiers who fought in the battlefields and perished during China's bloody War of Resistance, and the 12 million civilians who died, would be remembered as war heroes by future generations, not this single cohort of middle-aged book stewards doing their job.

Yet Du was not a typical librarian. He had been chiseling away at an important project for years. Its ultimate goal was to create a universal catalog system for China and the world. The most important piece was to first create a filing system for Chinese-language materials using the Chinese script. Du was among the first to respond to Lin's index proposal in 1917, and ever since he had his eye on developing a more intuitive shape-based system using the most common spatial patterns in character composition. The idea was to save the user the trouble of memorizing even Lin's nineteen strokes or twenty-eight stroke pairs, developed from his five basic stroke types. To make that possible, Du first had to analyze character script both as parts and wholes.

Though he began soon after seeing Lin's proposal, it was not until 1932, fifteen years later, that he was ready to explain his own ideas in full. In a treatise on using Chinese script as an index, Du began by revisiting how the ancients looked upon characters in motion. He made the case that Chinese characters were not meant to be treated or seen as purely static shapes, as stale forms on paper.

Treating each character as the two-dimensional depiction of a three-dimensional object, he tried to reconstruct how the ancients reflected what they saw in the script and how that related to their angle of viewing. The three hundred or so pictographic characters like "sun" 日 or "mountain" 山, Du noted, clearly place the perspective of the spectator opposite the scenery. "Man" 人 is a snapshot of a person walking, viewed from the side, and "horse" 馬 looks like it is galloping by, with four hoofs underneath. The character for "ox" 牛, he noted, was clearly composed from a posterior view. One can well imagine the habitual vantage point of a cowherd, who spent more time watching the gentle beast from behind, sideswiping its tail while grazing, instead of viewing it head-on. Written characters like these offered proof of having been composed from the visual perspective of an observer.

No bovine rear end had ever been more consequential. Even if no character actually leaped off the page or galloped by, the habitual ways of seeing characters began to shift for Du. The Chinese script was no longer flat images on a page but multidimensional objects caught in motion. Pictographs varied in points of view, according to the plane of observation. This kind of insight later freed up other indexers to explore shape in various ways—in three dimensions, from the top, side, or back. Some indexers proposed six, eight, or as many as twenty-four ways of doing so. Du, though, had a greater application in mind. He was going to use a mere eight shapes, or spatial patterns, to capture the physical composition of characters and build a library catalog system.

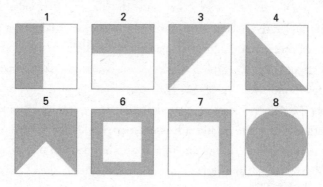

Du Dingyou's shape-based character
analysis in eight shapes.

What Du was seeing in his mind, and on the page, was not so hard to understand. He was rediscovering in the Chinese script what had long been forgotten in the Western alphabet. Few now see an ox in the letter "A," a house in the letter "B," or water in "M," as the Phoenicians once did in 1000 B.C.E., before the Greeks took over their alphabet two hundred years later and transformed it into their own writing system. Though the alphabet long ago shed its pictographic roots, the Chinese script always bore that mark of its origins, no matter how faint.

Du revived this pictographic element in order to impose a spatial perspective on the written script. Analyzing characters in a square space is akin to how children learn to write the alphabet on the ruled pages of a notebook. The lines give an immediate sense of the spatial proportion by which a letter is composed. Du came up with the typology of eight such spatial categories, then used a statistical analysis to gauge how frequently characters were used based on this shape structure. Most characters, he determined, belong to the first two shape categories he identified, 1 and 2, where the character can be neatly split in half. This can be done vertically, as in 咽船墙街, or sliced through sideways: 安呈英芙. An astonishing 85 percent of characters belong to these two categories. Next came the diagonal divisions, 3 and 4: slant and reverse slant. Visualized as two stacked triangles, a slant character contains a diagonal stroke that bisects the upper from the lower triangle: 尻瘟著虎. Reverse slant is just like slant, mirrored in a downward slash: 遠迴彫毯.

Shape category 5 is more complicated: The pyramid pattern layers or nestles its components like a Russian matryoshka doll. Characters in this category do not fit into an angular area or quadrant but are partitioned according to an overlapping or draping pattern, like a Christmas tree: 奋奉巷馨. The common wisdom that any Chinese character fits into a square space—hence one of its many aliases, "tetragraph"—was too coarse a concept for Du. He detailed their internal structure and refined the idea of components as shifting and modular. No character was too arcane or obvious not to warrant a close look. Du found that a squared pattern can be further broken down in shape categories 6 and 7, distinguished by enclosures and partial enclosures. As with categories 3 and 4, these two patterns are complementary. Full enclosure can be understood as putting squares within a square: 圖四目國. A border encases, at least in part, all the components, like a fence or divider. The graphic makeup of the character for "nation," 國, for instance—reappropriated in the early twentieth century from its former meaning of "kingdom"—is explained as a border that has to be defended by the people with spears, hinting at the intertwinement of violence and state power behind the modern concept of nationhood. Instead of being fully enveloped, characters in category 7 have a discontinuous border: 可 同 開 函. The opening can be on any of the four sides of the square and still brings to mind the contours of a full enclosure. Finally, there are characters that simply do not lend themselves to easy division. Du assigned these outliers to the indivisible category 8, the exception that makes the previous seven rules: 文 事 中 史.

Du, in essence, introduced a principle of modularity. His approach analyzed characters' shapes as inversely defined by the square space they occupied. Character components were treated as pieces of a puzzle, except that the same piece could be used in different places. With this, then, he built a card catalog system using shapes to search for any character as you would with letters for a word.

A Western card catalog is most likely organized by the author's last name. To find "Smith," you go first to the "S" section, skip anything

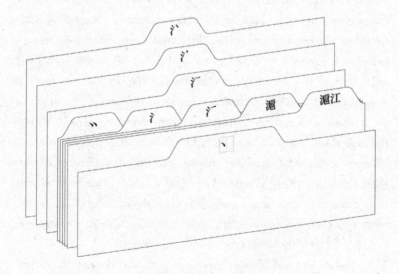

Du Dingyou's library card catalog system, using
components and stroke parts.

before "Sm," then slow down to look bit more carefully once you are in "Smi." Once you see "Smit" you will know you are very close, but if you see "Smits" then you have gone too far. And "Smith" is just between the two. It is like looking up a word in a dictionary. Instead of building with letters to find a word, Du treated the components of a character as you would an alphabetic ordering of successive letters. Instead of following the linear progression of alphabet letters, however, you follow the order in which the strokes of a character are normally written calligraphically within the imaginary square space, which can contain four quadrants: from top left to bottom left, then top right to bottom right. These quadrants, which are heuristic rather than part of the written character itself, constitute the square space that Du divides up into the eight possible patterns. He started with the basic stroke of the character *hu* 滬, ╲, in the left half of the square partition, and built out the character from there.

You can add another ╲ to make two splashes on the left, which is a component shared by a number of characters, like 江, 況, and 澌. That would be akin to looking in the "Sl" section in an English dictionary before you get to the "Sm" ("l" comes before "m" in the alphabetic order, just as the top splash stroke precedes the bottom splash when written out in Chinese). When you get to three splashes, 氵, now you are in "Smi" and getting warmer. That component happens to also be the radical for "water." Once you get to the top right portion, the specific stroke called for is another splash—but slightly different from the three on the left. Keep going and eventually, building stroke by stroke, this successive logic leads you to the character, 滬. If 滬 is not what you want, you would have branched off earlier at, for instance, 氵, 氵′, 氵ˋ. But the same process and logic holds.

Unlike Zhang and Wang, Du wanted to further develop the successive logic of alphabetism in Lin's shape analysis, rather than to turn to numbers like Wang Yunwu or to invent new spatial geometrics like his young unsuccessful challenger Zhang Feng. Looking ahead to the future of humanity past wars and conflicts, Du believed that the greatest challenge would be to enable nations to learn and understand one another's ways in order to mend past wrongs. His biggest worry was that, when that day came, no one would be able to find the right book on the right bookshelf. And if the Chinese script could facilitate that process of communication and open up China's tradition to outsiders, it would be a foundation on which to build deeper understanding. Others may have viewed the library as a mere physical repository for dusty old books, but Du saw it as a birthplace of world peace.

The thought stayed on his mind the day he fled Guangzhou. This was not a librarianship for the fainthearted. At the end of the seventy-two hours, Du and his colleagues made it to the crowded dock, joining the mass of refugees shoving and hauling their earthly belongings. They boarded six boats on the south side of the Pearl River, just under the bridge. Staring along the winding gray water down to its southward bend, flowing toward an uncertain future, Du knew he was fighting two wars.

THE FIRST FEW WEEKS were rough. Each person had to cram their body and belongings into about a foot and a half of space. Stashed in their carry-on rattan bags, grabbed in haste, were last-minute provisions: a change of clothing, towels, a toothbrush, soap, a bottle of antiseptic, a gas mask, antibiotic balms. These feeble talismans, they knew, were more for psychological comfort than any real defense against a flying shell fragment that could slice through an arm or a leg. They kept mostly silent, forging a deeper camaraderie out of a suppressed, shared sense of doom. Someone would despair from time to time, touching off everyone's unsteady nerves.

As far as the others could see, Du was immune to such outbursts of human emotion. They remembered how he did not think twice about saving books over people; some found his tenacity abhorrent and inhuman. Yet wartime adversity only inspired him to be more resilient. He assigned himself the task of buoying everyone's spirits. Even before setting out, he was already thinking about how to keep the mood light and upbeat. He started with practicalities. To transport the books over such great distances, how many and what size should the boxes be? He was not expecting modern accommodations at their final destination, so whatever they brought for transport had to last. And might not the travelers themselves enjoy a good book or two along the way, to take their minds off the war and to lift their spirits? How much nicer would it be if the reader had a decent surface to sit on while doing so? So Du designed an all-purpose modular structure, a "unit case" 32 by 12 by 7.5 inches that could fit neatly on a horse's back and was convertible into a bed, bench, and table. He named the design Doo's Sofa, and duly reported it to the *Bulletin of the American Library Association*, to the editor's great delight.

Despite his outward resilience, Du was not without vulnerabilities or delicate passions. He harbored an innate sense of fairness and justice almost to a fault, and was fond of maxims that offered positive reinforcement: "Use your intelligence for good and all that you seek will be for good; use your intelligence for evil and all that you accomplish will be for the bad." One thing he always stuck to was the principle of efficiency, a maxim he practiced daily, it seemed, even in the way he wore his hair—all slicked back in one grand sweep, impervious to being parted to either side or in the middle. The only vanity he allowed himself was a pair of black-framed Harold Lloyd glasses, perched across his down-triangle face like a supportive crossbeam.

Most of all, Du did not believe in shortcuts. Taking pride in having never enjoyed a day off work, he naturally looked upon the shenanigans of the 1920s index fever with disapproval. Keeping himself above the fray, he nonetheless had opinions. Where would Wang Yunwu's Four-Corner Method be anyway, he once grumbled, were it not for shape-based analysis? Wang did not address shape as a holistic entity. He simply rubbed out the straight edges of a properly shape-based analysis, Du sniffed, leaving only the corners as important. In fact, Du had announced his own shape-based proposal the same year that Wang unveiled his Four-Corner Index Method. Du published with a rival press, which sold his manual at seventy cents per copy. Wang, mobilizing the scale of the Commercial Press, was able to undercut that price by offering his at a slashed rate of twenty cents.

Du knew full well that his place was not in the limelight or front line of profitable commercialism. His niche was in the back-end support of library systems. After all, he had not followed a path like Lin Yutang's or Wang Yunwu's. His enlightenment did not happen in the comfortable setting of American or European universities. He earned his credentials via a cheaper route in the Philippines, at the time the far outpost of America's Pacific reach. There, he was able to get an American-style education at a fraction of the cost. He found a mentor in Mary Polk, an American librarian who helped to spearhead the development of library science in Asia. At that time, the field was only a few decades old and was an obscure subject of study, far less useful or glamorous than engineering or any of the practical industrial arts that China then valued from abroad. Even in Manila, it was marginal. Library science was a pilot undergraduate major at the university. Du was the program's first graduate, earning two other B.A. degrees along the way.

The truth was that Du had always loved books. He wrote about the amorous affair in a confessional essay, cast in the voice of a lover addressing his beloved. It was replete with winks and nods to fights, reconciliations, and ultimately an enduring lifelong partnership. From the beginning, the sheer sight of books seemed to make him swoon. The pleasure of touching them even made him tremble. Shelving them was like tapping his fingers on the naked curve of a lover's spine. It was not the passion for reading them from cover to cover or probing the secrets between the soft folds of white paper that most enthralled him. It was the sorting, classifying, and indexing that fascinated him to no end. So much so that Du wrote profuse odes to the temple that consecrated this bond, the modern library. He even created a special Chinese character for the book depot, or library 圕 (pronounced *tuan*). The character for "book," *shu* 書, is lovingly guarded by the enclosure *wei* 囗.

His dream at the Sun Zhongshan University had always been to build a world-class athenaeum, next to which he planned to build his idyllic house, where he would spend his days tending to his books and garden. The war cut that aspiration short. At the end of the long journey out of Guangzhou, Du found himself in exile with his books in a small village in a remote inland province in the southwest for the next year and a half. There, he would shed tears as he recorded the siege of Guangzhou. Not all was lost, he consoled himself. He had rescued some of China's most precious written volumes from the enemy's hands. The Japanese may have advanced inside China's borders, but on this particular occasion their destructive intent had been foiled on his watch. After the war, he would continue to rebuild his country's library system from the ground up, becoming the founding father of modern library science in China. He would propose a new universal classification catalog, combining East and West, modeled on his personal hero Melvil Dewey's decimal system.

As for the character index race itself, it left behind a critical legacy of studying characters by parts. The race prompted people to figure out a way to treat character parts as a finite set of modular units, like the twenty-six alphabet letters, and in an order that was predictable, systematic, and that could be analyzed statistically. It also treated all parts equally, openly dethroning the age-old privilege of radicals. Though library science was where component analysis found an immediate home, its full ramifications would not unfold until later in the century, when the need for Chinese character encoding in computers would once more revive the issue.

Though the character index race kept going strong into the 1940s, the war would redirect the tide of language reform, which was about to become a central point of contention between two rivaling parties. Both the Nationalists and the Communists recognized that literacy was the critical issue in mobilizing the masses. This was not just because every man, woman, and child had to rally to fight the Japanese in China's eight long years of lone resistance, but also in light of the opposing parties' coming death struggles with each other. By the 1940s, the Communists and the Nationalists were vying to consolidate their power via the war platform. Their multiple alliances to fight the enemy never lasted. With each breakdown of their temporary united front, their sense of betrayal and mutual hatred deepened. Language reform opened up a cultural arena for their contestation. The character index had built a new conceptual foundation, but the language war would soon shift back to Romanization. Research in that area had never ceased, and the timing was right to push it forward. The perils of war and the need for mass mobilization highlighted once more the urgent state of illiteracy among the populace. Whoever solved that problem would win the hearts and minds of China's multitude.

Meanwhile, in a sliver of a window between the civil war and the early years of Mao's founding of New China—officially known as the People's Republic of China—something wonderful happened for Lin Yutang. He did it. After decades of pouring his heart and soul into the project, he finally built his typewriting machine, one that set a precedent for a not-so-distant future of computing, shared by both China and the West.

. . .

ON A RAINY AFTERNOON in the early summer of 1947, three decades after he made his splash in *New Youth*, Lin hurried out of his apartment at 7 Gracie Square along the East River in Manhattan. Under his arm was a wooden case that he had carefully wrapped with thick waxed paper. It was a newly minted prototype of his Mingkwai Typewriter, "Clear and Quick," as he christened it. He had just welcomed his baby home, as he told a friend in a letter. The fourteen- by eighteen-inch machine was the first Chinese typewriter made for anyone's use, Chinese or Westerner, because Lin had designed it with a special keyboard. Any typist could type on it, even if he or she did not know a single character in Chinese. Every piece of information for locating a character was encoded on those seventy-two keys, which were simply labeled with character components instead of alphabet letters. It was no bigger than a standard QWERTY keyboard, and save for those Chinese inscriptions, it looked just like your average Western typewriter.

Lin was as excited as a schoolboy, because he had spent decades developing the Chinese keyboard to be used in the simplest, most straightforward way possible for printing up to ninety thousand characters. The answers to the questions of how to define a component and which to select for the number of spaces available on a keyboard came straight out of the principles he stated in his first essay on the Chinese index scheme in the pages of *New Youth*. Strokes were to him the true bones of Chinese character writing and carried the secrets of its compositional logic. Lin took advantage of the long-established calligraphic conventions of how strokes were written and in which sequence. He now repurposed that to redesign a complete retrieval system. The original first-second stroke pairs were now simply identified as the "top component" of a character—because the starting stroke always starts at the upper left-hand corner of the character—while another twenty-eight stroke combinations were identified as belonging to the "bottom component," which are the ending strokes that finish in the lower right.

Many indexers from the 1920s to the 1940s had tried to identify components that had even better objectivity and universal value, but only Lin came up with the logical consistency the task required. It was an elegant solution, as simple as it was evident. While not everyone can agree on what the four corners of a character are, anyone can see what is at the top or bottom. Instead of messing with lines, points, and planes, or all four corners of a character, or relying solely on a statistical analysis of shapes, he combined all three into a clear lookup system.

Unlike Devello Sheffield's or Zhou Houkun's typewriters, Lin's machine did not require an external cheat sheet pasted atop the machine or multiple separate trays that stored slugs of characters according to the frequency or priority of use. All the mechanisms of selection and retrieval were factored into the design of the keyboard.

Lin filed an application with the U.S. Patent Office in April 1946 and looked for American companies that would develop the machine for commercial sale. It was his life's dream, even more so than being the world's most famous Chinese writer. He had authored dozens of books in English, had been nominated for the Nobel Prize more than once, and was a leading intellectual figure and satirical essayist in China. But nothing was more precious to him than the package under his arm that day. The Remington Typewriter Company had asked to see the prototype, and Lin was going to give a demonstration with the help of his daughter Lin Taiyi.

They walked into a conference room where a small group of Remington's top executives waited. Lin gave a general introduction to the Chinese language and noted that, even though one-third of the world's population used the Chinese script in one context or another, there was no easily operable typewriter. His machine was the solution. The top three rows held thirty-six top strokes, while the next two rows included twenty-eight bottom strokes. To operate, the typist visually identifies the correct top and bottom keys that made up the desired character and presses down both keys simultaneously. At that point, a type roller inside the machine matches those two movements to five to eight possible combinations, or characters. The qualifying characters show up in a projected window perched on the top of the machine, the "magic viewer," which allows the typist to identify the correct character from the displayed list. Once that has been decided, the typist presses one of the eight keys at the bottom row—where the space bar would normally be—marked by the numbers one to eight. Each number corresponds to a character in the display window. The typist presses the right key with the right number, and that releases the hammer to print the desired character on the paper. Much to Lin's chagrin, however, nothing happened when his daughter pressed the keys in the Remington office. There was a glitch.

The malfunction was easily fixed, but Lin had lost his chance with Remington. Inventing the machine was easy, it turned out, but commercializing it was hard. The demo that afternoon was the first of Lin's several attempts to sell his prototype for mass production. He mobilized every contact and network that he had accrued as a writer, and newspaper headlines raced to announce his invention. His influential friends sent their congratulations; his house was heaped with telegrams and flowers. Chinese students, merchants, and residents in and around New York flocked to see the famous writer and inventor. The revolutionary Chinese typewriter had finally arrived for the world to see—and to use.

After Remington took a pass, Mergenthaler Linotype Company considered the prototype. Like other big companies, they feared that, because China was embroiled in an all-out civil war, conditions for production and sales were too uncertain. No one wanted to risk a loss, as it would take a significant investment to launch Lin's machine. The parts, especially the keyboard and the characters, would have to be customized. Meanwhile, unbeknownst to the world, Lin was also almost bankrupt. The invention had drained all the royalties from his several bestsellers, and a rebuffed loan request almost cost him his friendship with his publisher, Richard Walsh, and his wife, the writer Pearl Buck. Lin did not really have to spend all that time and all those resources building the machine, because what really mattered was just the keyboard. But he wanted to see the idea he had long nurtured take external form as an independent object—a gift to the Chinese people, he called it.

Sure enough, the typewriter took on a life of its own, but not in the way that Lin had expected. In 1948, Mergenthaler offered him a contract for a preliminary study for manufacturing, five thousand U.S. dollars per month for up to two years. Lin accepted and had nothing further to do with the machine. At the time, however, the Cold War had begun and the United States and the Soviet Union were racing to make advances in cryptography research and machine translation, the automated translation of human languages by machines, one of the first areas of research in artificial intelligence. Both superpowers saw clearly that whoever controlled the computer would control the future of information.

After Mergenthaler bought the rights from Lin, the U.S. Air Force acquired the keyboard in an effort to study machine translation and disk storage for rapid access to large quantities of information. Chinese had been identified as one of the priority languages of study. The USAF handed Lin's keyboard to an engineer named Gilbert W. King, the director of research at the IBM research center in upstate New York. King later moved to Itek, a defense contractor in Massachusetts, where he coauthored a seminal scientific paper on machine translation. He also unveiled the machine they built as a result of studying Lin's keyboard—the Sinowriter, a device for converting Chinese-character texts into machine input codes for processing Chinese into English.

Lin's keyboard provided pivotal evidence for how Chinese can be used in a photographic system of storage and optical retrieval. His reorganization of the Chinese script, by assimilating it to an alphabetic logic, put it in position for the upcoming digital age, almost forty years before China even had a computer. Computerized Chinese using Chinese characteristics would be the character index race's lasting legacy. Little did anyone know at the time that the Chinese script was much further along the path of modernization than they could have ever hoped. As Lin's keyboard made its lone way to the core institutions of America's computer and military research, it would not lie gathering dust. After IBM, it would have a still greater role to play.

For now, though, the Cold War was pushing internationalization higher up on the agenda of the recently established Communist China. In the years between the time that Lin filed his patent application and its approval in 1952, China underwent its last big political transformation of the twentieth century. Still glowing from its victory, its new leader would declare Chinese language reform the incomplete revolutionary road forward. A strong state's hand now guided China's linguistic path. In the name of the people, the Communist government looked to literacy as a promise they could deliver. Under Mao, important legacies would be created. They would leave an indelible mark on the modern face of the Chinese script.

FIVE

WHEN "PEKING"
BECAME "BEIJING"
(1958)

SIMPLIFICATION AND ROMANIZATION

In February 1955, twelve men convened to plot the future of the Chinese script. Among them were a onetime Esperantist, a former anarchist, a linguist, and several bookish academics. While some of them would be immortalized in the pages of Communist Party history, it wasn't the lure of fame that had drawn them to the project. As young men in the 1910s, many of them had attempted to overthrow the elite literary language and promote the vernacular. Having survived several failed revolutions, decades of factional infighting, a near conquest by Japan, and the Second World War, they knew all too well that dreams can be quickly and violently upended. Nevertheless, the call to duty from the Committee on Script Reform was one that all these citizens were ready to answer. Bespectacled men with furrowed brows, they became the Committee on the Scheme for Chinese Phonetic Writing, better known as the Pinyin Committee.

Some of them had been with Chairman Mao at Tiananmen Square for the founding ceremony of the People's Republic of China, or PRC, in 1949. On a crisp October morning, standing before an ocean of colorful banners, China's new leader greeted a well-orchestrated crowd, carefully vetted and trucked in before dawn, while loyal supporters like Zhou Enlai loomed behind him. Wearing a worker's cap and his namesake five-button suit, Mao reportedly uttered one of his most quotable sayings: "The Chinese people have risen!" The crowd roared.

Although Mao did not actually say that phrase—as restored footage of the event revealed decades later—the speech that he delivered was in a rustic Hunanese accent as thick as the earth he stood on. Mao did not speak a word of Putonghua, the common speech derived from the northern-based Beijing Mandarin. Yet Mao went down in history as, among other things, the political figure who guided the Chinese language through its two greatest transformations in modern history. The first was character simplification, which would reduce the number of strokes in more than 2,200 Chinese characters. The second was the creation of pinyin, a standardized phonetic system using the Roman alphabet and based on the pronunciation of Putonghua ("pinyin" means "to piece together sound"). Mao would lead the country through these dramatic changes, but not by example; he would never get used to writing simplified characters in his lifetime, or even Roman letters.

Following Mao, the Communists had fought and won a civil war in the name of the people—workers, peasants, and every member of the exploited underclass. At the founding of the PRC, more than 90 percent of the country was still illiterate and communicated in regional dialects. Romanization would be Mao's way of delivering his promise to the people, and the people to their linguistic destiny. It would be a new bridge to learning Chinese characters, employed in aggressive anti-illiteracy campaigns. The Committee on Script Reform was appointed to orchestrate the effort.

Mao Zedong had first started to think about the question of language modernization when he was a humble assistant at the Beijing University library in 1918, processing newspapers on a meager salary and rooming with housemates. He returned home to Changsha in the spring of 1919, just weeks before the May Fourth Movement broke out in the streets of Beijing. The movement sparked the ambitions of twenty-five-year-old Mao, an avid reader of radical publications like *New Youth*. He could only look on from afar at the time, writing passionate letters of support to those who led the cause in the capital. He was stirred by their cries to sever ties with the feudalist past and inspired by their declared war on the dead, literary language that had been deaf to people's spoken tongues for centuries. Though he would soon turn Changsha into his own base for radical ideas, Mao was not at the center of any movement. He was little known.

Thirty-six years later, holding the future of the Chinese language in his hands, Mao could recruit whomever he wanted to reform the Chinese language, and the twelve men he chose had the requisite experience and expertise. They would take charge of the planning, testing, and dissemination of the reforms. The Chinese script revolution was going to make its greatest language leap forward yet—with Mao's strong directive from the top.

For Mao, Romanizing Chinese for the Chinese was an essential element of national and political self-determination. He and his advisors took a two-pronged approach to literacy: harnessing the Western phonetic alphabet to make Chinese easier to access for the Chinese and foreigners alike, and reducing the number of strokes in characters to lower the threshold for reading and writing Chinese characters. Working in complementary ways, Romanization and the simplification of Chinese were intermediary measures for preserving the Chinese language while stamping out illiteracy.

CONTRARY TO POPULAR BELIEF, the credit for simplified characters in modern times cannot go to Mao and his committee alone. The first concrete proposal for character simplification was made in 1920, under the Nationalists' rule. The linguist and reformer Qian Xuantong, who extolled Lin Yutang's character index system, advocated for reducing stroke counts overall. Simplification had already been in practice for centuries outside the formal courts and halls of learning. About 80 percent of current simplified characters existed before the mid-twentieth century, and of those about 30 percent had been in use before the third century.

Simplified script was formed by popular usage and frequently found in account books, invoices, medical prescriptions, and performance scripts for actors—all documents for which it was more expedient to abbreviate characters than to write them out fully. Street vendors and entertainers skimped on strokes to make transactions and note taking easier on the spot. Some of the simplification also originated in calligraphy. The cursive and running styles favored fast, efficient, and minimal connections between strokes under the swift motions of the brush. Other simplified characters came from shamanistic and secret writings. Daoists used simplified characters to summon the spirit of past sages, while the Taiping rebels of a nineteenth-century sectarian Christian cult, led by a Chinese man, Hong Xiuquan, who believed himself to be God's second son and brother to Jesus, were the first to promulgate the official use of simplified characters in their documents, written records, and self-issued currency.

An important monument in the history of simplified Chinese writing, which otherwise features so few women, is a secret script, still used today, created by women themselves. Nüshu, literally "women's script," was a simplified writing system that used fewer strokes and gave women both literacy and a means of private communication with one another. It came from a small area in the southernmost tip of Hunan Province, where diverse ethnicities have historically resided. The script has been used for centuries and is believed by some to be as old as the oracle bone script, which contains the earliest examples of simplified writing. Women used this secret script to bypass the limits placed on them in traditionalist society and to create a world of literacy for themselves. Like children, they had limited access to written language and were restricted to the domestic realm, so nüshu was used mainly as an in-group, private form of communication. Its very existence puts a crack in the otherwise continuous presentation of writing as a mark of authority, the state, and patriarchal rulers.

Women's secret script powerfully took its inspiration from the stitching in embroidery. It incorporated crisscross patterns into the interweaving strokes of its slender, tightly vertical form, rather than the usual, more complicated and square structure of characters. Alternative or secret scripts in general were considered cultish, unsanctioned, and heterodox. They diverged from the orthodox full character forms and for that reason were occasionally purged by the authorities. Women's script, for instance, was persecuted as witchcraft for a time after the founding of the PRC.

The New Culture Movement of the 1910s and 1920s took a different approach. Its goal of revitalizing vernacular speech aimed to bring speech to writing, galvanizing a generation of young intellectuals and industrial inventors. They followed the pledge of earlier reformer and poet Huang Zunxian: "Let my hand write what my mouth speaks." Vernacularism was promoted, and at times idealized, as key to the survival of the Chinese language and people. That vision inspired a comprehensive effort to excavate past and present writings for examples of everyday language. Once people started looking, they discovered a vast treasure trove of simplified characters. Seeking to capitalize on this new knowledge, the leading cultural progressive Hu Shi—a classmate of typewriter inventor Zhou Houkun—called for the reorganization of national learning in 1919, which turned the reassessment of China's written tradition into an urgent cultural imperative. Hu acknowledged the vital work of the character index movement along the way.

In the early 1920s, after the first call for simplified writing, the Nationalists began to systematically collect, vet, investigate, and collate simplified characters. But the ceaseless political turmoil of the 1910s, 1920s, and 1930s made systematic reforms impossible. The cost of building new typographical matrices to print the newly simplified characters was a serious material constraint. Combing through the Chinese lexicon for earlier examples that could be useful was also demanding work. An official set of 324 characters for simplification was not proposed to the Ministry of Education until 1935, after more than a decade of full-scale research. Jiang Jieshi (Chiang Kai-shek), leader of the Nationalist government, tried three times to push through simplification schemes. Having grown up with traditional characters, the conservative senior members of the Nationalist Party would not hear of touching a single stroke on a written character—not while there was still breath in their bodies, they vowed. Jiang had to back down to avoid offending and disrespecting his party's elders. One of them purportedly got down on his knees to beg Jiang to spare the life of the Chinese script. Mired in protracted objections and logistical obstacles, the project folded.

While the Nationalists dawdled, the Communists took up the cause of simplification and made it their own. During the War of Resistance against the Japanese, they began to print simplified characters in the local newspapers that were circulated in the areas under their control. The use of these characters fanned out into the rest of the country after

1949. Simplified writing attracted more and more attention as discussions and debates grew. Eventually the Ministry of Education selected around five hundred simplified characters to be reviewed by experts and linguists. The task was handed over to the Committee on Script Reform for further investigation once it was established in 1952.

The committee completed the first draft of the official simplification scheme by late 1954. A list of 798 characters was formally introduced the following January to great enthusiasm. The Ministry of Education delivered three hundred thousand copies of the *Preliminary Draft of Han Character Simplifications* to various cultural organizations and educational institutions around the country for comment and feedback. More than two hundred thousand individuals weighed in with opinions. The Committee on Script Reform alone received more than five thousand letters. Up to 97 percent of those polled approved of the preliminary simplification scheme.

The party cadres were euphoric. Bringing back simplified script to the masses, after centuries of denying it official sanction, was true to the egalitarian principles of socialism. In the days after the scheme appeared in print, one linguist recalled, comrades congratulated one another wherever they met, rejoicing in the fact that the people's voices were finally being heard. At the time, the People's Liberation Army was still engaged with the Nationalist forces across the Taiwan Strait. It eventually ousted Nationalists from their last strongholds on two small islands, less than twenty-five miles off of mainland China, with intense shelling and bombing. Was that not yet another harbinger that a new era had dawned, the comrades would ask while greeting one another. The simplified script was the cultural monument of New China's triumph over the Nationalists.

The simplified form of every character that survived the committee's scrutiny was disseminated widely in print to familiarize the populace with its new look. While the government could not control how people wrote characters by hand or in private, it could change conventions by regulating how a character appeared as a font on a page. This measure was not easily reversed—in order to be printed, each simplified character required a brand-new typeface. Casting copper typefaces was costly, time-consuming work given the country's traditional, even primitive, printing process. So the choices had to be deliberate. Inevitably, there were conflicting ideas about what parts of characters ought to be reduced, which resulted in more revisions in subsequent versions of the simplification schemes.

It would take several more rounds before the character-simplification scheme reached its fixed form with 2,235 characters in 1986—and that number would continue to increase with subsequent adjustments. Though the bulk of the reduction concerned individual whole characters, a number of simplifications focused on components or radicals, with the idea that their new form could be plugged into any character that used the same part.

Among the beneficiaries of character simplification were China's workers and peasants. Their testimonies, volunteered or encouraged, lent the scheme its greatest legitimacy in the eyes of the people. After the release of one of the drafts, a humble typesetter came forward and testified to the scheme's infinite improvement. After decades of picking out character typefaces and arranging them for print, he was grateful to have characters that were easier to recognize. Variant forms were consolidated into one simple form, and someone like him would never have to agonize again over the six different ways of writing the character for "window." Another comrade typesetter recalled how before the reforms she had been on her feet eight hours a day, moving type trays back and forth. Now, with restrictions placed on the number of characters as well as the number of strokes in a character, she could do her work sitting down for part of the day. Mao said that the masses were the true heroes and their opinions must be trusted, and they felt that their daily experiences with wielding the Chinese script were part of the nation's grand struggle for socialist modernity. It was Mao's cultural workers who brought literacy to every man, woman, and child, from typesetters to soldiers, custodians to factory workers.

While there were reservations and objections to the simplified script—largely for cultural and aesthetic reasons—the rate of illiteracy began to decline under the twin implementation of character simplification and pinyin. By 1982, the literacy rate for people over age fifteen nationwide had risen to 65.5 percent, and it reached 96.8 percent in 2018.

Whatever support there was for character simplification among the Nationalists dwindled after 1949. After losing the mainland to the Communists and retreating to Taiwan, the Nationalists appointed themselves the true guardians of traditional culture and have kept the traditional written characters intact to this day. By distancing themselves from character simplification, they left room for the Communists to claim it as a central platform for New China.

The wounds of this contentious past are still fresh and reopen from time to time. The political weaponization of simplified scripts since 1949 on both sides of the Taiwan Strait, which divides mainland China from the proclaimed Republic of China in Taiwan, has only sharpened the differences between the old and new scripts. Proponents and opponents of simplification continue to hurl jabs and insults at one another. The character for "love" (愛 in traditional form and 爱 in simplified form) is a favorite example. The simplified version replaces the component for "heart" 心 with "friend" 友. What is love, the champions of traditional characters ask, with no heart? One online critic argues that "since the simplification of Han characters, one can no longer 'see' one's 'relatives' (親 vs. 亲). . . . The 'factories' are 'emptied' (廠 vs. 厂), while 'flour' is missing 'wheat' (麵 vs. 面). 'Transportation' has no 'cars' (運 vs. 运). . . . 'Flying' is done on one 'wing' (飛 vs. 飞)."

Advocates of simplified characters, in turn, have come up with their own character tales to tell. They argue that simplified "love" is more expansive and modern, extending generously to friends and comrades rather than being narrowly guided by the selfish heart. Another case is "masses." After some strokes were judiciously pruned away, the character is now composed entirely—and rightly—of "people" (眾 vs. 众). "To destroy" no longer has the superfluous radical of "water" (滅 vs. 灭), which served no semantic or phonetic purpose. And as for the character for "insect," who wouldn't want to avoid the creepy-crawly pests as much as possible? At least one is better than three (蟲 vs. 虫).

Both sides have their own clever retorts to reinforce the line drawn in the sea: Taiwan, the preserver of tradition and heritage (shared with Hong Kong and Macau), and the PRC, the custodian of revolution and class. It's an ongoing family feud that few outsiders can fully understand.

CHARACTER SIMPLIFICATION was the more conservative of the two major language campaigns launched under Mao. It was about reorganizing and fine-tuning what was already within the culture's writing practice rather than creating something wholly new. Romanization was more radical; it would give the Chinese script a different face in the world.

The roots of Romanization in the country ran deep—back to early encounters with Western missionaries and their various experiments beginning in the 1580s. The French, Spaniards, Portuguese, Russians, and Poles each had their own way of transcribing the Chinese they heard. Since the late nineteenth century, the dominant system in English was Wade-Giles, first developed by the British diplomat and official Thomas Wade in 1859 and later refined by his colleague at Cambridge University, the Sinologist Herbert Giles, in 1912. It was a godsend for Westerners, who could finally spell out Chinese in Roman letters in order to pronounce it.

Wade-Giles wasn't perfect, and complaints were as old as the system itself. Based on the southern variety of Mandarin, it did not reflect China's later standardized national pronunciation. Its placement of dashes and apostrophes also could be forced and confusing. Even native Chinese had a hard time remembering its awkward rules. It moreover didn't have a way to differentiate between same-sounding characters that were semantically different. Still, Wade-Giles was adapted to other European languages like Danish, German, Spanish, and Turkish and intended to satisfy all their Chinese transcription needs.

The Chinese wanted to create a Romanization system of their own—one that suited their speaking habits. Students returning from Europe in the earlier part of the twentieth century had advocated for Esperanto (invented by a Polish ophthalmologist in 1887); entertained the use of Volapük, meaning "language of the world" (cobbled together from mainly English, German, French, and Latin by a German Catholic priest in 1879); and considered Idiom Neutral, devised in 1902 to combine the best of Esperanto and Volapük. But these artificial languages, lacking native speakers, never really succeeded in replacing natural languages anywhere in the world. Other phonetic alternatives seemed more intuitive, using more native markers of sound, like Wang Zhao's *Mandarin Combined Tone Alphabet.* Bopomofo, first proposed in 1912 and then officially promulgated in 1918 as the National Phonetic Alphabet, would remain the most widely observed auxiliary phonetic system on the mainland until the introduction of pinyin. By the time of Mao's youth the country had not yet settled on a single Romanization scheme.

While using Bopomofo was more natural for Chinese people, it was not an obvious choice for foreigners. Its symbols, when first introduced in 1908, looked more like archaic script than modern-day characters. Only those already culturally familiar with calligraphic strokes and the nuance of reverse-cut tones found Bopomofo intuitive. The learning threshold for nonnative speakers was high. A single Romanization system that appealed to foreigners as well as to the Chinese was needed to enable China to further industrialize and thereby internationalize its socialist vision.

In the 1920s and 1930s, two competing Romanization systems emerged: the Nationalists' Gwoyeu Romatzyh, or National Romanization, and a later arrival, the Communists' Latinxua Sin Wenz, or Latin New Script. Each political party touted its system as an instrument to win over the masses, especially the huge, barely literate peasant population in the countryside.

The pursuit of a national Romanization system first got under way in 1923 during the Nationalist period. A research committee was formed under the aegis of the Ministry of Education, and it gathered all the most prominent intellectual progressives from the New Culture movement at the time, including Lin Yutang, Qian Xuantong, and Zhao Yuanren. Clever and ingenious like his friend Lin, Zhao had a voracious and eclectic appetite for Eastern and Western traditions, from linguistics to physics to mesmerism. He was the first to translate Lewis Carroll's *Alice's Adventures in Wonderland* into Chinese and was as comfortable composing a piece of music as he was inquiring into hypnosis. From the same class of young Indemnity Scholars as typewriter inventor Zhou Houkun, Zhao would become the most well-known Chinese linguist of the twentieth century. He had a distinct flair in his approach to the study of the Chinese language and set dialects to musical notes to better classify their different tones. A staunch proponent of standard Mandarin, he later wrote textbooks and recorded his own enunciations of model Chinese on gramophone disks, which were distributed nationwide as Mandarin learning tools. Having spent time in the English alphabetic milieu in the United States, Zhao had been thinking about how to represent Chinese in the Roman alphabet as early as 1915. He would now become National Romanization's most learned and eloquent expert, as well as the main architect behind its system.

There were those who feared opening the gates to full-scale alphabetic—and thereby Western—domination. But the connection between a sound and a symbol, Zhao assured the skeptics, was more arbitrary than natural. Just as the French, Germans, and Italians pronounce and spell with the same set of alphabetic letters differently, and keep their own national tongues intact, so, too, could the Chinese use alphabet letters as a medium of convenience. A native speaker who does not know how to read but can already speak would be able to identify what is being written on a page by sounding it out. And learning the ideographs themselves would be made easier if one could learn them at first by sound—via the phonetic letters of the alphabet—instead of sight. Romanization would be a crucial bridge to widespread ideographic literacy.

That reasoning did not convince everyone. Other skeptics wondered how well, if at all, the alphabet could serve the ideograph. It does not take a linguist to recognize an obvious problem: there are more characters than available sounds in the alphabet. There is only so much phonetic or pitch nuance that can be conveyed with twenty-six letters for an ideographic lexicon of thousands. The problem exists on two levels.

First, there are an inordinate number of characters represented by the same spelling, or homophones. In English, the same pronunciation shared by two words—"kernel" and "colonel," "borough" and "burrow," or "muscle" and "mussel"—are exceptions, but in Chinese homophones are much more prevalent. The Romanized spelling of "*yi*," for instance, is shared by nearly two hundred characters. It could mean "one," "cloth," "to lean," "100 million," "a ripple," "she," "a squeal," and so on.

Second, characters with the same spelling may have a different tone—or sound pitch. Once you have the homophones down, you must further distinguish them by the tone. One can well recognize the world of difference in pitch between "yes?" and "yes!" even though it is not indicated in the English spelling of the two identical words. Tones in the Chinese languages, in contrast, are far more important for understanding what is being said than simply indicating a question or an emphasis. They help to further differentiate between characters that otherwise sound identical.

Tones have always been notoriously difficult to capture and notate on paper, even for the Chinese. Without an objective system that fixed sounds to characters permanently—like the Western alphabet with letters—tones shifted over generations of speakers. Reverse-cut had drifted very far from Wang Zhao's Beijing Mandarin by the early twentieth century; people no longer knew what tones some of the characters stood for. The entire system needed fixing.

Tones also vary from place to place, depending on the dialect—there are four distinct tones in standard Mandarin, six to nine in the Cantonese dialect, five in Shanghainese, and five to six in Taiwanese. Imagine trying to indicate the tones of an English that is simultaneously mixed with not only the inflections of Queen's English, Cockney, Scouse, Yorkshire, Brummie, Northern Irish, and Scottish, but also all the northern and southern varieties of American English, plus Australian English, Singlish (Singapore English), and Hinglish (Hindi and English).

Just as English has a great number of nonnative speakers around the world who bring additional regional sound varieties to the language,

Chinese spans a no less impressive geographical and linguistic realm. The difference between two dialects in China can be greater than that between Spanish and Italian. The tonal variety that has to be corralled into a single phonetic system under a single standard is daunting.

Both homophones and tones eluded foreigners for a long time. They have had long-standing difficulties distinguishing between spoken tones, leaving a trail of woes and warnings to others. It was fictionalized to full satirical effect in 1769 in a letter from an alleged missionary to a lady in Europe:

> I was told that *shu* means book. I expected that every time the word *shu* appeared, it would have to do with a book. Not at all: *shu* reappears, meaning tree. So there I am, divided between *shu* book, and *shu* tree. And so it goes on: there is *shu* great heat, *shu* storyteller, *shu* dawn, *shu* rain, *shu* charity, *shu* habituated, *shu* to lose a bet, etc. I would never finish if I wanted to give all the meanings of the same word.

Wade-Giles did not purport to solve all the problems. The design behind the system was modest: not to indicate accurately the pronunciation of Chinese for the Chinese but to come up with a transcription system that foreigners could use to learn the language. It took centuries to get the phonetic representation of Chinese down in a Romanized spelling system that most foreign users could accept. Faulty as Wade-Giles was, the alternative was worse—not being able to Romanize Chinese consistently at all.

Zhao was sympathetic to such woes. The alphabet medium was indeed a poor host and needed some help in accommodating the Chinese language. For one thing, none of the Western schemes—Wade-Giles included—ever thought of phoneticizing characters in groups. Western phoneticizers seemed hampered by a common misconception of Chinese characters: that they were monosyllabic, singular, self-standing entities. They grasped a character as an equivalent of a word. When the script reformer Lu Zhuangzhang, a contemporary of Wang Zhao, developed his phonetic Quick Script in the early 1890s, he had proposed linking the Romanized letters of characters together by using dashes. This is, in fact, how Chinese has always been spoken and used, in pairs if not phrases, which makes immediately clear which character is meant in what context.

The pair of characters that stand for "butterfly" 蝴蝶 (*hudie*), or in "awkward" 尷尬 (*ganga*), for instance, always occur together because neither character would make sense without the other. The characters for "east" 东 (*dong*) and "west" 西 (*xi*) together mean "thing" or "object"—but only when they are alongside each other. Many character usages work like compounds in English, such as "schoolchildren" or "sunflower." Not grasping how Chinese characters occur in phrases rather than as independent characters makes all *shu*s look alike, when in fact they are each distinct in context.

While tones imparted nothing but torment to Westerners, Zhao considered them one of the Chinese language's most expressive qualities. To demonstrate, he used thirty-three different characters to construct a ninety-six-character parable about a certain gentleman, Sir Shi, who had a wildlife fetish and mistakenly tried to eat ten lions carved from stone. The story is vividly conveyed in succinct Chinese:

> 石室詩士施氏, 嗜獅, 誓食十獅。施氏時時適市視
> 獅。十時, 適十獅適市。是時, 適施氏適是市, 施氏
> 視是十獅, 恃失勢, 使是十獅逝世。氏拾是十獅
> 屍, 適石室。石室濕, 氏使侍拭石室。石室拭, 氏始
> 識食是十獅屍。食時, 始識是十獅屍實十石獅屍。
> 試釋是事。

Romanized without tone marks or indicators, however, it becomes a long string of monotonous gibberish:

> Shi shi shi shi Shi shi, shi shi, shi shi shi shi. Shi shi shi shi
> shi shi shi shi. Shi shi, shi shi shi shi shi. Shi shi, shi Shi shi
> shi shi shi, Shi shi shi shi shi shi, shi shi shi, shi shi shi shi
> shi shi. Shi shi shi shi shi shi, shi shi shi. Shi shi shi, shi shi
> shi shi shi shi. Shi shi shi, shi shi shi shi shi shi shi shi. Shi
> shi, shi shi shi shi shi shi shi shi shi shi shi. Shi shi shi shi.

The translation is:

> Stone house poet Sir Shi was fond of lions and vowed to eat ten
> lions. The gentleman went from time to time to the market,
> looking for lions. At ten o'clock, it happened that ten lions ar-
> rived at the market, and Sir Shi also just got there. Thereupon,
> looking at the ten lions, with the momentum of ten arrows the
> gentleman brought them to their deaths. He picked up the ten
> lion corpses and returned to his stone house. It was damp and
> he ordered his servant to wipe it down. The stone chamber hav-
> ing been cleaned, the gentleman started attempting to eat the
> ten lions' bodies. As he ate them, it dawned on him that the ten
> lions' corpses were actually the bodies of ten stone lions. Go
> figure.

Zhao's point was that without tonal differentiators, Romanization can never work for Chinese, because all *shi*s would look identical, as though repeated ninety-six times in the parable. This example illus-trates the most important feature of National Romanization: Zhao pro-posed signaling the tone with extra letters so that they are built into the very spelling of the character. That was how Zhao distinguished his Romanization scheme. He did not use additional diacritical or special marks outside of the twenty-six-letter alphabet, but he did use additional letters to serve the same purpose. Since the system was designed to Romanize the national language, Mandarin, it represented Mandarin's four tones by using a specific letter to indicate whether the spelling is to be pronounced in the second, third, or fourth tone (the first is simply the basic spelling with no additional letters). The Romanized form of a character like "*guo*," for instance, can be sounded through all its four tonal phases as follows: "guo" (first tone), "gwo" (second tone), "guoo" (third tone), "guoh" (fourth tone).

In 1928, a precious window opened for National Romanization to receive the official endorsement it needed. In June, the Nationalists' Northern Expedition concluded its two-year unification campaign with its occupation of Beijing. Though internal power struggles within the Nationalist Party itself would continue, the new government did portend a period of relative stability after more than a decade of political mayhem. The Nationalists relocated the capital to the city of Nanjing. Beijing, the "northern capital," was renamed Beiping, "northern peace"—or "Beeipyng," as National Romanization would have it.

The Ministry of Education promulgated National Romanization as the official scheme nationwide. Classes, textbooks, schools, and recordings of the national language standard pronunciation soon followed. Schoolchildren practiced its tones aloud in classrooms and adults adjusted to the new spelling standard in evening schools.

Despite an optimistic beginning, the so-called Nanjing decade would not remain peaceful. Just six days before their military campaign ended, the Nationalists purged their most important allies, the Communists. The CCP at the time had yet to define its overall strategy as a party and was still building its membership base. The CCP had worked hand in hand with the Nationalists in the countryside for years, earning the trust and support of the peasant masses while wrestling power away from the warlords who established their own fiefdoms after the 1911 Revolution. The two parties were able to set aside their ideological differences so long as they shared a common enemy. Once victory was in sight, however, the Nationalists made their intentions clear. Armed with guns and broadswords, they massacred thousands of Communists and suspected sympathizers in the streets of Shanghai.

For the next decade, as the ruling government of the republic, the Nationalists would make every effort to use their powerful military to quash the Communist Red Army. Language would be key in the struggle, as each party competed to grow cultural and political legitimacy. The Nationalists touted National Romanization as the first comprehensive Romanization system devised by the Chinese for the Chinese and in the modern standard Chinese language. It would accomplish what centuries of foreigners and Chinese alike had failed to do—to phoneticize Chinese in a single, complete system.

The Communists, however, came to hold a different opinion as to how to Romanize and especially whom such a system would serve. When the research on National Romanization began, the Chinese Communist Party was barely two years old. As the party grew stronger, they came to challenge Nationalist rule in the cultural arena. The Communists took issue with the fact that National Romanization was led by intellectuals, not the people, and that it enshrined Mandarin as the national standard, which meant accommodating only its four official tones while excluding all other dialects, some of which had up to seven or nine tones. The Nationalists failed to prioritize the masses, the Communists proclaimed. They were elite to the core, enforcing a top-down decision on the people.

The stakes were high for a power struggle that would forever reshape China's political landscape. Both parties raced to secure the loyalty of China's most important power base—the peasants. The Communists were out to upend the Nationalists, and it was an ardent, pale-faced young Marxist who investigated the scope of the problem.

IN 1921, TWENTY-TWO-YEAR-OLD Qu Qiubai was dispatched by a Chinese news syndicate from Beijing to the Soviet Union with a mission to report on the post-Bolshevik regime. The journey would become a personal quest as well as a political pilgrimage for this rookie journalist with delicate features and a touch of melancholy. Qu unexpectedly met many compatriots on his way to Moscow, among them Chinese laborers and shopkeepers ensconced in the Far East cities of Irkutsk and Chita. The Chinese had been settling in Siberia for decades, working as small-time traders, merchants, or laborers. Some Chinese described Chita as a passive colony because of the sheer number of Chinese who lived on the other side of the Sino-Russian border. In Chita, Qu met with the local leaders of the Association of the Overseas Chinese and befriended their constituents. The association had twelve branches and seventy thousand members throughout the region. He had no trouble finding a tea shop on one of Chita's side streets and even spotted a Chinese flag in the train station.

Like China, the Soviet Union covered a large landmass and had just undergone a violent revolution. Its social landscape was riddled with poverty and filled with lament. Having come from the fallen gentry, growing up poor and separated from his family, Qu was drawn to the Chinese migrants' plight. He was in search of a cause greater than his troubles. He wrote with great compassion and sympathy about the strangers he met and grew indignant at the sight of ragged peasants on the filthy streets of small towns and border cities. As if life had not already dealt them a harsh-enough hand, their destitute existence was made more precarious by the banditry rife in the region.

The ills of capitalism and class exploitation, he wrote passionately in the reports he sent home, would reach a breaking point, and nowhere more so than in China, the next stage of class struggle. What he witnessed in Moscow, after Chita, strengthened his conviction that a world socialist revolution was at hand. He decided to join the Chinese Communist Party.

Qu returned to China in 1923 and served in the party's propaganda department. As a journal editor and essayist, he helped promote its campaign and rose through the ranks. After the former editor of *New Youth*, Chen Duxiu, was relieved of his duty as party secretary as the result of a conflict with the Comintern, an international organization that propagated world communism, Qu filled the post temporarily. It quickly became clear that Qu was more of an idealist than an ideologue, because he was not terribly adept at internal politicking. His ideas struck his comrades as more impassioned and philosophical than concrete and executable. In 1927, when the Nationalists broke their alliance with the Communists, the Communists founded the Red Army and quickly mounted three failed uprisings. Qu was sent back to Russia in 1928 with many of his fellow Chinese Marxists to regroup under the tutelage of their Bolshevik brothers.

By this time, the language question occupied the forefront of the Soviet Union's policy toward its own national minorities. The newly unified Soviet Union included swaths of Central Asia that did not speak or read Russian. Among the groups in these regions that already had a written tradition, Arabic had been in use for almost a thousand years. Some of the national minorities in Turkic Central Asia had no script at all. Pacifying and assimilating these groups would require careful strategy from the Soviets. Reducing illiteracy with Latinized scripts became a key part of a general campaign to educate and control the population.

After the Bolshevik Revolution of 1917, the Central Asia Turkic republics began testing the Latin alphabet as a medium for their spoken languages. Many Turkic groups saw Arabic script as increasingly insufficient to meet the practical demands of modern life, much in the same way that Chinese reformers had viewed character writing as a disadvantage in the technological age. As a Soviet Tajik poet explained, the Latin alphabet flew at the speed of an airplane, while the Arabic script limped along like a weak donkey in pain. Others saw the conversion to Latin script as a matter of sharing in humanity's survival, because written records provide continuity from the past into the present.

The Soviet Central Committee supported the Latinization of the Arabic script in pursuit of a multinational language policy. The idea was to give each group its own right to linguistic self-determination within the newly unified Soviet state. Fifty-two languages were targeted for conversion to Roman script and about seventy were eventually Latinized, spanning an area that stretched between Norway and Korea.

In truth, Latinization was also a way to divide and conquer. From the Russians' perspective, Central Asia was about as savage and backward as a place could be—and they found its inhabitants difficult to tell apart. The Azerbaijanis were often referred to as the Tatars, Uzbeks as the Sarts, and Tajiks as the Uzbeks. If the Soviet East were to be brought to heel, the Russians thought, it would have to be purged of its Islamic influence. It was convenient to seize on the Arabic script as an object of backwardness in need of reform. And as long as the Turkic republics had their own separate writing systems—in Latin script, not the Turko-Persian Arabic that a few groups were already accustomed to—it would be harder for them to form a pan-Islamic alliance that could challenge Soviet rule. Only later, in the late 1930s, would language policy shift from Latinization to Cyrillization. Once these groups were sufficiently distant from their mother tongues, Russian control and influence could strengthen.

The Soviets were eager to include the Chinese laborers of the Amur region as a test group in their anti-illiteracy Latinization campaigns, hoping to extend their influence even further into Asia. These were the Chinese laborers whom Qu had met during his first trip to the Soviet Union. Their illiteracy rate was almost 100 percent.

The Soviet campaigns were instructive for the Chinese Communists, at the time young political upstarts. During his time in China serving the CCP, Qu had been immersed in Chinese language debates and consequently had a more informed perspective on language reforms when he returned to the Soviet Union. Yet Qu was not a trained linguist. He solicited the help of the Russian linguists Vsevolod S. Kolokolov and Aleksandr A. Dragunov. He drafted a proposal for the Latin New Script in February 1929 and distributed two hundred copies among Chinese workers. A revised version, with further input from Kolokolov, was published that October and reprinted again the year after with three thousand additional copies in distribution.

The Chinese laborers cheered the effort. Night schools opened to teach them how to recognize simple phrases like "boiled water" or "I sell dumplings," as well as ideological questions like "To what class do poor people belong?" More than five thousand factory workers and peasants were able to read and write letters to their families by the time they graduated, thanks to the comrades who volunteered their time as instructors and administrators. Between 1931 and 1936, scores of Latin New Script textbooks and several literary works were circulated and taught. The demand was overwhelming. The language reformers could not train teachers or print textbooks fast enough. A weekly newspaper wholly printed in Latin New Script, *Yngxu Sin Wenz* (*Support the New Alphabet*), was published in Khabarovsk, with its forty-third issue appearing in late 1934.

Instruction in Latin New Script was touted as a hallmark event in an era of socialist brotherhood and mutual aid. The Soviets saw it as an opportunity to finally address the problem of illiteracy among the community of one hundred thousand Chinese laborers within their territory. As for the Chinese Marxists, they now had a linguistic instrument with which to reach their revolutionary goals: If the Chinese could read easily, they could be radicalized and converted to communism with the new script.

For Qu, it was inevitable, even imperative, that Latinization would replace written characters. Unlike National Romanization, which was designed by a small coterie of academically minded intellectuals and based on fancy linguistic theories, he remarked, Latin New Script was a practical phonetic script that served every dialect and every class.

Qu painted the Nationalists—and their National Romanization—in as poor a light as possible. Not only had they catered to Mandarin speakers, but their Romanization program was too complicated for the layman to grasp. He characterized National Romanization as a self-congratulatory intellectual exercise that excluded most everyday speakers. Qu would not have seen the humor or cleverness in Zhao's lion-eating Sir Shi—just evidence of the privileged class's excess. Only the Communist austerity of Latin New Script, straight from the mouths of the peasants themselves, could counter the Nationalists' bourgeois policies. Championing the cause of all speakers of the Chinese languages, divided by class rather than geography or religion, Qu and others believed they were standing up for the factory workers, coolie laborers, and toiling peasants who would drive the coming world socialist revolution.

The 1929 draft of the Latin New Script showed its intent for the future. It contained a few alterations to the alphabet. It did not utilize the letters "q," "v," or "x," which Qu at the time thought weren't useful for spelling Chinese. He added a couple of modifications, "é" and "ń," for distinguishing nasal sounds, and made provisions for a few compound consonants that were common in spoken Chinese: "zh," "ch," "sh," "jh." The idea was to stick to the existing letters of the Western alphabet so that no new letter had to be created or employed. Special note was given to three thorny sounds, "ji," "qi," "xi," which were enunciated differently depending on whether a speaker was a northerner or a southerner. They were rendered in Latin New Script as "gi," "ki," "xi," which was transmutable to accommodate either speaker.

Qu clearly tried to work within the existing pronunciations of the alphabet, with some attention given to the spelling of the syllables. The second draft, with the Russians' input, was more complete. It contained all twenty-six letters of the alphabet, which were correlated, as individual or combined letters, to the sounds one can find in the phonetic symbols of Bopomofo.

The Russian linguists also worked out the finer details of orthography—whether a polysyllabic word comprised of two or more characters in Chinese should be connected or written out separately, syllable by syllable, and whether to transliterate foreign words or leave them in their natively spelled form. In this regard, the Russians were working within the framework of the Unified New Turkic Alphabet and wanted their Chinese counterparts to be more or less consistent with that framework. Yet the Chinese were already thinking of how the system could be implemented back home. Exceptions were made to allow the Chinese to keep digraphs—"ch," "sh," "zh," "ng"—rather than representing them with cedillas—"ç," "ş," "ⱬ," "ŋ."

The Chinese laborers concentrated in the far-eastern cities of Khabarovsk and Vladivostok were the main test group, along with Blagoveshchensk and Artyom. The draft was presented and debated at the First Conference on the Latinization of Chinese Writing in Vladivostok in 1931. Qu was absent, having already returned to China for another assignment. But two of his comrades, Xiao San and Wu

ㄅ	b		ㄍ	g		ㄓ	zh		ㄧ	i		ㄞ	ai
ㄆ	p		ㄎ	k		ㄔ	ch		ㄨ	u		ㄟ	ei
ㄇ	m					ㄕ	sh		ㄩ	ü		ㄠ	ao
ㄈ	f		ㄏ	h		ㄖ	r		ㄚ	a		ㄡ	ou
ㄉ	d		ㄐ	j		ㄗ	z		ㄛ	o		ㄢ	an
ㄊ	t					ㄘ	c		ㄜ	e		ㄣ	en
ㄋ	n		ㄑ	q								ㄤ	ang
ㄌ	l		ㄒ	x		ㄙ	s		ㄝ	ê		ㄥ	eng
												ㄦ	er

Bopomofo matched to alphabetic sounds.

Yuzhang—known by their Russian names, Emi Siao and Burenin—presented and explained the scheme.

The conference opened in the Chinese theater in Vladivostok on September 26, 1931. Around fifteen hundred Chinese immigrant workers attended, along with eighty-seven delegates from all over the Soviet-Siberian and far-eastern regions. More than four-fifths of the delegates were Chinese, and most of them were factory workers from Shandong. Vladivostok had borne traces of Chinese presence since the 1870s. Street signs like Pekinskaya Ulitsa, or Beijing Street, and the Chinese Theater were evidence of how the Chinese had built their niche in the port city. The theater itself was a setting for their cultural life, host to Beijing opera troupes who would set the homesickness of the audience to song and gesture. After the opening, the conference moved to a smaller space at the Chinese Workers' May First Club for technical discussions.

People expected something entirely different than the National Romanization they knew. Surely, after so much effort devoted to maligning it and highlighting its shortcomings, Qu's scheme promised to be different. Significant revisions had been made with the help of Soviet friends. "There is no such difficulty that the Bolsheviks cannot overcome," the Russians exclaimed. "We are to accomplish a great deal to fulfill the grand mission of Latinizing the Chinese script." But it apparently did not have enough of the Soviet touch. The truth was that Latin New Script had simply coopted the most central principle of its mortal enemy, National Romanization.

Already in the 1929 draft, Qu noted the importance of marking the different dialectal tones in the spelling of the characters themselves, of which he named five. In the revised version, Qu called them "double consonants," spelled to cue "emphasis on the vowel." This amounted to no more than using additional letters to mark tones, much like National Romanization with the four tones of Mandarin. Instead of "guo," "gwo," "guoo," "guoh," Qu proposed "-en" for the first tone, doubled vowels for the third tone, double consonants for the fourth tone, and so on.

When Zhao devised the tonal spelling system for National Romanization in the 1920s, his hallmark contribution was to build the four tones of Mandarin into the spelling itself. But Zhao in fact had in mind a more relative range of accents, not restricted to Mandarin. By criticizing its elitist pretensions, Qu made National Romanization's bias toward Mandarin seem more rigid than it was. Simultaneously, he did more to spread the core principle of National Romanization than its supporters could have on their own by borrowing its tonal features for the Latin New Script.

Meanwhile, other forces brought about National Romanization's demise. Just a week before the conference on the Latinization of Chinese writing in Vladivostok, the Japanese invaded Manchuria. With that, the Nanjing decade ended, and the struggle for national salvation entered another period of chaos. The Japanese aggression had interrupted the Nationalists' consolidation of power. For the Latin New Script, it created an opportunity.

Within a year of being reintroduced in China in 1931, Latin New Script spread widely through the war effort. Between 1937 and 1942, Latin New Script provided a bushfire of resistance to Japan's cultural and military encroachment. The script proved effective and easy to learn and spread to key cities across the country, from the urban speakers of Beijing to the Miao ethnic minority in Guizhou. Young children were taught the new script in school and urged to teach the adults at home. Small neighborhood study groups self-organized to promote the learning of even just three or four characters a day. Latin New Script reached far abroad to Chinese communities in Xinjiang, Lyon, and San Francisco and spilled over into Southeast Asia—where two-thirds of the overseas Chinese population resided—and eventually made its way to Jakarta, Kuala Lumpur, Penang, Singapore, Bangkok, and the Philippines.

Latin New Script rose in tandem with the growing influence of the Chinese Communist Party. Though its members and the Nationalist Party would unite once more in 1936 to face a common enemy, the Japanese war had given the Communists an opportunity to build a popular base of support. The Pinyin Committee drew on Latin New Script as pinyin's immediate precursor, and Qu and his Soviet sojourn came to be well known.

Qu, however, did not live to see his efforts' lasting success. He was captured by the Nationalists in February 1935. Repeatedly refusing to switch his political allegiance, he was sentenced to death. On June 18, 1935, after penning his last verse, he asked a prison guard to take a photo of him before his execution, which was personally ordered by Jiang Jieshi. On his way to the execution grounds, he sang the Communist anthem and Soviet Red anthem in Russian and calmly accepted his fate. He was thirty-six years old.

Created during one of the most dramatic periods of China's internal political struggles, the Latin New Script prepared China for another language revolution: pinyin's consolidation of Romanization efforts in the 1950s. But there is a hidden prelude to this national story of linguistic struggle. Pinyin had another direct antecedent, long forgotten in narratives of national unity and class politics. Far from Beijing, on the fringes of its control and its struggle for national self-determination, a young Muslim villager built a crucial early link between the Chinese language and the Roman alphabet.

DRAW A HORIZONTAL line across the map from Beijing to Bishkek, and then follow it westward past China's border into Kyrgyzstan, a gateway to Central Asia. Through the Gansu Corridor you can trace the path of Genghis Khan, who led his nomadic warriors across the steppes, leaving terror and destruction in their wake. The corridor was one of the most lawless places on earth, a region of competing influence between Russia and Britain in the nineteenth century and a choke point for taming China's frontier.

Near Bishkek (formerly Frunze) and in Tashkent, the first Latinization scheme of spoken Chinese was developed, entirely independent of China. It shared no common roots with the initial late-Qing script reforms in southern China or the nationalization campaigns of the republic. The story begins on an unremarkable day in 1924, when at the end of a dirt road eighteen miles east of Frunze, a young Chinese Muslim embarked on a journey from the tiny village where he grew up. Iasyr Shivaza was leaving home for the first time. His eyes sparkled with defiance and his thick head of hair was brushed back, leaving two high cheekbones in plain view. He was going to start school at the Tatar Institute for Education of the Minority Groups in Tashkent.

Shivaza belonged to a Chinese Muslim ethnic minority called the Dungans, at the time a tiny population of mere thousands in the Aleksandrovka collective settlement in the Chu Valley. They lived alongside Kyrgyz, Russian, Uzbek, and Tatar neighbors. Within China's borders, Chinese Muslims were called Huis, as they still are today—"hui" 回 meaning "return" because of the pilgrimage to Mecca. The Huis are considered more Sinicized than the Muslims of Central Asia, like the Uighurs. On the other side of the border, under Soviet influence, Huis came to be called Dungans. Shivaza's family came from the poverty-stricken province of Shaanxi. His ancestors were illiterate peasants who had never learned to write Chinese characters. Following the Muslim rebellion in northwestern China in the 1870s, his grandfather took the boy who would be Shivaza's father and fled across the border, along with thousands of others. Apart from the few belongings they carried, all they brought was their spoken tongue, a Gansu-Shaanxi dialect that shared many characteristics with Mandarin. After crossing the border, this Chinese dialect had absorbed loanwords from Arabic, Turkish, Russian, and other languages and came to be known by the Soviet linguists—the first ones to study it—as Dunganese.

The son of a poor Communist blacksmith, Shivaza was handpicked by the Communist youth organization to go to Tashkent. An opportunity like that did not come very often to a remote village like Sokhulu, where Shivaza grew up reading Arabic from the Koran under a mullah's stern whip. Every day the students learned three to four Arabic letters and practiced writing them in ink on pieces of bone. The following day, after reciting them back to the teacher, the students would lick the ink off the bones to create a clean slate. Shivaza learned to write his own language in Arabic script. Physical punishment was the daily fare, and the young Shivaza was particularly rebellious and unyielding. As he was trying to find his bearings at the new school in Tashkent, little did he realize that the comprehensive strategy to tame the Soviet Union's wildest frontier was about to engulf his native tongue.

In February 1926, a congress opened in Baku, Azerbaijan, to discuss the fate of the Arabic script in expressing Turkic languages. Highly regarded linguists and writers from all corners of the Soviet Union— Crimea, Kazan, Yakutia, Bashkortostan, Azerbaijan, Uzbekistan— gathered at the Ismailiyya Palace. They met behind its yellow Venetian Gothic façade of lancet arches and Moorish domes to discuss how the lack of standard orthography impeded communication between the different groups. Lubricated by a generous supply of alcohol and cigarettes, they deliberated the issues in ways that strongly echoed how the Chinese saw their own writing system.

Though they had different reasons for Latinizing (the Russians wanted to eradicate the Arabic script, while the Turks hoped to repel Russian dominance), the delegates agreed to adopt a new writing system. It was necessary, they argued, because it was about 15 percent faster to write Arabic in the Latin alphabet than even in the Cyrillic alphabet—the other alternative at the time—and four times as fast to read (comparisons of Chinese to the Latin alphabet yielded similar results). Arabic was never well suited for the Turkic tongues anyway, because of the lack of vowels in the former and the importance of vowel harmony in the latter. Survival in an accelerating modern age depended on abandoning the old, ill-fitting writing system.

What the delegates did not know was that the Soviet language planners had bigger goals for Kyrgyzstan's Dunganese. They saw it as a possible wedge for opening a door to the East: "We must not forget that behind that small nation, we have great national mass in the East—behind them stands China." And behind it stood the 20 million people of Korea, who would be the next converts to the Soviet Union.

Through China's lost ethnic tribe, Russia intended to vastly extend its influence in Asia through linguistic assimilation.

The Baku congress ended with a resolution to Latinize, and the Unified New Turkic Alphabet was forged soon after. Among the first to feel the effects of its resolutions were Shivaza and his classmates in Tashkent. They were recruited to devise the first Dunganese Latin alphabet on the model of the New Turkic Alphabet by writing out their spoken language in Roman script. Though decades removed from when his grandfather first settled in the valley of Chu, Shivaza still spoke the Gansu-Shaanxi dialect his ancestors had used. Growing up, Shivaza heard the same diminutive "r" sound one could still hear in the streets of Beijing, a soft cadence in its local dialect. He learned old phrases from the bits of folklore his aunt told him when he was young. The lore and legends tied the Dungans to a past that was distinct from their Turko-Islamic neighbors. Caught up in the Turkic and Russian debates about linguistic survival and self-determination, Shivaza had a personal commitment to linguistic adaptation. He saw a unique opportunity to save and preserve his people's tongue, a chance for Dunganese to survive between the cracks of nations and empires.

Dunganese had one less tone than Mandarin, but its Gansu tones were unmistakable and understandable to a Mandarin speaker. Shivaza captured them as closely as he could in a draft of a Dunganese Latin alphabet, using the New Turkic Alphabet as a template. He also relied on help from the other young Dungans at the institute as he forged the first Latin system for their spoken Dungan dialect. A couple of his classmates would become the first Soviet scholars of Dungan studies as a result, but linguistic scholarship was not to be Shivaza's ultimate calling. He was discovering his own talents as a writer and poet.

The Dunganese Latin alphabet Shivaza helped to devise was submitted to the second meeting of the Turkology Congress in Tashkent in January 1928. It followed much of the New Turkic Alphabet and added a few more symbols adapted from Cyrillic. Another proposal drafted by the Kyrgyz Committee of the New Alphabet was also under consideration, but Shivaza's scheme was unique because it had originated with the Dunganese native speakers themselves. After its success at the meeting, Russian linguists formally took over the project and continued to study and refine the Dunganese alphabet at the Institute of Oriental Studies of the Russian Academy of Sciences in St. Petersburg. Taken out of the young Dunganese students' hands, it became part of a state-sponsored language project.

The fate of the Dunganese Latin alphabet now rested with Russian language experts in St. Petersburg, who forged a critical link between Dunganese and Latin New Script. After Shivaza's original draft was submitted to the Tashkent conference and turned over to the Institute of Oriental Studies, it went straight to Kolokolov and Dragunov, the Soviet linguists who helped Qu Qiubai finalize his draft. It had been the Soviets' plan all along to use Dunganese to achieve the Latinization of the Chinese language and to sponsor China's own Romanization as part of the alphabetization of the Eurasian continent.

Two powerful nationalist and internationalist narratives overshadowed Dunganese. One was the story of how world socialism rose to meet capitalism on the Eurasian continent. The other told of how the Chinese nation was reborn from the ashes of empire. The Soviets believed that they helped to bring Latinization to China. For them, the Latinization of Chinese was a consequence of the 1917 Bolshevik Revolution. The Chinese saw things differently—they thought Latinization had sprung from the blood and sweat of their own nationalist struggles since the nineteenth century. There was no place to credit marginal groups or their role in linking these histories. Dunganese was written out of this linguistic history altogether. Shivaza, though one of Chinese Latinization's pioneers, was not invited to the first conference in Vladivostok in 1931, where Qu's draft was debated. Instead, he attended a follow-up conference in 1932, which focused on the use of the Latinized alphabet by the Chinese inside the Soviet Union. By then, his original link to the Chinese Latinization project in China was already obscured.

For Shivaza's part, preserving Dunganese remained an unflagging personal mission. He became Kyrgyzstan's national poet and continued to teach Dunganese at a school in Bishkek, where he wrote or coauthored about eighteen Dunganese textbooks. He never ceased to encourage the Dungans to observe their own traditions and to remain in their communities. Though a deep friendship with the Chinese writer Emi Siao finally brought him to Urumqi and Beijing in 1957, Shivaza's trip to his motherland would be his first and last. He got to speak before his Chinese comrades, but while they were moved by the familiar sounds in his spoken Dunganese, he did not find any evidence of the union he thought he had been missing. He remained where he felt most at home, on the cusp of two language worlds, until his death in Frunze in 1988.

LATIN NEW SCRIPT proved to be the script that could rally the people. It brought the country closer to the final stage of its last linguistic transformation. On the eve of the founding of Communist China, a letter to Mao from the language reformer Wu Yuzhang—who had presented Qu's Latin New Script in Vladivostok—put character reform at the top of the agenda. Mao, who knew Wu from the Communists' struggles in the 1940s, passed the letter along to three of his advisors in education and literary affairs. On their recommendation, the Committee on Script Reform Research—the direct precursor to the Committee on Script Reform that would oversee the pinyin task force—was formed.

The members of the committee had all participated in the research and promotion of National Romanization, Latin New Script, or both. All of them were certain that phonetic orthography would replace character writing in just a few years. It was the dawn of the new era they had been waiting for. After more than eighty years of efforts that spanned the end of the dynastic reign, a republican government, dozens of revolutions and uprisings, two world wars, and an all-out civil war, language reformers—along with the rest of the country—were ready for the last conversion to a national scheme.

Yet the 1950s came with their own set of politics. Despite the proof of progress in National Romanization and Latin New Script, it was not a settled matter that Latin letters would be the way for pinyin, China's very own national phonetic system in the new era. There were more ways to phoneticize, or "piece sounds" together—what "pinyin" literally meant—than one. In 1951, Mao seemed to support phoneticization and reaffirmed the priority to reform the written character, but he remained vague about whether it would actually take a Latinized form: pinyin should be "nationalistic in form," complementing the Communist creed of "socialist in content." No one would blame the committee members for puzzling over what the chairman meant. Was a "national" form the same as "Chinese," and thereby to be forged from Chinese character parts rather than alphabet letters? Did that mean no foreign script at all, or that any script could be coopted in the service of Chinese pinyin? Perhaps Mao had in mind something like a sound notation system using traditional character strokes as phonetic symbols? But even so, should the Chinese script be kept for all eternity? If it were changed, should it stick to the logic of its own shape or be replaced altogether by phonetic symbols? One member, Ma Xulun, with proper deference, cautiously offered the interpretation that Chairman Mao had indeed ordered the phoneticization of the script, but as for the how, "it is not quite yet his final directive."

The party's initial preference was to derive something from the existing Chinese script. That was the topic of discussion at the committee's first meeting. The majority of the members wanted to use the sound scheme of Bopomofo as a blueprint and keep the basic premise of deriving any phonetic symbols from the character script itself.

The committee searched high and low for other examples of sufficiently national forms. As this was a language campaign for the people, the Pinyin Committee solicited ideas and proposals from the public. More than 650 proposals flooded in, coming from soldiers, factory workers, teachers, merchants, and even Chinese living abroad. Many were character based, using existing ideographs or an entirely new set of invented symbols. Others employed Latin or Cyrillic scripts. And some were more experimental, employing shorthand, geometric symbols, and even Arabic numerals.

From February 1952 to the end of 1954, the Committee on Script Reform Research worked to deliver what the chairman wanted. The primary emphasis was on a Chinese script-related written form that would seem to fulfill the criteria of "national form" most closely. They submitted a draft proposal in late 1954, with six possible forms: four drew from the Chinese script, using either characters or the symbols of Bopomofo. Two other minor proposals used Cyrillic and Latin letters (with five added letters).

Mao was not satisfied. He weighed in with yet another directive. The idea of pinyin was to simplify how sounds were put together, and the selected character strokes in the Chinese-based proposals were still too many for the purpose of phoneticization. He noted disapprovingly that some of the proposed symbols were even harder to write than Bopomofo. Pinyin script did not have to be in a rigid square ideographic form, and perhaps it should take lessons from the calligraphic style of running script, where the brush moves so fast that it does not completely leave the paper, so that the strokes connect more. This principle allowed the writing itself to be fluid and executable in one direction using connected strokes.

The committee went back to the drawing board. Its members might have heard that Mao himself was also receiving different advice from the Soviets, still the mentor to the young Communist China. After Stalin died in 1953, other Soviet advisors in China—including linguists—tried to pressure Mao into using the Cyrillic script instead. They wished to bring Mao's China further under its influence, just as they had hoped to do via the Latin New Script.

It became clear that the question of whether pinyin would take ideographic, Latin, or some other form would find no easy answer. So the newly renamed Committee on Script Reform announced an expert subcommittee in February 1955—the Committee on the Scheme for Chinese Phonetic Writing, or the Pinyin Committee—to find one. The committee was comprised of the twelve men whose work would unfold under the public eye. They split into two groups: one continued to sort through Chinese character-based symbols and assess their feasibility, while the other worked specifically with Roman letters—a de facto move away from Mao's vaguely defined "national form." Not the least of the considerations was how well the symbols could be reproduced in a linear fashion for typing, telegraphy, and typesetting. No final decision had been reached after a dozen more meetings, but there was agreement that the Latin alphabet, with some modified additions, would be put forth as the International Phonetic Alphabet of the Chinese script. A draft of the Latinized pinyin scheme was completed in February 1956.

Once again, an important litmus test was the public's reaction. The committee was more specific this time when they put out the request for feedback. An announcement in *People's Daily* solicited responses from all official entities at the municipal, provincial, and regional levels—including the ethnic autonomous regions. The draft consisted of thirty-one letters: twenty-five of the twenty-six alphabet letters (leaving out "v"), one Cyrillic letter, two newly created symbols, and two Latin letters from the International Phonetic Alphabet. The draft was announced and disseminated throughout the nation.

Discussions followed throughout the country. No less than ten thousand people nationwide participated. Workers from the postal service and telegraphic services, the military, railroads and transportation, and the education of the blind evaluated the proposal. By the fall, the Pinyin Committee had received more than 4,300 letters of commentary. A significant number of people vetoed the draft, and still more criticized it. Despite the successful past use of National Romanization, Latin New Script, and all the compelling arguments for decoupling Latin alphabetization from any negative associations with the West, many of those polled could simply not accept adopting a foreign writing system.

Was it not worth preserving, some asked, the very script that had grown up in tandem with the Chinese people over the millennia, enriched by their individual lives and experiences, their thoughts and struggles with reality? The Chinese script was born of the masses and sprang from the seat of the culture's emotions. No matter how complicated Chinese script was, a foreign script, with its own roots and origin, would always look strange and unfamiliar to the Chinese people. Curvy and windy to write, not to mention hard to pronounce, the Latin or Cyrillic alphabets would not be easily embraced by the general populace. Another argument looked to the future rather than the past: given that society would ultimately develop into a unified Communist world, where a single language and script would be desirable—and a final script revolution on a world scale inevitable—should one not think twice before rushing to go with the Latin script?

The desire to preserve the Chinese script in some form in the future pinyin system was hard to extinguish. But the state's will burned stronger, its pursuit of its own goal not to be deterred. Other difficulties also became apparent. Some authors among the hundreds of proposals, not satisfied with their first attempts, continued to send the committee's office a steady stream of revised symbols, graphemes, and homemade cursive scripts. The committee's daily task was to sort through the piles, only to start all over again the next day. Duty bound, the task force pored over every single submission and resubmission, carefully noting where more technical details were needed or how to fill in a conceptual gap in the author's explanatory notes. Every proposed notation was scrutinized like a possible diamond in the rough, lest the right one accidentally slip by.

The committee held more meetings and invited more participants from the publishing industry, education, culture and arts, and science and technology. It solicited more responses from language workers in dozens more cities outside of Beijing. Finally, a verdict was reached: While Chinese characters would continue to undergo the simplification process, the Chinese pinyin scheme would be in Latin letters as an auxiliary tool for learning written Chinese and propagating Common Speech, or Putonghua. The Latin script was deemed the best candidate for serving not only the existing Chinese writing system, but also the engineering of new writing systems for China's ethnic minorities. Fifty-five such groups, besides the dominant Han Chinese, were officially classified in Mao's era, and a number of them did not have their own writing systems. Latinized script would be their answer.

The final pinyin got rid of invented symbols and used all twenty-six letters of the Roman alphabet (though the letter "v" was reserved for spelling foreign words or the speech of ethnic minority groups in China). Pinyin also observed the exact order and orthographic conventions of the Western alphabet. There was just one small intervention: to facilitate the transition to using Roman letters, each letter was matched to a phonetic symbol in Bopomofo. The letters "q" and "x," nominated to replace the old "*chi*" and "*hsi*" in Wade-Giles, required the most straightening out. Place and person names were particularly important for correct postal delivery and communication with foreigners.

The Chinese character pinyin was approved in late 1957. The timing was felicitous, as in early 1956 Mao had called for "a hundred flowers to bloom, and a hundred schools of thought to contend." It was a much-touted but short-lived period of openness where all members of society were invited to comment on the government's policies, and as such was also the period when the Pinyin Committee was able to get people from all over the country to feel they were part of history in the making. People believed that their voices mattered, even though many of those who spoke out in matters of the party's political policies inadvertently put a target on their backs for future purges and persecutions. Mao reaffirmed the primacy of class struggle in a speech in June 1957, quashed dissent, and promptly sent over a half million intellectuals who disagreed with the party to labor camps or the countryside for reform. The so-called Anti-Rightist Campaign lasted for about two years. But in a brief safe window in early 1958, Premier Zhou Enlai upheld the goals of writing reform. The final pinyin proposal went to the National People's Congress in February 1958 for ratification. Pinyin was born.

The mood was euphoric and fervently patriotic. The change would impact more than 500 million people. Nothing like it had ever been attempted in the history of the world. Nationwide instruction began that fall. In the first year alone reportedly 50 million people learned pinyin. And that was just within China. Internationally, pinyin would be the name and spelling by which Chinese would henceforth be known—and no foreigner would ever be able to interfere again. Existing foreign-made Romanization systems like Wade-Giles, it was hoped, would be phased out from international usage once China started to circulate its own system. No longer would the Chinese have to tolerate Wade-Giles's confusing use of apostrophes. Nor would they have to live with Wade-Giles's "Peking"; henceforth the capital would be known in pinyin as "Beijing."

Decades later, Zhou Youguang, one of the twelve men from the Pinyin Committee, reminisced about the momentousness of their task. An original member of one of the subgroups that drew up the first draft of Chinese Romanization, Zhou lived to be 111 years old and came to be celebrated as the father of pinyin. But he knew better than anyone that it was a collective effort; everyone gave their utmost. It was a time of idealism and hope, after all, when New China promised a better path for its people and intellectuals and workers alike were roused by the bright rhetoric. "Mao promised us the rule of the people," he recalled. And pinyin gave the people their voice.

The year that pinyin was born—1958—also began Mao's bid for radical industrialization in the Great Leap Forward, which would last until 1961. China set goals to make giant industrial advances, increasing steel and building production capacity. Mao confidently predicted that in fifteen years the PRC would catch up to England, the leader of the Industrial Revolution. What happened after the hundred flowers period, however, was a dark harbinger of what was to come. Those who spoke their minds were branded as rightists and mercilessly punished for not toeing the party line. As a multiyear agricultural, ecological, and economic experiment, the Great Leap Forward would see between 16.5 and 45 million people perish from man-made famine— and things would only become worse. Those who expressed their dissatisfaction with the pinyin reform would be swallowed up in the years of persecution that followed. A scholar who simply spoke out against the hasty procedures in the character simplification campaigns was driven to suicide a decade later during the Cultural Revolution. Many more would not survive.

Pinyin would become the new linguistic platform on which China engaged the world from that point onward, its new international medium. The simplification campaigns were declared a success and began to spread beyond the PRC's borders. In 1971, as relations thawed between China and the United States, the People's Republic of China replaced the Republic of China (Taiwan) as the official representative to the United Nations. Simplified script was recognized as the country's Chinese writing system, and Singapore, followed by Malaysia, both with large overseas Chinese populations, adopted the PRC's simplified script. Pinyin itself was accepted by the United Nations as the country's official Romanized representation in 1977.

As China entered a new era of internationalization, a new technological integration challenge loomed. It would dwarf the earlier challenges of telegraphy. As much as the Chinese script revolution had accomplished up to this point, it would still need to make several more steps to keep pace with the coming computing age. Now with a second identity in alphabetic form, the Chinese script had never been in a better position to propel China forward. The question is how far and how fast it could make that next leap.

SIX

ENTERING INTO
THE COMPUTER
(1979)

CONVERTING INPUT AND OUTPUT

E ven without being able to see the July sun, Zhi Bingyi felt its smoldering heat between his back and a thin, sweat-drenched straw mat. It was barely a centimeter thick and the only furnishing in the room. Time undoubtedly passed slowly for him in the makeshift cell, known notoriously as a "cowshed." It was 1968, two years into the Cultural Revolution. Shanghai was in the middle of an unseasonal heat wave, and its people cursed the "autumn tiger." Zhi had more to worry about than the heat. He had been branded a "reactionary academic authority," one of the many damning allegations that sent millions of people to their deaths or to labor camps during the Cultural Revolution. Was it still appropriate for Zhi to think of himself as one of the people? Hadn't he betrayed them, as he'd been told?

Just four years earlier, Zhi had gone to work every day as director of the newly established Shanghai Municipal Electric Instrument and Research Office under the government's First Ministry of Machinery Industry. It was one of the most secure jobs one could have. First Ministry was in charge of building heavy industrial machines in the early period of New China, and later split off a Fourth Ministry to oversee electronic communications technology. Zhi's specialty was electric metering—focusing on precision meters and electronic modeling by enhancing the performance of a device's various parts.

Quiet, cautious, and insistent, Zhi was also highly qualified. He earned a Ph.D. in physics from Leipzig University but declined a job offer in the United States in order to return to China. He taught at two Chinese universities and later helped to devise China's landmark twelve-year Plan for the Development of Science and Technology of 1956. The plan identified electronics, computer technology, automation, and remote control as target areas of development. It was a hopeful time for scientists and technicians who were deemed useful for their contributing roles in a state-guided socialist economy.

Since his arrest in July 1968, Zhi had been cut off from his research, the news, and his devoted German wife. He was used to working on equations and engineering problems with teams of colleagues. No longer. His only company was the eight characters on the wall of his cell reminding him that prisoners faced two options from their minders: "Leniency to those who confess; severity to those who refuse."

The question was not whether to confess, but to what and how much. Many prisoners learned to assume fault, reach deep into their souls, and scrutinize each memory for confirmation of possible wrongdoing—raising one's voice too sharply at a student; unwittingly spreading blasphemous Western ideology in research; not showing deference to a superior. Mao's earlier thought reform of 1951 had encouraged such techniques of ideological self-remolding, which were then rolled out on a mass scale during the Cultural Revolution. Huge handwritten posters with class slogans and condemnations dominated public spaces. University lecture halls, libraries, and laboratories were taken over by workshops, factories, and farms, following the political tenet of combining teaching, scientific research, and production. Some school grounds became host to public confessions as classroom instruction came to a halt. Students turned on their teachers, friends against friends, children against parents. Teachers were made to kneel before their students, now Mao's young army of Red Guards, confessing to their bourgeois thought crimes. The accused were interrogated by the crowd, who were invited to kick and beat the guilty. They were shouted at and spat upon and slapped when failing to recite Chairman Mao's sayings properly, while wearing heavy wood placards around their necks, hung on razor-thin wires that cut into their flesh. Not even the elderly or the sick were spared from these infamous "struggle sessions."

The purge of the intellectual class had just begun, and anyone who was educated had to bow to the tenets of class struggle and the will of the Gang of Four—the radical contingent of the Chinese Communist Party. Many were sent to the countryside to be reformed through backbreaking labor, picking through manure and tilling fallow fields in the heat and rain with little to eat. They were held to the strictest military discipline in camps that doubled as reeducation centers. So successful was Mao's anti-intellectual campaign that it inspired Pol Pot to launch a similar crusade in Cambodia between 1975 and 1979, killing anyone who wore eyeglasses—incriminating evidence of bourgeois intellectualism.

In the cowshed, Zhi stared at the eight characters on the wall. One day, he no longer saw the ominous message but instead the strokes and characters of which it was composed. He began to notice where the ink thickened, blotched, or trailed off at the ends of each character. Every stroke appeared to him anew, each an enigma with a fresh riddle. Though created by a human hand, he realized, each character was essentially repeating combinations of the same abstract strokes and dots.

Bismarck Doo would have seized on this finding to group the strokes by their direction, length, and physical likeness. But Zhi's next thought turned on a different idea. How would one translate and turn these human-made brushstrokes into a coded language that could be entered into computing machines? It was not the first time someone thought of rendering Chinese characters systematically into codes, of course. The same question had crossed Count d'Escayrac's mind more than a century earlier in another prison—the urine-soaked cell of imperial Beijing. And coded language was fiercely defended by Wang Jingchun as a question of national sovereignty in the marble halls of Paris in 1925 and attempted as telegraphic encryption by Zhang Deyi and Septime Auguste Viguier. But it never would have occurred to any of them to come up with a solution for a machine. Every solution of theirs had been oriented toward the human user—how to organize characters so they are easier for people to write and to learn, less taxing and time-consuming to memorize or look up. The question in Zhi's mind burned to a different purpose: How could one render Chinese in a language that computers can read—in the zeros and ones of binary code? Having been used to building computer models of his electrical devices, he would have come across the problem many times.

To bridge to the state of technology in the advanced world in the 1970s, China had begun to build machines that could handle mass-scale calculations, sieve through huge amounts of information, and coordinate complex operations. The data for calculating and controlling flight paths, military targets, and geographical positioning, or tracking agricultural and industrial output, had to be collected first. Yet all the existing records, documents, and reports were in Chinese. It became clear that in order to be part of the computing age at all, the Chinese script would have to be rendered digitally. Western computing technology was also moving in the direction of text processing and communication, not just running large-scale calculations. Converting human language scripts into digital form was the next frontier. The arms race during the Cold War was advancing the state of computing technology in both the Soviet Union and the United States. Getting Chinese inside the machine was critical to ensuring that China was not left out.

Requiring precise inputs, computing machines are unforgiving of inconsistencies and exceptions. All the characteristics of Chinese that stymied earlier innovators—the unwieldy size of the character inventory; its complex strokes, tones, and homophones; the difficulty of segmentation—created new challenges in the digitization of the script. Executable commands could only be in the form of a yes or a no, an on-or-off switch of an electric current running through the circuitry of a computer control board. No partial solutions or patches would help China get by this time. During Zhi's incarceration, China was in the throes of its biggest social and political upheaval yet and hardly had the resources to make such a bid for the future. But for a country so far behind the Western world, science and technology were not just a barrier. They were viewed as essential for helping China leapfrog out of backwardness and speed up the process of modernization. China was doubly invested in exploring the computing age. Of the countless obstacles that lay in the country's path, the Chinese language was the one that could stall the state's ambitious plans before they even got off the ground.

The challenge was multifaceted: to devise a code for Chinese that is easy for humans to remember and use and that can be entered into a machine via punched tape or keyboard; to find a way for the machine to store the massive amount of information required to identify and reproduce Chinese characters; and to be able to retrieve and restore the script with pinpoint precision, on paper or on a screen.

Zhi knew he could tackle the first, critical step: how best to input Chinese into the machine. That meant figuring out a way to represent each character in a language that the human operator and the machine could both understand: as a finite set of zeros and ones entered directly into the machine, or in the alphabetic letters on which computer programming languages were already built. The latter seemed more promising. Mapping characters onto the alphabet immediately led to other questions, however: How many alphabet letters would it take to uniquely encode a single character? Should the spelling of characters be abbreviated like acronyms? And what should serve as the basis of the acronyms—characters, components, or strokes?

Zhi needed a pen and paper to test each hypothesis, but the guards did not even give him toilet paper, let alone something to write on. He looked around and saw the only viable object in the room—a teacup. With that modest vessel of worship, Zhi began his own personal pilgrimage. Each day, with a stolen pen, he inscribed as many characters as he could onto the matte ceramic teacup's lid, testing out each character with a set of possible Roman letters, then wiped it clean. He squeezed dozens of characters at a time onto the curved surface, relying on memory to keep track of his incremental efforts.

He aimed for every character to have some kind of intuitive but unique relationship to the alphabetic code representing it. There were two known ways of doing so, by sound or shape. Zhi's predecessors like Bismarck Doo, Wang Yunwu, and Lin Yutang preferred shape-based analysis, taking strokes and components and rearranging them into classifiable categories, but the adoption of pinyin had made the phonetic approach the national and international language standardization policy.

While pinyin solved the problem of phonetic standardization, it did not make the old problems go away. For one thing, it made the issue of homophones worse, because so many characters were now spelled identically in alphabetic form. There were only so many ways to spell the pronunciations of different characters with the alphabet's twenty-six letters, and they ran out more quickly than the thousands of individually distinct characters. Zhi decided to utilize the best of phonetic Romanization and shape-based cues to make his own encoding process as predictable and logical as possible. The idea was not destined to rot in jail.

In September 1969, Zhi was released. After fourteen months, he had failed to prove himself sufficiently culpable after all. Or perhaps his written confession was plain and unremarkable. One reason for leniency would have been that Zhi did not have a damning connection to the elite academic scientific establishment, the Chinese Academy of Sciences. Despite Mao's original blessing, the academy's glories were almost wiped clean by the 1960s. It was the target of wide-scale persecution and a terror campaign that drove at least twenty academics and scientists to take their own lives in 1968 alone. Its membership was reduced to a fraction of the original, its constituents purged or jailed. Those who survived were sent to the countryside to feed pigs and plant rice. With the educated elite decimated, the country's high-level scientific research generally came to a halt, with the exception of technologies concerning national defense, which were largely developed in secret.

Upon release, Zhi was assigned to lowly positions as part of his rehabilitation: sweeping floors, shaping tools in a factory, standing guard at a warehouse. He found it a blessing to be a nobody and went right back to his encoding scheme. He used the warehouse as his study to stash the foreign journal articles and newspapers he had scavenged. He was excited to learn that Japan had been making progress on resolving the problem. Much like what had been done with Chinese typewriters, they were using radical parts of characters to locate, retrieve, and print them on the computer screen. But the Japanese keyboard included more than 3,600 characters, each taking up one key, which was impractical. A company in Australia was also using the radical system to retrieve characters. Using a more modest keyboard of 33 keys, they were able to access close to 200 characters at any time with the stroke of one key, which was an improvement over the Japanese, but still not enough characters for the Chinese. Then there was the United States, where experimental models were using 44 keys and—as Zhi would later learn—an even more ambitious project was under way to computerize Chinese printing at the Graphic Arts Research Foundation in Massachusetts. Scholars in Taiwan, meanwhile, were also developing their own input systems for traditional characters.

Zhi felt greatly encouraged. His solitary work was running parallel to these larger efforts. Most of them, though, still had not been able to free themselves from clunky keyboards. They were inputting whole characters or radicals because they did not have a truly standard Romanization system like pinyin—pinyin was not yet well-known abroad—or other more consistent ways of taking characters apart and putting them back together. While breaking down characters into components had worked well enough for specific character retrieval indexes and type-writer keyboard designs, it did not translate directly into programming such a process for a computing machine.

Zhi remembered the advantage of the shape-based approach, where character parts helped to identify the whole character directly. Bismarck Doo had shown how to use strokes to organize library card catalogs, and Lin Yutang's schemes had identified different sets of stroke patterns that followed the way characters were written. To integrate that useful principle into his encoding scheme, Zhi decided to index characters by their components—the simpler characters within each ideograph—using the first letter of each component's pinyin spelling.

The idea took another two years to flesh out. On average, characters can be broken into two to four components, and there are three hundred to four hundred components total. The majority of characters can be divided into two halves—vertical or horizontal—as Du Dingyou demonstrated in the 1930s, along with other possible geometries. This yielded a two-to-four-letter alphabetic code for each character, which meant each character required at most four keystrokes on a conventional English keyboard. The average English word length, by comparison, is close to 4.8 letters. Zhi thus made the alphabet work more efficiently for individual ideographs than it did for English. The system also cleverly worked around the problem of dialect difference and homophones. Because the code took only the first letter, rather than the complete sound of the character, most regional speech variations did not matter. The four-letter code worked like an acronym of the different parts of the character. Zhi essentially used the alphabet as a proxy to spell by components rather than words.

He sequenced each character's components in the order they would have been written by hand. Coding by components gave context and important cues that reduced ambiguity and the risk of duplicated codes. The chances of having the same components—or even components starting with the same letter—occur in the exact same order in two different characters are low.

Zhi's way of indexing the Chinese character by its alphabetized components made it easier for humans to input Chinese—as long as you knew how to write the language—and created a more systematic human-machine interface. For instance, in his system, the character for "road," 路 (*lu*), which has thirteen strokes by hand, can be broken up into a mere four components: 口 (*kou*) , 止 (*zhi*), 夂 (*pu*), and 口 (*kou*). Isolating the first letter of each component gives the character code of KZPK. Or take the character 吴 (*wu*), a common last name, which can be quickly decomposed into two parts, 口 (*kou*) and 天 (*tian*), yielding a character code of KT.

Alphabetic spelling, once mediated by Chinese in this way, is no longer a phonetic but a semantic spelling system, where each letter actually stands for a character rather than a sound. This method of indexing can also be extended to represent groups of characters. Take, for instance, "socialism," or *shehui zhuyi*: 社会主义. By tagging the first letter of each of the four characters in the phrase, the phrase can be coded in a four-letter sequence, SHZY. Or consider another frequently invoked phrase, the seven characters that make up "People's Republic of China"—Zhonghua renmin gongheguo: 中华人民共和国. It can simply be typed in as ZHRMGHG.

Zhi's coding system could also include properties that are not strictly phonetic. Additional letters could add the pronunciation of the whole character or its shape pattern to the basic four-letter component-based code. The character 路 has the phonetic pronunciation of "*lu*" and, because it can be divided into two vertical halves, has a *zuo you* (left-right) structure. Both features can be indicated in the extended code KZPKLZ. The more precise you can be about encoding the information of a character, the more useful that code can be. These extensions of Zhi's system would be important for Chinese-language applications in machine translation and retrieving information from stored data.

Zhi formally introduced his "On-Sight" encoding system in the Chinese science journal *Nature Magazine* in 1978. He described his system as topological—extrapolated from the geometry of parts. With four-letter codes using all twenty-six letters of the alphabet, there were enough combinations to generate 456,976 possible unique codes. Zhi claimed for his system an efficiency similar to that of Morse code—quick, intuitive, and transparent.

News of Zhi's feat spread, galvanized by the political fervor for science and technology that broke out after Mao's death in 1976. On the front page of Shanghai's *Wenhui Daily*, on July 19, 1978, the editor euphorically announced, "The Chinese Script Has Entered the Computing Machine."

Computers could finally "understand" square-shape characters. After more than a decade of isolation, China could at last have a shot at communicating with the world and managing its own flow of information digitally. Zhi's invention also provided a much-needed boost in morale. Mao was gone, and the Gang of Four had been charged with treasonous

Zhi Bingyi, "The Chinese Script Has
Entered the Computing Machine."
Wenhui bao, July 19, 1978.

and counterrevolutionary crimes. China needed healing and its people
a reason to believe that the party could still lead them forward. Deng
Xiaoping, China's new leader, soon announced his Four Modernizations
program. Three of the areas were agriculture, industrialization, and national defense; the fourth, science and technology, would determine the
ultimate success of the three and be the party's new ideological touch-
stone.

Zhi's code made it feasible for human operators to input Chinese
into computing machines. But that was only one-third of the digitization process. In Zhi's time, computer terminals lacked the interactive
graphic screens that are common today, so they were programmed to
perform automated tasks by taking commands from the user. A user
would enter a letter or character code on a keyboard, which would then
be converted by the terminal to a corresponding address code. The
address code tells the computer's character generator what bitmap—a
grid of tiny squares—it should output, either as pixels on a computer
monitor or dots of ink (a dot matrix).

Two hurdles still stood in the way of developing an input-output system for Chinese. The number of input code schemes would soon proliferate across China and around the world. There was nothing like the universally shared internal code that today allows a MacBook to talk to a PC. Making sure that a document file or a text message can be read by its recipients, regardless of where they are, what kind of device they use, and in what language they speak, would be another daunting task, one that would occupy an international group of dedicated computer engineers well into the twenty-first century.

Zhi's innovation set off an explosion in Chinese encoding research, rivaling the zeal and fanaticism of the previous character index race, aimed at solving the other remaining challenge for Chinese language processing. By this time, not many of the former script reformers and character indexers remained; most were dead or in exile. Many were self-identified Nationalists: Wang Jingchun had passed away in Pomona, California; Lin Yutang was teaching in Taiwan and Hong Kong in the 1960s and 1970s; and Bismarck Doo was convalescing in a sickbed when the Cultural Revolution erupted, his beloved library shut down as all university education across the country ceased. In the intellectual wasteland of the Cultural Revolution's dark decade, Zhi relit the torch. He had shined light on the path for solving the input problem. The next big piece of the puzzle was how to turn Chinese characters into digital outputs.

In April 1973, the deputy director of China's state-owned Xinhua News Agency and a team of advisors traveled to Japan, where they visited the headquarters of Kyodo News in Minato. The purpose of the visit was to observe Japan's cutting-edge computers for news editing, communications, image-data management, and typesetting. The Japanese news agency had no trouble publishing newspapers in *kanji*—Chinese characters—for daily consumption.

The Xinhua team watched with envy and embarrassment. They saw the typesetters wearing white lab coats and working at keyboards without fuss or exertion. Their workspaces were as clean and orderly as a hospital ward. Back home in China, printing and communication were still largely dependent on hot lead type. Not much had changed for centuries. The pressrooms were dirty, deafening places where typesetters hurriedly picked through thousands of character types hanging from racks on one side of the room, while on the other side another set of workers arranged type for printing. Skilled press workers with enough physical stamina could arrange up to seven thousand characters a day, their hands blackened with ink and their health threatened by prolonged daily exposure to lead. The process was so chaotic that at the end of the day, it was often more efficient to melt down all the type rather than sort and return it to the racks.

At the time, 70 percent of all circulated print information in China was still produced using this archaic method. It was not uncommon for today's newspaper to arrive tomorrow in most cities in the country, and books often took an entire year to print. China was stuck in a mode of information dissemination that had long since become obsolete. In fact, printing methods had not changed much from the day when the young MIT typewriter inventor Zhou Houkun saw a demonstration of the office Monotype in Boston in 1912.

The Xinhua team went home and reported their observations. They had expected that Japan would be years ahead with its technology. There was little doubt that China's industry and economy were in desperate need of repair. U.S. president Richard Nixon's landmark visit in 1972 signaled the beginning of the Cold War's gradual thaw. Diplomatic relations between China and the United States resumed, and the loosening of restrictions on academic and scientific exchanges made visits like that of the Xinhua team to Japan possible. The following year, Deng Xiaoping was rehabilitated after having been denounced by the Communist Party and made to work in a tractor repair factory for almost four years. Succeeding Mao, he would turn the political focus to advancing science and technology as a way to redirect the party's energies. By rallying around economic reforms instead of class warfare, the nation could open up once more to the world.

How would that be possible, the Xinhua group pointed out, if daily newspapers in China could not be read on the day they were written? In other parts of the advanced world, the publishing industry had moved on to cold type. Dispensing with hazardous lead altogether, cold type used photographic techniques coupled with computing technology. Printing with lead and fire no longer sufficed.

After Xinhua's trip, the Fourth Ministry invited other representatives from Japanese companies and news agencies to China for further conversations. The visits convinced those in the ministry and many others that China was long overdue for its next print revolution. China had invented movable type in the eleventh century, about three hundred years before the appearance of the Gutenberg press, but the country had since fallen way behind. In August 1974, Xinhua and the Fourth Ministry, along with the First Ministry, the Chinese Academy of Sciences, and the National Publishing Administration, collectively petitioned the State Planning Commission and the State Council, asking them to make Chinese language information processing an official priority in the state's plan to develop the country's science and technology.

The petition came not a moment too soon. American companies were making rapid advancements in computing and modernized printing. Remington Rand had already built the first high-speed printer to be used with the first milestone computer system, UNIVAC, in 1953.

IBM marketed the first dot-matrix printer in 1957, with the first laser printer to follow in 1971. The first personal computer, produced by a small firm in Albuquerque, hit the market in 1975, and the Apple I computer was introduced the following year. The young industry expanded rapidly after the Apple II appeared with a color monitor and floppy drive in 1977.

Governmental scientific agencies in China took note of the plethora of new technologies and deliberated over which ones China should pursue. The country's most urgent priority was to build and coordinate state industries and production across the nation in a series of projected five-year plans. They saw the future of rule in automation, a technology to help reinforce the infrastructure through which governance can be carried out. In their joint petition, Xinhua and the Fourth Ministry urged concerted action. They noted that the Western computing industry was shifting its emphasis from building large room-size mainframe computers to smaller, personal machines for language processing and communications. Moving into text and human language processing, the technology was on the cusp of reshaping the management, speed, and control of information. Newspapers acutely felt the need to modernize. Responsible for disseminating the party's messages to the people, Xinhua had to typeset a large body of information within a short period of time on a daily basis. As long as computing machines could not process the Chinese language, the petitioners warned, the party's moral and political message could not efficiently reach the people. Digital technology would be of little use to China if the Chinese script could not fully cross that threshold. It was up to the Chinese themselves to bring the Chinese script and computing technology together.

The State Planning Commission reviewed the petition and did some calculations. It discovered that more than two hundred thousand tons of alloy lead and 2 million sets of copper molds were being consumed every year in the mechanical printing industry to cast type molds for Chinese characters. Each of those molds required time, sweat, and manpower to complete, rearrange, and melt down. Every step of setting type, lining up margins, or adjusting page layouts had to be done by hand. Modernizing that process had vital political and economic implications. Editing would be as easy as pressing a few keys on a keyboard in front of a computer screen instead of reassembling metal blocks of characters and laboriously arranging them into lines. A wrong character could be deleted on the display screen by pressing a single key rather than removing the mistaken type, melting it down, recasting the hot metal—and repeating the process all over again.

What Xinhua and others had pointed out as areas of concern were indeed where China was the weakest and farthest behind. The commission concluded that the country would be better off using the metal materials consumed in mechanical printing for building the new equipment necessary for basic digital publishing. This required putting the heads together from a vast number of research units, institutions, and agencies to identify and divide up the research and coordinate resources and effort. The project was swiftly approved and dubbed Project 748, named after the month and year of its founding in August 1974.

Project 748's overall goal was to create an entire computing environment for the Chinese language tailor-made to process the Chinese script, not just to copy Western computing wholesale. Three target areas were identified: electronic communication, information storage and retrieval systems, and phototypesetting. It quickly became apparent that two of the three areas were still far beyond China's current technology. Given the relatively high cost of computers in China, electronic communication in general was uncommon, let alone personal computing. Only selected state agencies and research institutions were given permission to build mainframe computers or to house them, and their equipment was largely dependent on imported parts if not entire machines. Information retrieval was also a distant goal. Back then, information retrieval meant something more basic than typing a query into a search box on Google or Bing. It was literally about where and how to store data information and how to call it up as a file or other format. Both electronic and informational retrieval would take longer-term planning.

For the time being, the only area that was both urgent and achievable was phototypesetting. This method of typesetting involved taking a snapshot of the character to be printed, then transferring the film image to printing plates. It would be a big improvement from arranging type blocks and reproducing their engraved images by hand. Developing Chinese-language phototypesetting was complicated by the same problem China had always had with its written language—there were too many characters to use and choose from. Figuring out how to store and retrieve them—and how to computerize the process of printing them—was essential for exchanging information with the world outside of China as well as disseminating it domestically.

Every unique, physically complex Chinese character now had to be translated into electric signals that could—with the computer—be automatically retrieved, manipulated, stored, and typeset. China wasn't starting completely from scratch. A couple of generations of modern typesetting technologies had already been developed and commercialized in the West. The first generation of machines worked on the same principle as hot metal presses and relied on mechanics rather than electronics. One example was the Monotype machine that inspired Zhou to devise a Chinese typing machine in the 1910s. The second generation set type by photomechanical means, exposing type directly from a photographed master film onto printing plates. It was a bit more automated than the Monotype but still drew on rudimentary electronics. A third generation was just coming out and attracting wide attention before Project 748 got under way. A German machine, Digiset, developed in 1965, projected light onto photosensitive paper by bombarding a phosphor-coated cathode ray tube with electron beams. The coating turned the beams into spots of light that formed an array of dots: a dot matrix. This third-generation phototypesetting technology was approaching full digitization, storing images of letters and words in the computer's memory or on magnetic disks.

Even a phototypesetter like Digiset did not quite offer what the Chinese needed. Because characters contain more codable information than letters by virtue of their physical complexity, and because there are so many of them, when it came to storage—inside or outside the machine, digital or analog—size remained a roadblock. Chinese scientists and engineers had to invent a way to compress the size of characters that would avoid slowing down a computer's processing speed or taxing its memory, both of which were limited at the time.

China's technological capabilities were nowhere near the early days of Silicon Valley. Despite a determined but scrappy socialist "can-do" spirit inculcated since the Great Leap Forward, the material conditions in the country for building computing technology were poor. Available computing machines in China at the time were used primarily for numerical tasks and were restricted to research facilities or university settings. National defense was heavily developing automated computing technologies, but their research was proceeding in secrecy. Outside of that protected industry, shrouded from public view, the visible state of affairs was rather bleak.

When academic delegations of Western scientists began to visit China again in the 1970s, they were stunned by the wide shortages of basic components like magnetic tape—which had already replaced punch cards and paper tape in computers in the West. No large-scale effort to miniaturize hardware had yet been undertaken, let alone to mass-produce it. In the labs, scientists prepped their programs and data on paper tape and then waited their turn at the machine, as if they were queuing up for a telephone booth. While imported foreign computers were available in small quantities, most Chinese components and peripherals had to be developed from scratch, and it was not uncommon to measure and build the machine components by hand. One common practice was to buy a foreign machine and reverse engineer it. It was estimated that China's technology was more than a decade behind that of the United States.

Despite the gap, China's goal was to achieve full technological parity with the West by the year 2000. Slogans and signs promoting this aim were disseminated among the populace. The message was even found on candy wrappers. The New Long March it was called, summoning the specter of Mao's Long March from almost half a century earlier. "Putting proletarian politics in command," a common phrase at the time, meant that every decision concerning science and technology was a political one. Every entity and organization had a "revolutionary committee," composed of members from different classes, so that every action and decision could be arrived at dialectically in light of its political ramifications and ideological goal. An example that impressed foreign visitors at the time was a Shanghai factory that manufactured door handles. Run by women comrades, mainly housewives, it switched production overnight to make magnetic cores, transistors, and computer mainframes. Suddenly, housewives were working alongside scientists and engineers—it was a perfect socialist picture of comrades working arm in arm. At the same time, production was driven not by demand or the market but by the planned directives of the party. And the party was resolved that China would succeed and be self-reliant wherever possible.

Part of the drive for self-reliance came from a hard lesson learned from the Soviets in the 1950s. When ties between the two nations were still strong, the Soviets helped the Chinese to build the first large-scale digital computer in China, August-1, drawing on the details of their working model for the mainframe computer Ural-1. That milestone, widely celebrated, was, however, singular. In 1960, when China officially parted ways with the Soviets over ideological differences, the latter pulled out fifteen hundred military and scientific advisors and withdrew all economic and technical assistance—including blueprints. This left hundreds of critical state projects unfinished—a devastating blow that nearly derailed China's fledgling industrialization.

China vowed to survive and strengthen itself against all odds. At a time when the country did not have the capacity to even build cars, scientists later recalled, they were expected to build an atomic bomb. Impossible as that seemed, China shocked the world when it tested its first atomic bomb in October 1964, followed by its first nuclear missile and hydrogen bomb in quick succession. It established itself as a nuclear power in two and a half years—a process that took the United States seven and a half years and the Soviets four. If that was not enough to bolster national pride, China also managed to launch its first satellite in 1970. The 381-pound aluminum gadget broadcast China's de facto national anthem—"The East Is Red"—as it spun through space, thirteen hundred miles away from Earth. By 1973, China was the third country in the world with the capability not only to launch but also to retrieve its satellites for repeated study and use.

While much of the country was embroiled in political purges, national defense and computing remained priorities in research and development. China began building its own integrated circuits as early as 1968, the same year as the Soviets. Although outside print materials and news were forbidden to the masses, scientists and engineers had privileged access to foreign technical and scientific journals—the only kind of Western knowledge that was considered not spiritually polluting. Amid the atmosphere of cautious opening up, desperate ambitions, and scant resources, a greater scarcity existed—talent.

. . .

PROJECT 748 WAS LUCKY to have found the thirty-eight-year-old engineer Wang Xuan, who knew the state of China's computing research from the inside out. Wang had always wanted to combine his interests in hardware and software research ever since he helped to build an early mainframe computer in 1958, partaking in the feverish race to make a technological jump during the Great Leap Forward. He was known for his maniacal work ethic. Twelve-hour shifts were common, as were skipped meals. By winter 1960, the Great Leap Forward had begun to show its grave toll. The initial euphoria of overnight progress was replaced by the devastating reality of droughts, floods, and famine. Wang's meals were rationed; often his dinner was nothing but a small portion of porridge with some pickles. Over time, his body swelled under the fatigue, but he continued to work relentlessly. In 1961, he fell ill, with consequences that would plague him for the rest of his life.

In the early 1970s, Wang Xuan was working as a researcher at Beijing University. One day he would become a legend, with biographers immortalizing every aspect of his life and his groundbreaking development of laser phototypesetting. But at the time his research on software and new computing systems was sneered at by his colleagues as impractical, far divorced from the reality of China's technological capabilities and needs.

Wang Xuan was home on sick leave, living on a modest stipend, when he first heard of Project 748 from his wife, Chen Kunqiu—an equally formidable academic and mathematician with whom he worked closely. In spring 1975, Beijing University formed a task force to investigate the possibility of automating overall operations and management on campus, and Chen was appointed to the committee. They looked into phototypesetting, the predominant printing technology then being tested by Xinhua News, in collaboration with Beijing University's competitor,

Tsinghua University, a couple of miles away. But the machines at Xinghua and Tsinghua broke down often. Instead of printing characters in neat rows, their output was often out of alignment. They could read Chinese but couldn't consistently output it in its original form.

Given the state of China's phototypesetting technology, Wang Xuan found the goal of Project 748—to build out a full Chinese computing environment—far-fetched. But he did see a niche of opportunity in digital storage. His wife, Chen, worked with him to flesh out his idea and introduced it to her colleagues in the math and engineering departments, eventually pulling in others from library information processing and publishing to join in a team effort. Beijing University put together a proposal out of the group's preliminary report and submitted a request to be included in Project 748.

While Zhi Bingyi had proposed a fully functional Chinese input digital system that could process the Chinese script, he didn't address the question of storage. Whether you were trying to delimit a character set for encoding, store characters on a disk or in internal memory, or design a library of fonts, it was like trying to put an elephant in a small tent. Wang Xuan's solution was to leap past third-generation phototypesetting in the West, which had begun storing images of typefaces at least through a partly digitized process. Rather than figure out how to adapt existing storage methods for Chinese, he homed in on one specific area of innovation still seeking a breakthrough: the compression of the digital typeface itself. His was going to be a fourth-generation phototypesetting machine, editing Chinese characters and typesetting with lasers.

The solution was specific to the Chinese language and its digital storage requirements. An enormous number of dots are required to reproduce the complex contours of Chinese characters in a digital image. China's publishing industry in the 1980s employed more than ten different fonts and sixteen font sizes, due to the varying needs of newspaper layouts and book designs, and digital storage then was not anywhere near where it is now. Without somehow compressing the amount of data in each character, the storage required for all of those fonts would be unachievable, even on Digiset's magnetic disk.

Aesthetics, too, mattered. How characters looked at the end, when restored as output, was paramount to the success of printing. Since characters contain components that are positioned at very specific angles in relation to one another, a slightly off piecing-together would look odd and be distracting to the reader. Some of Qi Xuan's contemporaries in the 1910s did not like his three-key keyboard input method because it could not guarantee the way characters would be reassembled in type form on paper. The Chinese attached a great deal of value and significance to the way characters looked. The thickness or thinness of the strokes and how parts sit in relation to one another, depending on the font and the calligraphic style it was modeled on, had to be in aesthetically pleasing proportions that took mastery to achieve. That was important for Lin Yutang's typewriter as well, though in a simpler way. He spent an inordinate amount of effort figuring out how the components could come together seamlessly when printed. Wang Xuan provided a solution to the same problem but with the added challenge of digital intermediation.

It was not easy to turn his solution into reality. Project 748 operated on a shoestring. It drew on the state's will to succeed and the work and sacrifice of its staff more than anything else. Wang Xuan's operation was far from state of the art. His research team was at first housed temporarily in a run-down campus building east of the university's library. It offered a shabby two hundred square feet of space with no heat in the winter. The draft was so severe that Chen sat with a hot water bottle in her lap throughout the cold months, while working out the software part of the project as lead engineer.

Meanwhile, anyone who was part of Project 748 knew that there was no disappointing the will of the party. The scientists worked cautiously, dutifully, and with a pragmatic focus on delivering results. Items on the project's agenda were assigned to different research units to create the pressure of competition. Zhi Bingyi, then head of the Shanghai Institute of Electronic Instruments Research, a possible competitor, visited Wang Xuan's lab in 1976 to learn about their research. At that time, Wang had no real thoughts of turning his idea into a consumer product. All the same, his colleagues warned him not to divulge any key technical information and risk giving away their competitive edge.

Attempting to stay ahead of the mounting pressure, Wang Xuan applied all his diligence and ingenuity as he took on the challenge of data compression. He systematically resolved one problem after another and began shaping a technology that would most efficiently represent high-resolution Chinese characters.

He needed a succinct way to represent the exact shape of each character—every stroke and dot, in exact proportion—in a language of commands and instructions that the computer could decipher. The dot-matrix approach of reproducing an image pixel by pixel was inadequate because it required too much memory. What he needed was a shorthand code for describing the shape of a character's strokes. But he had to be careful. Too much compression might come at the expense of the quality of the character's final appearance; too little would preserve the clarity of the script but not resolve the problem of size. Others had tried to store Chinese fonts on an external magnetic disk, but it took too much time— several milliseconds—to retrieve a single character this way. To avoid these inefficiencies, Wang needed to devise a mathematical formula to turn each character's geometry into arcs, curves, and line segments, a finer simulation than representation by strokes, let alone components.

Wang Xuan's first step was to separate character strokes into two types: regular and irregular. Regular strokes contained straight-edged segments like vertical, horizontal, and folded lines. Irregular strokes were made up of curved lines. He then assigned each line a numerical code, essentially compiling a collection of instructions for describing the physical contours of the character. He represented the curved lines as a series of mathematical quantities called vectors, which indicate the starting point, length, and direction of each line in a shape. Importantly, vector images scale—they can be made larger or smaller without changing the amount of memory required simply by adjusting the values in the formulas. Finally, through a reverse process of decompression, Wang converted the vector images back to bitmaps of dots for digital output.

The results of the compression scheme were better than he could have hoped. Characters were reduced by a ratio of as much as 1:500. It seemed too good to be true, but he checked the results numerous times from every angle. There was just one final catch: The high-resolution Chinese character generator he had designed required a powerful computer chip as the central control unit. China had been manufacturing its own chips in small quantities since 1968 and trying to build an indigenous semiconductor industry while importing foreign chips in the 1970s, but the quality of the Chinese chip was far from what he needed. Most of the best chips were produced overseas in America, which were not available in China. Wang Xuan agonized over a solution.

His project had reached a critical point. Without a powerful chip, he could not optimize his typesetting system's performance. He needed that last piece in place but did not know where to find it or have the technology to build it. Resources were still scarce, and by now it was 1979. Then, out of nowhere, an unexpected guest appeared—and showed him the way out.

WHILE THE WESTERN RESEARCHERS and academics who began to visit China in the early 1970s opened up an essential channel of scholarly exchange, the ones who did the most to bring both sides of the Pacific together—and knew China from the inside—were the often less-visible Chinese American scientists. They were typically educated in the United States and had stayed on, but they were still driven by a spirit of intellectual cooperation and academic openness to assist in China's technological development. At a time when the world knew so little of what was happening inside China, people-to-people diplomacy was carried out by these individuals.

In the late fall of 1979, one such Chinese American professor arrived in Beijing. Officially, he was there to help Tsinghua University set up its first microprocessing lab, modeled on the one he ran at MIT. Francis F. Lee was ten years Wang Xuan's senior and a native of Nanjing. He spoke English with a crisp British accent, thanks to his father, a well-known Western-educated linguistics professor at Wuhan University.

Lee left China during the Communist takeover in 1948 to study at MIT. He received his B.S. in electrical engineering a mere two years later in 1950 and enrolled in a Ph.D. program. Full of energy and talent, but also struggling to support his wife and children on his fellowship stipend, he left MIT without finishing his degree. Instead, he joined the forefront of computing research, working at leading electronics companies like the Radio Corporation of America (RCA) and then the UNI-VAC supercomputer division of Remington Rand. Over the next decade, he developed a precursor to cache memory, which stores past data and performs operations within the computer itself. Along the way, he became a naturalized U.S. citizen. In 1964 Lee returned to MIT, swiftly finished his Ph.D. in sixteen months, and was immediately hired by the university with tenure as a professor of electrical engineering and computer science.

Wang Xuan welcomed Lee to his lab and explained his research on character data compression. He printed out photographic film with character images. Lee was impressed. He told Wang he had assigned one of his Ph.D. students at MIT to work on Chinese-language typesetting as well and immediately invited Wang to come develop his project in the United States. MIT had the resources and equipment, he noted, not to mention talented people who had been working on the exact same problem. Wang could take his work to a different level.

Wang thought long and hard about it. At the time, China was in the middle of a massive talent drain. Project 748 was desperate to hold on to its staff. In one case, a supervisor and project manager literally got down on his knees, begging his engineers not to abandon China to seek more comfortable lives abroad. But begging couldn't repair the distrust and emotional trauma of the Mao years. Scientists feared what would happen if their work failed. Many who were involved in Project 748 were more used to informing on one another than helping one another as colleagues. One factory supervisor had to recruit someone who had once outed him for public confessions and self-criticism. Everyone was used to being watched and betrayed by their coworkers, neighbors, and even family. As soon as the atmosphere in China began to relax and travel to the West was possible again, many of its best scientists and engineers seized the opportunity to leave—some never to return.

Wang Xuan, however, declined Lee's offer. He felt that his work was deeply rooted in China; he could not leave the organization or his collaborators after having achieved so much with so little. Lee understood. Was he himself, after all, not also bound to his country by a love and concern that would not fade despite the ruling regime, despite his having lived and thrived in the United States for decades? He had come back to help his fellow Chinese build a microprocessing lab, to open up a path for scientific exchange, and to reinstate a shared intellectual space where knowledge could flow freely. In that spirit, he left Wang a parting gift. There was a chip much better than the one Wang had been working with, and the details were right there in Lee's hands—a pamphlet manual for the state-of-the art Am2900, a modular semiconductor chip for high-performance processing. It was still in the testing phase and not yet a final product. "Under Development" was stamped on the cover. Wang was getting a first look.

It changed everything. He greedily devoured every part of its circuit design, page after page. Ever since he got involved in building computers in college, Wang had always held himself to the twin principles of speed and aesthetics. Am2900 was the marriage of both. With it, he was able to achieve the final step of restoring a character from compressed vector data form to a printable bitmap.

What Wang didn't know was that there was more to Lee's generosity than met the eye. Lee was in Beijing to help Tsinghua University's microprocessing lab, but he was also there for a different purpose—to build relations on behalf of a Cambridge-based American organization, the Graphic Arts Research Foundation. GARF had been pursuing the very same technology that Wang was trying to invent. Lee was an outsider and yet also was not. A Chinese American who was perhaps more Chinese than American—or perhaps the other way around—his path and curiosity had been shaped by an earlier plot twist, back across the Pacific, in the quest to computerize Chinese.

Founded in 1949 by a small group of scientists and publishing professionals, GARF was a nonprofit entity that sprang from a collaboration with a photoelectric typesetting printing company, Photon. The company had just one innovation, but it was an important one. Two telephone engineers from France figured out how to set type photographically without using any hot metal casting. They did this by taking pictures of letter images on a whirling glass disk in front of a stroboscopic tube. When a word or letter was placed in front of the light source, a camera picked up a fixed image of the word, which was then resized through a lens before a positive image of it was exposed on a piece of film. From this, the word image could then be photoengraved onto plates for printing. GARF pioneered phototypesetting.

As early as March 1953, GARF began to discuss developing the same technology for non-Western languages. Given all the scripts in the world that were still bound to the limitations of traditional movable type, GARF thought it had the missing ingredient needed to bring literacy and print information to the world. Of all the non-Western languages, the difficulty of Chinese made it the ideal litmus test.

The Chinese ideographic script was deemed the next—and perhaps ultimate—frontier for the alphabetic technology. What resulted was the Sinotype, the first keyboard machine for Chinese language typesetting. GARF credited the work of a New England engineer of Scottish descent for this breakthrough development. As a professor of electrical engineering at MIT, Samuel H. Caldwell earned his reputation as a computing pioneer during and after the Second World War. He worked on the differential analyzer—an early analog computer—and the logical design of switch circuits. Caldwell interacted with all the right people: cyberneticians like Norbert Wiener and important gatekeepers in the field like Warren Weaver and Vannevar Bush. Developing the Sinotype as the GARF research director would be his last big project.

In 1959, Caldwell published a paper with the Franklin Institute in Philadelphia that detailed the concept and specifications of the machine. It was the foundation's cornerstone invention. Nothing GARF produced before or since has rivaled it. Sinotype has been heralded as the first Chinese computer and Caldwell as the father of Chinese computing. Yet there was just one problem: Caldwell did not speak or read a word of Chinese.

When the president of GARF, William W. Garth, first approached Caldwell about developing the Sinotype behind closed doors in early 1953, someone else was in the room. It was Lee, then a young graduate student who had arrived at MIT from Nanjing only four years earlier. He was in his second year of Ph.D. studies, working under Caldwell, when the Sinotype conversation took place. At that meeting, Lee was given the task of investigating the properties of the Chinese language and its technical requirements.

Within a few months, Lee wrote an internal report for MIT's Research Laboratory of Electronics. He proposed to look at characters more methodically and extract statistical correlations based on distinct physical and topographical attributes. Lee suggested a modified keyboard of strokes to be used together with a simple encoder to generate the codes after the key had been pressed. Essentially, the Chinese character index method could be used to organize and retrieve characters and compute encoding to automate the process. The characters would then be stored as a matrix on a photographic negative plate and assigned their own unique X-Y coordinates. Lee showed how the Chinese script and the computer could come together; he provided both native knowledge of the Chinese language and the technical solution for its photocomposition.

Based on Lee's report, GARF found its niche. It spent aggressively on Sinotype research, approximately $1 million within the first few years. GARF was going to make the Chinese script its signature project. It secretly harbored even greater hopes: If it could make the Chinese script compatible with computing technology, it could do the same for any script system. The Chinese script could be the conceptual gateway to the digitalization of all nonalphabetic scripts.

Lee, however, did not stay. When he left MIT for a higher-paying industry job, the Sinotype project was left in Caldwell's hands. For a while, Lee appeared often in the foundation's internal memos and correspondence. He was explicitly acknowledged as the person responsible for Caldwell's Sinotype. To Caldwell's credit, he acknowledged Lee and another Chinese colleague, Yang Liansheng, a professor at Harvard, for helping to select the twenty-one strokes that ultimately came to be known as Caldwell's twenty-one-stroke-order system. Yet that fact never became well known to the public, and it was not mentioned in GARF's official brochure. Over time, Lee's and Yang's direct participation in the making of America's Sinotype was forgotten.

Instead, in a 1956 patent application filed on behalf of GARF for the Sinotype, now called the Ideographic Type Composing Machine, Caldwell discussed the work of Lin Yutang and his 1952 patent of the Chinese typewriter. In fact, Caldwell's twenty-one-stroke system—the heart of the Sinotype—was identical to Lin's original nineteen-stroke system in all but a few places. Caldwell extended the idea of strokes in a more general sense—regardless of first, second, or last in order—and streamlined and reorganized the variances.

The Franklin Institute article attracted quite a bit of attention. It was the 1950s, and the Cold War was getting chillier. Spreading the ideology of the free world to combat communism was taken seriously at every level. A small working group at the Pentagon, made up of members of the Department of State, the CIA, and the Operations Coordinating Board, thought the Sinotype might give the United States a great advantage in disseminating its messages directly in the Chinese-language world. They wanted President Eisenhower to announce the Sinotype publicly. Having control of the first Chinese language computer would be decisive in the ideological battle with communism. Yet after further investigation, the working group decided that more proof was needed that the Sinotype was the breakthrough technology that GARF said it was. In the end, the Pentagon decided that it was not lethal enough as a weapon of propaganda war. Technologies like machine translation for deciphering Russian or Chinese documents or cryptography were of greater consequence for America's strategic interests.

When Caldwell died suddenly two months after his patent was

approved in 1960, the Sinotype was left without its principal investigator. Dust gathered on Caldwell's original drawings for the next ten years. GARF's head, Garth, came close to resigning because no other idea could inspire the same excitement that had surrounded the Sinotype. "Since the conclusion of the Chinese machine contract, the Foundation has been almost inactive," he wrote in a mournful letter. "It will be a tragedy if the work started by Dr. Caldwell . . . in the complex writing forms cannot somewhere be continued." The project was handed over to RCA, while another version was run out of IBM. Prototypes were built and tested but nothing was produced on a mass scale.

In the 1970s, the engineers and leaders at GARF began to feel restless, as China tentatively opened itself up to the West. One of GARF's collaborators at Harvard, Roy Hofheinz, read Zhi's article in *Nature Magazine* and learned that a feasible Chinese language input had been found. Several companies, meanwhile, were also considering a push into China's market. GARF had other reasons to feel hopeful. Lee had returned. He became a professor of electrical engineering at MIT and took up a consulting role at GARF. He no doubt saw a certain irony in the situation—and it was not because he had initiated the research on Sinotype more than twenty-five years earlier. The truth, which Lee had only divulged to his daughter in a personal letter, was that while he was a student at MIT, apart from being recruited to work on a preliminary report on the feasibility of the Sinotype, he himself had also proposed a Chinese-language typesetting machine design to Caldwell. Caldwell rejected it on the grounds that "symbolic manipulation is not a suitable subject for electrical engineering." But Lee wasn't going to quibble over the past. What was important was that he had found Wang Xuan, who was well on his way to accomplishing what he had lacked support and encouragement to do at MIT.

From GARF's perspective, Lee was the ideal bridge to China. As early as 1976, GARF approved plans to send him to establish contact with Chinese universities. In January 1979, GARF also arranged to pitch its idea to a group of representatives from Chinese industry and government. GARF did not know about Project 748, which was not publicized outside China. But Lee must have known about it from an earlier trip to China with his wife and children in September 1974 to engage with scientists there.

Meetings between GARF and the Chinese went well. Both parties agreed that GARF would work with Zhi's On-Sight encoding scheme, incorporate it into the next prototype of the Sinotype, and return to China in early 1980 to sign an agreement for a multiyear collaboration. For a while, it looked as if all the pieces were coming together. Zhi's survivalist effort in encoding Chinese, Wang Xuan's relentless toil at Beijing University, Lee's unexpected intervention from America, and the Chinese state's resolve to modernize its science and technology together meant that the Chinese script was poised to be reborn in the digital age. With a more powerful chip, thanks to Lee, Wang moved ahead at warp speed with his laser typesetting technology, bypassing third-generation cathode ray tube devices. Whether Lee's aim was to help GARF or Project 748 is a question for which there is no clear answer. Perhaps his loyalty was to the idea itself rather than a particular organization or country. Like Lin Yutang, who brought his idea of a Chinese typewriter from China to the United States, Lee was a conduit through which ideas flowed in the reverse direction—and perhaps his and Lin's loyalty was first and foremost to the Chinese script revolution itself. As a result of Wang's breakthrough, officials overseeing Project 748 realized that China had little to fear from the West. As Wang later recalled, all along China had possessed a secret "weapon of assassination" against any foreign competition in computing technology—and that was simply the Chinese script itself.

．　．　．

ONE BY ONE, the foreign companies came knocking at China's door. While Germany's Digiset had established the standard for third-generation cathode ray tube machines, Zhi would later partner with the German firm Olympia to incorporate his encoding scheme into the Olympia 1011 electronic typing and word processing machines. The most aggressive play was made by the British firm Monotype, which had been leading innovation in this area. In the fall of 1978, the firm wanted to reaffirm its edge by tackling the problem of text capture, editing, and phototypesetting for the Chinese script. The tool would be Lasercomp, an advanced laser typesetting system.

Monotype had been selling equipment to the China Printing Corporation for decades, so it enjoyed a working relationship with the country and a level of trust. It pushed that advantage as far as it could go. In December 1978, it organized a demonstration of Chinese typesetting in Hong Kong. Just as GARF partnered to use Zhi's code, Monotype collaborated with a Chinese professor in Hong Kong, Shiu-Chang Loh, who had developed a shape-based keyboard with 256 customized keys. His invention provided a clear key sequence to uniquely represent each character, and the sequences themselves were decoded by the computer and matched with the right character in storage. Lasercomp provided special programs of code conversion that could restore the sequence back into the character.

Progress was rapid. Monotype gave more demonstrations in Shanghai and Beijing, and by summer 1979 its systems had been installed in the two cities with trained operators. In Lasercomp, characters were stored on magnetic disks and controlled by computers. These character images were then projected onto photographic paper or film. The only limitation was the storage capacity of the magnetic disk, which at the time ranged from 80 to 320 megabytes. That was enough to accommodate around sixty thousand Chinese characters—a number significant enough to catch Chinese officials' attention, and to alarm them.

The State Council authorized the purchase of Monotype's equipment and a continued joint venture to further develop the technology. But the leadership of Project 748 was already reassessing the situation. They began to realize that China had the advantage because it had what the world wanted—a vast market. But no matter how advanced Western phototypesetting technology was, as long as the machines could not better accommodate the extraordinary amount of storage and high resolution required by the Chinese script, they would not gain an edge in the Chinese market. Entertaining offers of phototypesetting technology from foreigners was not about opening up the market and becoming dependent but rather learning with the end goal of becoming self-sufficient, and even with an edge over the West. The commitment to this goal remained unwavering for decades. In a letter to the State Council dated February 22, 1980, then deputy commissioner of the National Import and Export Regulatory Commission Jiang Zemin—who would become the general secretary of the Chinese Communist Party within the decade and then after that the president of the PRC—made it clear:

> Beijing University and its various units had attained notable results with their research on the Chinese language laser phototypesetting device. The technology is nearly mature and is on its way to be refined and perfected. . . . As for the application from the First Ministry and *People's Daily* and their request for $2,500,000 to collaborate with the American Graphic Arts Research Foundation, for the time being we shall set it aside. Various units should work with Beijing University to push forward the research on compressing and resizing Chinese characters.

The leadership had spoken. Wang Xuan subsequently enjoyed the protectionism of the state as he further developed his invention into a marketable product. In 1981, he built the first successful native prototype of a computerized Chinese script laser phototypesetting system, Huaguang I, which was introduced to the commercial market in China in 1987 and updated several times thereafter for the world market. Building on his research under Project 748 at Beijing University, he then established the company Founder Group in 1986, which became legendary for its innovations in Chinese language processing—from software development to personal computing. It was one of the first successful socialist capitalist ventures in Deng's economic reform era. It was a unique hybrid borne out of university research, state involvement, and the new practice of socialist capitalist entrepreneurship.

Books continue to be written about the legend of Project 748, the extraordinary people behind it, and the nation's proud moment in developing globally marketable Chinese computing print technology. The success of Wang Xuan's invention as part of the project would be celebrated for decades. Yet its singular achievement in Chinese information processing also made glaringly obvious the related areas in which Chinese language did not have an advantage. The original aspiration to build an entirely Chinese computing environment had encountered serious constraints. It was one thing to add on Chinese language processing capability to computers that were still Western in architecture, but quite another for China to create its own computers, from central processing units to operating systems and programming languages.

In the 1950s, while the spirit of socialist fraternity was still strong between China and the Soviet Union, that was the dream. Beginning in the early 1950s, Chinese scientists began to travel to Moscow and Leningrad to learn from their Soviet counterparts, and they devised China's own first twelve-year science and technology development plan in 1956. The Chinese Academy of Sciences opened up an Institute of Computing

Technology, founded in the same year and the first such organization in the country. They pushed on with their efforts after relations with the Soviets soured. A woman engineer at the Institute, Xia Peisu, built China's first all-purpose electronic digital computer—Model 107—in 1960, developed from two earlier prototypes that were replicas of Soviet models, M-3 and BESM-II. Research continued in building transistors and integrated circuits, especially as technology related to national defense was made a priority, but mass-scaled computing was still far from getting off the ground. In 1978, Apple II and IBM personal computers arrived and began to dominate the world's market. The chances of China coming out with its own seemed even more distant. Deng came to power that same year, and the spirit of reform and opening up to the world took hold. Science and policy planners relented and decided that it was more expedient to go with Western computing architecture and hardware than to continue the struggle to build their own.

Meanwhile, those who helped to shape China's decisive turn to the digital age during these pivotal decades dispersed as quietly as they had come together. Caldwell did not live long enough to see the Sinotype succeed, while Lee continued an illustrious career and moved back to industry, where he garnered several patents and an Emmy Award for the application of his technology to motion pictures in Hollywood. He stayed in the United States with his family. Zhi remained a quiet and reserved man for the rest of his life, leaving behind no public statement on his private thoughts, except for these words from 1991: "Based on our country's history and my personal experience, I have come to profoundly realize that only the Chinese Communist Party can lead the Chinese people to build a socialist New China." He died from a stroke two years later. Wang Xuan continued to struggle with poor health and passed away in 2006. To this day he remains a towering figure in the story of China's economic and technological miracle.

It would seem that, having spent centuries leveling the ground between its script and the West's skewed view of it, China had finally arrived digitally on both ends—input and output. Yet all that progress was still measured from where the country had started rather than against the world's pace. Now that China's path seemed to be moving toward merging with the outside, the question of how to integrate with other standards loomed. Having made extraordinary sacrifices to get to this point, the Chinese would now have to think about how to interact with other languages and their codes in a shared digital space. The Hundred Years of Humiliation narrative was no longer sufficient or desirable for propelling China forward. It was time to test and collaborate with others in a truly global system.

SEVEN

THE DIGITAL
SINOSPHERE
(2020)

MAKING WAY FOR A
NEW UNIVERSAL

S wipe. Tap. Drag. Chinese smartphone users can mix those three motions with their thumbs at an astonishing speed on the touch screen—on the subway, waiting in checkout lines at the supermarket, between dates and appointments, at the office, or just to pass the time. Their frenetic finger-pecking might even be dedicated to searching for one of the many websites that offer remedies for thumb cramping—a known condition caused by overtexting. With such a complicated writing system, Chinese users are obsessed with finding the latest, fastest, easiest, and most convenient way to fire off short messages or navigate through zillions of Chinese-language websites and news feeds. There is a big market for bundling keyboard input methods with other products and services like search engines, games, and shopping apps. Effortless typing is a vital gateway for luring users, and companies compete by offering thousands of cute emojis and GIFs alongside the keyboard input. Whether on a phone manufactured by Huawei or Vivo or using a KK Emoji Keyboard or Sogou Input app, typing in Chinese is no longer an end in itself; it opens the pathway to other smart technologies.

One scarcely has to learn Chinese characters the hard way—by memory or by hand—anymore, it seems. After a few decades of consolidation and standardization, several major options for Chinese input methods on a computer or mobile keyboard cover just about everyone's needs. Someone from Taiwan may prefer the Big5 or the Bopomofo method—still alive and well—while those from mainland China generally use Sogou, the most popular third-party input method of 2020, which offers pinyin as well as voice and character-component input. Nonnative Chinese speakers may opt for the convenience of the pinyin input that came installed on their phones. As you type, an array of full characters pops up to anticipate the sentence or phrase you're composing. Voice dictation lets you bypass the keyboard or touch screen altogether.

Technology for inputting Chinese for electronic communication is improving all the time. We take it for granted that a Chinese message sent from Hanoi will arrive instantaneously on the screen of another electronic device—mobile, laptop, tablet, or desktop—in New York, Beijing, Mountain View, Taipei, or Seoul without a glitch. Every user in the world has become dependent on this frictionless and instantaneous global experience.

It took a century of effort—from the adoption of a national dialect to the engineering of efficient digital character encoding—for the Chinese to benefit from the reach of that precision. Today, that hard-won leveled ground is teeming with engineers and tech companies building the optimal infrastructure for communicating in Chinese with the most advanced technology. As more characters enter digital circulation, the Chinese language is being ever more widely used, learned, propagated, studied, and accurately transformed into electronic data. It is about as immortal as a living script can hope to get. That path to immortality was not easily attained, though. If any one organization acted as a conduit for the Chinese script's lasting survival, it was a Silicon Valley nonprofit devoted to the creation of universal standards.

AFTER ZHI BINGYI published his On-Sight system for encoding Chinese characters, more than four hundred competing Chinese input methods exploded onto the scene by the late 1980s, in a burst of creative and entrepreneurial energy driven by market reforms that encouraged innovation and for-profit pursuits. Keyboard designs using Chinese, parts of Chinese, letters, shapes, and symbols flooded the market and patent offices.

These different coding systems were designed by different vendors, typically for use on their own machines. Once machines started to communicate with one another, a serious problem emerged. When text files were shared between machines using incompatible languages or coding systems, the computer would spit up strings of question marks or empty squares on the screen in place of letters or characters. As the market for personal computers, document sharing, and email took off, mutually exclusive keyboard input and encoding systems were not just a growing problem for the Chinese. They were an impediment throughout a globalizing digital world that was connecting users faster than there was time to coordinate the different systems.

In the United States, early IBM and Unix machines developed in the 1960s and 1970s used different standards, too. Both systems assigned numeric codes to letters and symbols, but the codes didn't match. That meant, for example, that the character code 97 would output "A" on an IBM machine, but on a Unix system you'd get "/." Trying to transfer data between the two systems would result in a long stream of gibberish even though they were designed in the same country.

Corralling different encodings into one standard was a relatively straightforward process for alphabetic scripts. The first encoding standard that gained wide traction, the American Standard Code for Information Interchange, or ASCII, was developed in the early 1960s. The original ASCII code was a one-byte (or eight-bit) system: Each character (here meaning text data, to be distinguished from a Chinese character) took up seven binary bits of storage space with an extra bit for checking errors, limiting the system to 128 possible values. The designers of ASCII didn't really think they needed more. They assigned a two- or three-digit numeric code to each number, letter, and punctuation mark; special symbols like "%" and "#"; and control codes like "tab," "shift-in," "shift-out," and "escape." To accommodate diacritics in other Western languages—like the Norwegian "ø," German "ü," French "é," or Portuguese "ç"—a later version of ASCII adopted the eighth bit, expanding the number of potential values to 256. So foundational was this basic one-byte architecture, narrowly specified for Western alphabetic languages and in particular English, that it is still embedded in some of the most widely used software programming languages today.

ASCII was never meant to accommodate non-Western script systems containing thousands of ideographic characters, due either to its designers' limited worldview or their failure to imagine the code's wild success beyond the Western alphabetic world. Each Asian nation eventually developed its own two or more byte standard, starting with Japan in 1978. (Using two bytes to encode characters enables a much-expanded set of more than 65,000 possible codes.) Those national standards faced the same incompatibility issues that had plagued early English-language machines, on a much grander scale. Some of the same Han ideographs were contained in various national standards, but identical characters were assigned totally different codes. Another problem was that there was no universally fixed number of ideographs to determine the size of the character set. The number of characters instead varied from country to country: Japan had fewer, the PRC needed more, and Taiwan required the most so it could include traditional characters.

Without a universally usable code, ideographic characters were barred from broad digital dissemination or use outside their local or national community in Hong Kong, Macau, Taiwan, Singapore, Malaysia, the PRC, or Vietnam. From the Chinese perspective, this meant losing the Chinese voice in the global arena. Having "discursive rights" (*huayu quan*) became a much-touted concept at this time. It meant not just having the right to a seat at the table, but also the power to establish and promote one's own narrative as the master or universal narrative for the world to abide by. China borrowed the idea of "discourse" from the West, adding to it its own perception of how the West wielded discursive power to impose its worldview on other nations. The ability for China to export its language for universal use was seen as an important condition for changing the narrative, giving it a platform to tell its own story. To use language as soft power, it was essential to take charge of one's own communications technology.

Meanwhile, that technology was reaching a new level of sophistication. In the 1970s, text processing was becoming widely used by businesses around the world. American companies were eager to market personal computers, operating systems, and hardware and software globally. Corporations like IBM already had subsidiary companies in every major city in western Europe. Consolidating a single unified encoding standard that included ideographic characters was important for an American computing industry seeking to secure a global competitive edge. Though no one could have foreseen how lucrative this eventual multitrillion-dollar industry would become, they knew standardized encoding was vital for reaching the growing number of individual users at home.

In the 1980s a group of software engineers and linguists in Silicon Valley began to explore how language scripts could be made to communicate with one another, so that a file in French could arrive and be read in Taipei just as easily as a Chinese file could be read in San Francisco. The solution they came up with in a 1988 working paper was called Unicode. In the words of its author, Joe Becker, every coded language script would be "unique, unified, universal." But Becker had not come up with the idea on his own. He'd been thinking about the challenge of how to handle all language scripts on any computer anywhere in the world for some time. In college, he came across the 1963 article by Gilbert W. King that drew on Lin Yutang's typewriter keyboard to discuss the possibility of machine translation. Although Becker did not know who Lin was, let alone how his keyboard connected the United States to China's efforts to modernize its script, his early thoughts about Unicode converged with the Chinese script revolution.

Becker first witnessed Han script encoding in the late 1970s in Japan while working at Fuji Xerox. Becker saw how Japanese electronics companies like Fujitsu and Hitachi had met with the same problem as IBM and other companies in the United States. They all had their own encoding for the *kanji* script. When the Japanese industrial standard came out in 1978, it offered a solution for Japan, but not for how Japan would exchange Han script with China, Korea, or Taiwan.

National character sets enabled computers made by a country's different vendors to communicate with one another. But because those national sets were developed without coordination across East Asia, the same ideographic character in Korean *hanja*, Taiwan traditional *hanzi*, PRC simplified *hanzi*, and Japanese *kanji* clashed with different coded versions of itself. Some characters were encoded multiple times or assigned to different code points in different national character sets. This led to many duplicates and great inefficiency. If Becker's idea of Unicode was to create something truly universal, it would have to accommodate non-Western scripts and reconcile the discrepancies between the different national character sets.

After his stint in Japan drew to a close in 1981, Becker returned to the United States, where he and Lee Collins, a young software engineer with linguistic expertise in East Asian languages he'd met in Japan, set to work. In 1986 Becker's team began to build a database at Xerox to map the Han characters encoded in the Japanese industrial standard to their counterparts in Chinese. They started floating the idea of Han script unification, as that was the obvious step forward. Such an endeavor would involve merging characters from different national sets with identical or similar structures and the same meanings, eliminating redundancies and duplicates. Their task was to determine which characters were shared by the various East Asian users and which ones were unique to them. Because of the distinct challenges of East Asian scripts, collating them was a prerequisite to integrating Han characters into the Unicode structure. By the end of 1987, Becker had the working concept of Unicode. Not long after, Collins moved to Apple. That was when the Han script unification project became a collaboration between Xerox and Apple, as the two companies began to coordinate their work on software development.

Unicode was envisioned as a master converter that would map all the existing national encoding standards of all languages. It would bring all human script systems, Western, Chinese, or otherwise, together under one umbrella standard and assign each character a single, standardized code for communicating with any machine.

It was a lofty aspiration—and a practical one. The Unicode developers thought their project was above politics because it was a technical solution to a problem of machine interchange. What Becker and his colleagues did not realize, however, is that the technology of language scripts is always political. The Asian countries whose scripts were being unified had much more at stake than incompatible inputs and outputs.

.   .   .

IN THE EARLY 1960s, the Library of Congress decided to embark on a massive automation project. It would build a universal catalog system, the kind that the Chinese librarian Bismarck Doo had dreamt of decades earlier but powered by computers. The Library of Congress began converting its paper catalog to a searchable digital index. With this machine-readable system, a user would be able to look up a title in a library thousands of miles away and at any time of the day, as long as he or she had access to a computer. Millions of catalog cards were made obsolete. The project turned the bookish craft of library cataloging into the sleek discipline of information science.

East Asian library collections in the United States expanded rapidly during the Cold War. Driven by an urgent mission to contain the global spread of communism, academics, librarians, and the government worked together to build up a knowledge base about China. In the 1960s alone, East Asian libraries acquired as many new holdings as they had during the course of the entire previous century. Digitizing these collections would be a challenge, because machine-readable databases could not accommodate non-Roman script languages like Hebrew, Arabic, Persian, or any of the East Asian languages.

A number of American foundations finally took action. In November 1979, the American Council of Learned Societies (ACLS) sponsored a conference titled East Asian Character Processing in Automated Bibliographic Systems at Stanford University. Among the approximately thirty attendees were the Library of Congress and the Research Libraries Group (RLG), a U.S.-based library consortium. Representatives from other American foundations as well as Japan, Korea, and Taiwan also attended. The RLG had already laid the groundwork for the conference with prior visits to Japan and Taiwan. Japan was the rising technological and economic giant in the region, poised to battle the United States in car manufacturing and electronics. It was the first Asian country to launch its own complete standard character set, including Chinese characters, or *kanji*. At the conference, the Japanese tried to capitalize on their advantage in the region by proposing that the Library of Congress adopt their industrial standard. The automation specialist from the Library of Congress named the Japanese standard as having "solved the problem in a way quite compatible with existing standards for international interchange." The RLG and others seemed perfectly willing to go with that assessment. That made Taiwan nervous, for its representatives at the conference saw this opportunity as bigger than just digitizing libraries.

From the start, automation was about establishing a standard to be used around the world, one that would represent all Chinese script use as it was practiced by the multiple users in the region. Whoever established an ideographic encoding standard stood to control the future of Han script information processing, and Taiwan saw itself as the only legitimate keeper of the tradition. Since retreating to Taiwan in 1949, the Nationalists had deemed themselves the true bearers of Chinese cultural heritage, with traditional written characters—unmarred by simplification—as the written emblem that sanctioned their cultural legitimacy. Still, the Chinese and Taiwanese orthographic systems were more alike than they were different. While today there are officially 8,105 simplified characters in circulation (increased from 2,235 in 1986), the rest of the Chinese lexicon—in Taiwan as well as the PRC—remains in the traditional form. Tens of thousands of archaic, traditional characters are very rarely used, some appearing no more than a handful of times in all written records. Whatever the number, Taiwan appointed itself their caretaker.

Cultural legitimacy wasn't the only thing at stake for Taiwan. When U.S. president Jimmy Carter withdrew diplomatic relations with Taiwan in 1978, the island needed to win and keep friends. It sought to gain a new economic edge, transforming itself from an agricultural economy of rice, pineapples, and sugarcane into one centered on electronics. The island had never felt more politically isolated; they saw establishing the Taiwanese character set as the international standard as an opportunity to become competitive in the international computing industry.

Taiwan's delegates quickly pointed out that Japanese had only a few thousand ideographic characters in *kanji* (Japan's standard encoded 6,349 of them), whereas tens of thousands of characters were needed for Chinese. Other Chinese librarians from the United States present at the ACLS conference also expressed reservations, even though it would have been easier to just go with Japan's already established industrial standard. Taiwan seized the moment and vowed to go one better; it had the resources and computing industry necessary for devising a standard that would truly benefit all Chinese users. The meeting attendees agreed to defer a final deliberation on Japan's proposal. Taiwan got a reprieve, in exchange for a promise: It would deliver a Chinese character set for consideration by the following March.

A small but critical window opened. The Taiwanese delegation returned home and mobilized government resources to summon a team of computer scientists, librarians, and philologists to work on a Chinese character set. It was an important effort to secure the island's future standing. After three months of working around the clock, the proposal was finally finished. Moments before the Taiwanese delegates boarded the flight to Washington, D.C., in March 1980 for a follow-up meeting with their American counterparts, the glue used to bind the pages of the final character set proposal was reportedly still wet. Contained in those pages was a preliminary sample set of 4,808 Chinese characters, intended to provide a blueprint for subsequent expansion.

At the meeting in D.C., discussions of Taiwan's character set lasted for hours. A special committee, made up of librarians from the Library of Congress and encoding experts from the RLG as well as the

American National Standards Institute, was then formed to verify the results. Taiwan's months-long effort was not for naught. The committee decided to use their set for the American libraries' digitization of East Asian materials. They asked Taiwan to expand the set to include more than 22,000 ideographic characters to accommodate all Chinese, Japanese, and Korean script needs.

The PRC learned of the RLG's acceptance of Taiwan's standard only after the sample set was approved. Taiwan's team had in fact deliberately kept its work quiet. Their goal was to give Taiwan a prominent international platform, and they feared the PRC would protest or intervene if it realized Taiwan's strategy.

The PRC rushed to develop the first version of its national standard, partnering with Japan. The character set contained 6,763 Chinese characters, with an additional 682 for the Latin, Greek, and Cyrillic alphabets and the Japanese *kana* syllabary, for a total of 7,445. The PRC tried to lobby to replace Taiwan's character set with its own, made up of both simplified and traditional characters. (It did not provide the traditional forms of characters that had already been simplified.) The PRC's engineers and computer scientists thought they could claim an edge over Taiwan by providing the simplified characters essential for digitizing documents from the Chinese mainland.

Taiwan, however, anticipated this move. Its character set also included simplified characters—but clearly labeled as "variants" of the "correct" forms of the Chinese script. Long established in Chinese lexicology, "variants" referred to characters that shared the same semantic meaning and even pronunciation but differed in shape. Within Chinese Han characters, the distinction created a hierarchy. The variant category traditionally included characters that might have been improperly copied at some point or that were idiosyncratic regional adaptations of characters in popular use. The Taiwanese set also treated Japanese *kanji* and Korean *hanja* as variants, but those were clear cases of foreign adaptation of Chinese characters, so the distinction was accepted. For Taiwan to put simplified characters under this category sent a clear signal: They were attempting to establish simplified characters as the anomalies of the true form.

The last thing the American librarians wanted was to get bogged down in regional squabbles, which they had no way of adjudicating anyway. They wished to engage Chinese encoding primarily as a technical matter, a piece to plug into the grander scheme of library catalog automation in the United States.

In September 1980, the Research Libraries Group made an important announcement. Together with the Library of Congress, it planned to catalog and enter all Chinese, Korean, and Japanese materials into a shared online database for all library networks. The announcement gave a boost to Taiwan's standard, as it now had a guaranteed reach and platform that it could not have dreamt of as a local standard among several in the region. The project was supported by several major foundations. After a few revisions, Taiwan's character set would serve as the basis for American bibliographic automation for East Asian languages, encoding sixteen thousand characters and variants. It would also become the recommended industrial standard for American computer vendors, even though officially it was not a national standard—because Taiwan was not recognized as a nation.

With the Americans' approval and endorsement, Taiwan's coded characters were given an incontestable advantage. Other Han standards would have to reckon with Taiwan's coded characters as they developed their own systems. With the expansion requested by the RLG, Taiwan's character set became the backbone of the RLG's unified East Asian character set. According to the rules of this set, any given character, despite having slightly different versions in Japan, Korea, Taiwan, or China, would be coded only once, which minimized errors and economized encoding space. This enhanced and improved character code was then adopted by the American National Standards Institute for national use. By the end of the 1980s, American computer vendors began to develop software that could support this character set, which was poised to dominate the way library collections would be automated across the United States.

The impact of this decision would be felt far beyond library science. In the summer of 1988, Joe Becker and Lee Collins met with key people from the RLG at the latter's annex in downtown Palo Alto to discuss the criteria for unifying Han characters. Apple then purchased the RLG's ideographic character database for further study, and it formed the first draft of the Unicode Han character set. When Unicode introduced its first standard, it included the RLG's repertoire of by then 15,850 characters, which were passed down to subsequent versions of Unicode. Still embedded in Unicode's DNA today is the Han script's much older regional strife in Asia, which raged even as Unicode was being designed—and still hasn't subsided today.

WHILE THE PUSH for library automation in the United States led to the first attempt to unify the coding of all Han characters, developing individual national ideographic character sets remained the greater concern in East Asia. No one wanted to be coerced into using another country's standard in place of their own, especially because language usages and needs in different Han script countries were not identical. Each country emphasized their differences all the more. After Japan came out with its own industrial standard character set in 1978, Taiwan and the PRC doubled down to develop their own sets.

China especially felt the need to assert and protect its position as the script's original and rightful steward, as it saw multiple stakeholders rise from neighboring countries. To the east was Japan, to the northeast Korea, and across the straits Taiwan, whose use of traditional characters was also shared by Hong Kong and Macau. China believed it had the greatest stake among Asian countries, since it possessed the greatest number of native Chinese speakers. Any conversation about Han script unification would fail, the Chinese felt, without them shaping the conversation. At the same time, China was not in the position to lead in this area; its computing technology was in its early stages and personal computers were uncommon. It needed to collaborate. Despite the delicate cross-straits political climate, mainland Chinese computer scientists and engineers reached out to their counterparts in Taiwan. They appealed to them on the grounds that if the Chinese themselves did not figure out a common solution, they would have little hope in communicating with the rest of the world.

The Taiwanese scientists and engineers required no further persuasion. They, too, saw that Chinese-speaking Han script users were in danger of being outflanked by other Han script users in the region. China and Taiwan would be stronger together. Despite their political differences, they still shared the same cultural roots and had a closer affinity with each other than with any other East Asian neighbor. So the researchers in Taiwan began collaborating with their counterparts in the PRC.

Meanwhile, a solution was being introduced from the other side of the Pacific. After the Unicoders decided to pursue Han ideographic unification, building on the RLG's earlier work, they inevitably brought American computing's industrial ambitions and dominance to bear on the region's dynamics. Unicode's Han character repertoire went far beyond that of the RLG's bibliographic sets, providing comprehensive coverage of newer national as well as industry standards. Collins was in charge of developing the unified set and flew to meet with his Chinese counterparts in Beijing in 1989, just months after the student demonstrations in Tiananmen Square. It was a politically and internationally tense moment for China. But the American and Chinese computer scientists and engineers were in agreement about prioritizing the task at hand and taking the long view. Under Unicode's umbrella, different versions of Han characters in East Asian usage would be unified according to rules drawn from Japan's and China's own experiences in working out their national standards. The Americans and the Chinese were embarking on something unprecedented together, enabling a shared text-processing world of emails, texts, and files, where every language and script could be represented. It was going to change the future of electronic communication and the Chinese language's place in it.

For China, it was also a way forward. Embracing Unicode was part of an answer to ending its technological and economic isolation. Unicode would allow China to take advantage of an existing international infrastructure, a platform far superior to anything it could build on its own at the time. While dovetailing with China's own interests, Unicode did not, however, win unanimous support in the region. From the beginning, Japan was skeptical. After all, behind the nonprofit Unicode Consortium stood the industrial and commercial interests of American computing giants. It was unfair, the Japanese complained, that an international standard should be predominantly determined by American corporate interests. Moreover, Japan's own linguistic affairs should be left to the Japanese.

Others felt the same. South Korea thought unification ignored the fact that written Han script traditions had in essence evolved into separate cultural systems in East Asia. One basic question was what would be included as a most common character in Unicode's official character set, defined by ISO 10646, also known as the Universal Coded Character Set—and "common" for whom. Unicode purported to represent all human scripts, but some characters are more frequently used in Japan than in China or Korea. Moreover, Korea's own history of Han script use, going back to the fourth century, predated the PRC's simplification campaigns in the twentieth century. From Korea's perspective, traditional—not simplified—characters should, if anything, be the basis of the unified character set. All East Asian parties agreed that Unicode needed more input from the regional stakeholders. As native users, they should have the greatest say in the Han script's future. In February 1990, a special working group was proposed, composed of members from countries and organizations in the region, to study this encoding. Three years later, this joint research group—representing native speakers from China, Korea, and Japan—would become the Ideographic Rapporteur Group, joined by Vietnam in 1994.

Jointly supervised by the Unicode Consortium and the Geneva-based nonprofit International Organization for Standardization, which sets the industrial standard for everything from the curvature of your wineglass to the sweetness of toothpaste, the IRG has been meeting twice a year for more than a quarter of a century. The Han script is the only writing system that has its own international working group. At first glance, the group does what Chinese language reformers inside China have been doing since the late nineteenth century: scrutinizing thousands of characters, their every joint and ligament, and debating their etymology and morphology.

But the rapporteurs' work has a different purpose. Their concern is not to phoneticize or index characters, nor to break them down into simpler parts or render them into alphabetic form. Instead, the IRG's job is to determine whether each character will be assigned its own code in the ever-expanding Unicode character set—or whether a proposed character is "unifiable" with an already encoded character from any of the original national character sets that were collated for Unicode 1.0.1, released in 1992.

The principle of unification underlies IRG's work. But the concept is not as straightforward as it seems. Take a character that has morphed into different forms over the centuries but still means the same thing in Japan and China, like 読 (yo) and 读 (du). Would the forms be unifiable on the grounds of having had the same origin? Or not, because they look different? One clear rule is that all the major and commercial national character sets that Unicode originally sourced for its 1992 version would remain untouched—known as the "source separation" rule.

Still, Unicode 1.0 wasn't perfect, because the original national standard sets were not entirely consistent with this rule. Duplicate characters, or characters that ought to have been unified but weren't in the original national and regional character sets, continue to surface and plague the IRG. On top of that, more characters, far beyond what was originally included in the different national character sets, are being dredged up from archaic and more specialized sources. Han characters continue to be discovered in archaeological excavations, ancient texts, minority languages, local dialects, etc. The rarest characters have been by and large the names of places and people. Chinese parents invest great significance in the characters they choose for their children—the more unique and auspicious, the better. Unusual characters like "soaring dragon in the sky"—龑 (*yan*)—which contains the characters for "dragon" and "sky," would seem much flatter if the parents could only use plain "dragon"—龙—a far more common and already encoded character. The etymological lineage and history of these uncataloged characters often have not yet been sorted out for computer encoding, and that pre-vetting takes up time.

Characters have to be researched and submitted for review by IRG members before a meeting. At the meeting they are projected onto a screen so their structures can be carefully examined for accuracy, and then, after a lengthy period of discussion and debate, approved or denied entry to the system. There is currently a backlog of characters awaiting review, so many that in 2019, the IRG renamed itself—after twenty-six years—the Ideographic Research Group, recognizing that its work had long ago surpassed its original intent of temporarily working with the Unicode Consortium and ISO as they sorted out the East Asia ideographs. Dealing with the Han ideographs has become a critical and ongoing task. So many more thousands of characters are being proposed just from the PRC alone that admitting Chinese or Han ideographs is no longer a finite responsibility with a clear end date.

IN THE SIDE WING of Building G at the National Library of Vietnam in Hanoi, the ceiling fans hummed, pushing hot air from one end of a long room to the other. It was a late October morning in 2018, and delegates from the United States, South Korea, Japan, Hong Kong, Taiwan, Vietnam, the PRC, and a few independent participants were already in their seats when I arrived. Dressed in a casual mix of plaids and T-shirts, they made small talk as they searched on their laptops for a solid internet connection. It was the fifty-first international meeting of the IRG, a mini-U.N. in the encoding world.

Our Vietnamese host had left copies of the National Library's official brochure scattered around the room, introducing its collection of more than five thousand Sino-Nom—or Chinese-language—books. It was a polite nod to the Chinese script's millennium of influence in the region. In Vietnam, the Chinese script no longer resembles the Chinese script, just as the French baguette at the hole-in-the-wall café a few blocks away, our lunch spot, is no longer a French baguette. Since it was introduced to Hanoi in the late 1880s, the French baguette has been changed to suit local taste—made fluffier so you can stuff more pâté, roasted pork, beef shanks, chicken, pickled radish, cucumbers, cilantro, and chili flakes in between its two halves, slathered with mayonnaise. Yet the ways the Vietnamese have altered that icon of French cuisine are nothing compared to what they have done with the Chinese script over the span of ten centuries. Apart from importing Chinese characters wholesale as Japan and Korea had, the Vietnamese also used the Chinese script's compositional principle—part semantic, part phonetic—

as the basis for building their own ideographic script, *chữ nôm*. It looks like an extended application of square-shaped Chinese characters and does not stray far from the character mold.

The attitude in Vietnam toward the Chinese script's thousand-year legacy has gone through its ups and downs. At one point Chinese was deeply revered. When Vietnam fell to the French in the 1880s, it has been said that one could hear the gentle sound of Sinoscript writing brushes falling to the ground. It was the end of high culture, nurtured by the once-great Chinese Empire. Yet in 1946, Ho Chi Minh, seeing the Chinese influence in light of anticolonial struggles, spoke of the Chinese legacy in a less poetic light: "The last time the Chinese came, they stayed one thousand years. . . . I prefer to smell French shit for five years, rather than Chinese shit for the rest of my life." The politics of the Han characters for other countries in East Asia are still real and present.

Some of the old rivalries may have receded, but others remain. Those in attendance at the IRG meeting represented the users and stakeholders of the Chinese script around the world. One delegation was missing from the room—North Korea. After attending the meeting a few times, it had mysteriously stopped coming more than a decade ago.

A cheery Japanese delegate handed out free T-shirts from a plastic shopping bag, reminding everyone of the team spirit needed to get through the days ahead. "He brings them every year, and they're always in black and the same size," whispered the person sitting next to me, Ken Lunde, a tall Swedish coder from Adobe who wrote the definitive book on Chinese, Japanese, and Korean (CJK) information processing. It was important to be egalitarian, even in shirt size. Seated on my other side was Lee Collins, now in his early sixties—relaxed, sharp, and unruffled.

The largest contingent in the room was from mainland China, with nine delegates representing the government, industry, and academia.

Having filled their teacups, the PRC delegates walked back to their chairs. Polite and unhurried, they exchanged a few quiet words with one another while dunking their tea bags. The Taiwan delegates—all two of them—sat across the room. Mr. Bear, as he called himself, was the most senior veteran there. Squat and avuncular, he had been involved in the development of the earliest precursor to Taiwan's current computer encoding standard, Big5, back in the 1960s. The cover of his laptop flashed a yellow warning sticker that bespoke his seniority: "Beware. Bear Sighting."

There were still others, independent, self-funded, and here for no reason other than their love of the task at hand. For the next five days, they would present, argue, and deliberate on each ideograph that was in the queue for encoding. Two of the newer, younger members, one in a white shirt with "Artificial Intelligence" in boldface type above a human brain map, and the other with a pocket protector and a soft voice, were having a tête-à-tête next to the snack table as they peeled wrappers off pieces of candy—that was breakfast.

Meanwhile, Lu Qin, a fifty-eight-year-old computer scientist from Hong Kong, was ready to start. Tough-minded, warmhearted, and standing with a slight stoop, she has been attending the IRG for twenty-five years and has served as its convener for the last fifteen. Her hearty, abrupt sense of humor lends an occasional piratical air to her matriarchal presence. She gave a couple of quick taps on the microphone. Behind her against a wall of golden curtains hung a stiff two-tone sign in Chinese and English, officially welcoming us all to the IRG meeting. Lu gave an overview of the order of business, followed by a bureaucratic reminder for all to please think as an international body and rise above their individual and national interests. The next five days promised to be as efficient and uneventful as possible. Three thousand characters were on the docket to be reviewed—and that was a light load.

The first two days passed by quickly in their orderliness. By the third day, the IRG was deep into its vetting work. Character after character was projected onto a white screen, and people were commenting, voting, sometimes getting up and walking closer to the image. Collins was even-keeled, with a blue gaze that can turn quite intense when something catches his eye—like the ideographic character on the screen just then. Henry, the young guy from Hong Kong with the brain T-shirt, suggested that it should be separately coded from another character, or "disunified," as they say. One stroke was intersecting, not merely intruding upon, another stroke line. There were murmurs of disagreement. The delegates got out of their seats to take a closer look.

A small circle formed at the white screen and then a shouting match erupted. Collins and I stopped talking and turned around, as did everyone else in the room. It was between Mr. Bear and Henry. Forty years apart in age but inches away from each other in a face-off, they disagreed over a proposal for character unification. Henry wanted to speed up the process of confirming characters by putting variant characters under a different rubric of a coding sequence, basically a subset of an already encoded character. The variant character would not get its own code per se but would be included as a version of a set. It is similar to the way face emojis can have different skin colors. The issue is which color gets to be seen first—as the one that represents the whole category—before other variants are scrolled to.

To the Taiwan delegates, Henry's proposal sounded awfully like demoting Taiwan's ideographic characters from the "correct" status, or base character, supplanting Taiwan's decades of painstaking labor in collecting and preserving traditional script. With new characters being proposed, Taiwan carefully guarded its already encoded traditional characters as the legitimate ones that should stand on their own. Concerns of identity were at play, and emotions ran high. Mr. Bear, exasperated, finally exploded: "You are not Taiwanese—you would not understand!"

The room fell silent. Collins, observing the commotion, exchanged a few quick whispers with Lunde and a representative from ISO next to him. Nodding to one another, they shifted back in their chairs with their arms crossed, faces still, like they had decided to sit this one out. As far as Unicode was concerned, Collins explained to me over dim sum a couple of months later in Menlo Park, their job was already done. All the East Asian nationally encoded major character sets—previously devised by the countries themselves and set at a number that was sufficient for the characters they needed—were included in the original 1992 version of Unicode, at the time 20,902 Han characters. That was the original mission—to facilitate the practical matter of systems interchange, not to dredge up written records from the past. Around 90 percent of the characters added since Han unification, however, have been variants, many of them uncommon or ancient characters. One of the sets proposed by Japan at the Hanoi meeting, for instance, had been gleaned from the esoteric ninja manuals.

"Everything I told them not to do," said Joe Becker, whom Collins brought to lunch for me to meet, "they're busy doing." He chuckled. In the original 1988 Unicode document, Becker recommended that Unicode's highest priority was "ensuring utility for the future [rather than] preserving past antiquities." But the East Asian members of the IRG had their own retort: Unicode had already included in its encoding an ancient script—Latin. So Unicode had already broken its own rule. Moreover, whereas Latin is a dead language, Chinese is still evolving as the oldest living language with the greatest number of native speakers in the world. For all these reasons, inherited and ongoing, "We are never happy with our work," Lu said to me during one of the breaks at the Hanoi meeting, laughing off the frustration. Skirmishes like the one between Henry and Mr. Bear were nothing. "You should have seen it in the old days," she said in a lowered voice.

Lu had already hinted that something like this would happen when

I first went to meet her in her office in Hong Kong. It was the week before the Hanoi meeting, and I wanted to find out why telling Han characters apart can be so difficult and hence controversial. I knew she could explain why the IRG's task remains as vital as it was on the first day. Where the Chinese script is concerned, the greatest strife is in the smallest details. Whether an ideographic character gets a unique code in Unicode hinges on whether it is seen as an original character or a variant. Lu showed me on a piece of paper. She drew me three versions, or glyphs, of the character for "bone," *gu*. They represented how the character appeared in Hong Kong, the PRC, and Taiwan, respectively:

Hong Kong Glyph   Mainland China Glyph   Taiwan Glyph

Variants of *"gu"* in Hong Kong, China, and Taiwan.

A first glance will not reveal how these three glyphs are different. If you take a second, longer look, you'll realize that the little corner squares inside the characters close off in opposite directions: Hong Kong's and Taiwan's to the right, and mainland China's version to the left. Variations like this happened historically, and in other cases could be attributed to any number of medieval scribes, Confucian scholars, woodblock printers, or arbitrary ruling. As inscription moved from medium to medium, errors happened. Print technology may not have been precise enough to register the difference between a dot and a short dash and thus produced two versions of the same character over time; a woodblock once fresh enough to make a strong sharp corner eventually made a rounded one. These were mistakes that humans could detect and determine. But try to tell that to a machine. In the case of "bone," the PRC version required only a single stroke—in line with its simplification policy—while the Taiwan and Hong Kong versions required two. For the purpose of Han unification, it had to be decided whether to code all three glyphs of "bone" as one—thereby suggesting that they are all variants of the same abstract character. This is important. What determines a base from a variant, for the IRG's purposes, depends on which version had already been encoded, because its job is to make sure that there are no duplicate encodings for characters that essentially are the same. Even though the IRG is made up of mainly computer engineers and scientists, they find themselves having to take on a Sinologist's or linguist's work in proving whether a proposed character is unifiable with an existing character. This is where conflicts arise, because no one wants their character to be subsumed under someone else's—a stroke's difference may be the erasure of one's own character. In the case of "bone," since the physical difference is minimal, and does not alter the meaning of the character, the ideographs are coded as the same, according to one of the IRG's precise rules for unification. If two characters look alike, but are semantically different, however, they get separate coding.

Whether a character should be unified with another can be a hard call to make, but someone has to make it. The Chinese script so far has defied most attempts to systematize it in a complete way. Should there be a future technology for writing even more exacting than machine-readable codes, any judgment call made by a human user today might very well be seen as an inconsistency later, which would entail more corrections. But no matter, as Lu urges whenever the IRG delegates are locked in stalemates and heated arguments, "we must go on." And they do.

One could see the IRG's workload as essentially a denial-of-service attack by an unwieldy language: the Chinese script having its revenge on Western technology. But for the Chinese, this is important and essential work. They aren't intentionally trying to overwhelm the Unicode platform. They are motivated by a future where digital literacy might become the only form of literacy—and they are staking a claim in a technology-driven world so that their culture will continue to be known, disseminated, and celebrated. The IRG's workload continues to grow because Unicode is seen as a pathway to the universal platform of language power. Of the different stakeholders, China feels the greatest fear of its language not being broadly disseminated, understood, and accepted globally. Representing the Chinese language to the world in the right, user-friendly way is vital for its presence in the global information infrastructure.

Whoever controls information controls the world. That is the lesson that has been demonstrated with greater and greater clarity in the digital age. For the East Asia region, who gets to provide the most digitally comprehensive representation of Chinese characters first is important. Once a representation becomes embedded in the technological infrastructure—as with Morse code, the QWERTY keyboard, Romanization schemes, the Four-Corner Method, ASCII, Taiwan's character set for the RLG, and all other attempts to modernize Chinese—it gets reinforced via repeated use within the technological infrastructure until it is embedded within that technology. This recognition has touched off a race among Han script users. In 2009, Taiwan motioned to submit traditional Chinese script for consideration by UNESCO as a world intangible cultural heritage, to be recognized and safeguarded. For China, though, the Chinese script is neither a dead tradition nor a heritage that has been exhausted. It continues to live and change, with still greater potential for a broader reach to nonnative speakers around the world. Unicode is an official pathway to carry that vision into the future. It is like holding a permanent megaphone on a universal platform.

The apparently endless queue of Chinese characters still waiting to enter the digital world reflects where the Chinese script—and China—have landed after more than a century of failures, lessons learned, and hard-won modernization. The Chinese language finally got its foot in the door, and the country has been accumulating digital power ever since. China is currently positioning itself to set the next standard for what it means to be a global power—and it is far from done.

EVERY TECHNOLOGY THAT has ever confronted the Chinese script, or challenged it, also had to bow before it. Ideographic characters have pushed to the brink every universalist claim of Western technology, from telegraphy to Unicode. Having bent over backward many times to accommodate the technologies of the Western alphabet, the Chinese script, however, has not been altered in a fundamental way. Having survived, its presence has only been strengthened by those trials. There has been a resurgence of nationalistic pride and cultural interest surrounding the Chinese language. TV shows and national youth competitions, oral recitations and calligraphy have once more become extracurricular platforms for instilling in the young a sense of pride and confidence in their cultural heritage.

A frequent theme in global Chinese contemporary art over the past several decades and now a new niche in the design industry, the Chinese script has also flourished on the internet. Not only are hundreds of thousands of characters still being rediscovered and promised for encoding and dissemination at the IRG, but Chinese netizens have also found their own way of enlivening the language's unique expressivity in the digital realm—sometimes to the dismay of the authorities. Homophones, once the bane of Romanization, returned with a vengeance as a way of going around censors and discussing taboo subjects online. Even Arabic numerals, once the stigma of Chinese telegraphy, are being exploited as slang for their roughly similar sounds to certain Chinese phrases: 520 for "I love you"; 540 for "I promise"; 886 for "Goodbye"; 1314 for "Forever"; 7456 for "You're making me so angry"; or the onomatopoetic 555, which simply mimics the sound of crying.

Without knowing Chinese, few outsiders can interpret how these language games reflect the political and cultural temperature of everyday China. And more characters are still coming. The General Administration of Press and Publication (now the National Press and Publication Administration), which is a censoring body that regulates print and publication nationwide, launched in 2006 the largest digitization project of any single script—five hundred thousand new Chinese characters, to be extracted and collected from old written records. One-fifth of the characters are expected to come from ethnic minority scripts, while the rest would come from premodern sources. For the first time, archaic, classical, and obscure characters would be as available for usage as characters from more recent, modern repertoires, all a few key taps away on your phone or laptop. There would be no need to distinguish between common and uncommon characters where availability is concerned. The projected scale is massive. The sheer volume would no doubt add a few more decades to IRG's projected backlog. By one calculation, it would take them more than two centuries just to evaluate China's proposed characters alone. As of 2020, the number of Han characters that exist in Unicode (now at version 13.0) is 92,856. What is being proposed, if all approved, would dramatically increase that number.

While getting those characters ready for vetting remains an ongoing process, as the deliberations at the 2018 IRG meeting in Hanoi made clear, the information age has given Chinese a new platform and megaphone. And the initiative is not limited to elite technical spheres like the IRG. When it comes to the future global prominence of the Chinese language, every native speaker is a stakeholder. In 2017, a Chinese citizen wrote to China's current chairman with a request:

Dear Beloved Chairman Xi Jinping,

I am a lover of ancient books, and I have a dream: to realize the digitization of China's ancient books. . . . Our civilization goes back 5,000 years, and has produced a prodigious amount of books, divided into more than 20,000 categories. After more than thirty years of reform and opening up, China has managed an extraordinary achievement under the world's eyes. The second largest economy in the world, a secured number one position in foreign reserves, our country has accumulated massive wealth and human talent. . . . These accomplishments have provided very favorable conditions for digitizing ancient knowledge. . . . It is an arduous, complicated, and long-term task. History has proven time and time again that, without support from the highest level, a colossal project like this would not be possible. Which is why I risk intruding on your busy schedule and write you personally.

This concerned citizen, a lover of the Chinese language, cuts a familiar figure. More than 117 years ago, he was Wang Zhao, who risked his life to bring back to China a new spelling for the Chinese script. A few years after that, he was the determined Zhou Houkun, the young engineer who traveled across an ocean and a continent to study at MIT and invent a Chinese typewriting machine. At the same time, he could just as well have been Bismarck Doo, Lin Yutang, or Wang Yunwu, who fed their ambitions and poured their creative energy into bringing order to the Chinese character universe, turning the library into a laboratory for creating new systems of knowledge. None of them forgot that they were part of a long, native written tradition—not even Wang Jingchun while he was trying to fight for Chinese telegraphy on foreign terms.

The Chinese script revolution has always been the true people's revolution—not "the people" as determined by Communist ideology but the wider multitude that powered it with innovators and foot soldiers. Every devotee inside and outside China, like the laser-typesetting inventor Wang Xuan and the forgotten Chinese American scientist Francis F. Lee, had a hand in carrying it forward regardless of the difficulties and the perils of politics, wars, and international conflicts.

This revolution has been carried out by both the people and the state at different times. China has made science and technology their primary focus for more than sixty-five years, with computerization and Chinese-language information processing at the top of that list for most of the time. During periods of political and social upheavals, when all seemed lost, it was once again the people who carried the script's future on their backs. Even the wrongly accused like Zhi Bingyi managed to play their part in propelling the Chinese script forward during the darkest years. The technologization of the Chinese script gave hope to pulling China out of a state of industrial belatedness. It set an early precedent for how the Chinese Communist Party would develop its socialist institution–cum-entrepreneur model for innovation, paving the way for a unique path to reshape modern capitalism. Information processing was the tool that opened the door to the cutting edge, technology-driven future that China's decades of linguistic reform and state planning at last pried open.

As Chinese becomes one of the most geopolitically important languages in the twenty-first century, the Chinese state has wasted no time in cultivating the world's appetite for it. Its push to establish Confucius Institutes around the world has not been uncontroversial. Outside of western Europe and North America, China tries for a more receptive audience through its own brand of cultural diplomacy while promoting an alternative success model to Western democracy–led progress. While the country's global presence continues to incur mixed reactions, Mandarin fever has remained strong. Chinese language learning has been sweeping through the United States, from K-12 classrooms to college seminars. Chinese is already one of the most studied foreign languages in U.S. universities—second only to Spanish and often competing with French. Chinese textbooks have found their way onto every other continent, from Nairobi to La Plata, Dubai to Phnom Penh, Havana to Vienna. A concerted effort has been under way to sway the world's opinion in China's favor, propagating its cultural power alongside its economic and political forays.

Yet the most important consequences of the Chinese script revolution do not lie in these obvious manifestations. Beyond culture and tradition, Chinese script has been sharpened and upgraded into a technology that is intended to be a first step, a foundation for building an entire ecology of Chinese digital nationalism. China is aiming to reshape global standards, from supply chains to 5G. It learned the critical importance of infrastructure building from the incursion of Western telegraphy on Chinese soil. Instead of laying down rubber-wrapped cables, China is manufacturing fiber-optic cables and investing in space satellites, building a worldwide network of economic influence—overland, underwater, and into space. More than a century's effort at learning how to standardize and transform its language into a modern technology has landed China here, at the beginning—not the end—of becoming a standard setter, from artificial intelligence to quantum natural language processing, automation to machine translation.

The Chinese script has completely turned around its position in relation to the Western alphabetic script. There are currently more than 900 million internet users in China. As each of them searches through Chinese language websites, uses Chinese input methods, posts on social media, and buys and sells on Chinese websites every single day, they are making the Chinese internet smarter, faster, and ever more rich in data. As China's internet sphere grows, so does the potential loss for any outsider not being able to access it. China has more data and three times more users than the United States. The Chinese internet ecosphere has at its command the largest data militia in the world, each user a volunteer and participant. Powered by the Chinese script, a new digital Great Wall is being erected in place of the old one made of mud and brick. Unlike before, this one works both ways—it can open or close off its internet sphere to outsiders, as well as keep insiders in by controlling the information flow. In the current technological era, where power means access, the ability to direct and curate information literally reshapes reality and beliefs; it can bring about the conquest of the mind without a single soldier on the ground.

The country is poised to create its own Han script sphere of influence, once again, in the current millennium. China's domestic market can sustain its own internet sphere, even if decoupled from the alphabetic world. This time, the Han script sphere of influence would also mean much more than just a system of written ideographic signs shared by regional neighbors. The Chinese digital sphere of influence is not physically limited to the PRC or Chinese-speaking communities in the world; it can welcome others into its fold, as long as they subscribe to China's digital technology and infrastructure, thereby multiplying its footprint. Old-fashioned, bare-knuckled dominance alone is no longer central or sufficient for global powers of the twenty-first century.

An adage, recalled by Yiddish linguist Max Weinreich, goes, "A language is a dialect with an army and navy." The idea is that the way any language becomes dominant has less to do with linguistic attributes than the politics that drive it. The Chinese script revolution has scaled up that statement for contemporary relevance. The country's most decisive push will come in the next two decades, as it aims to take the lead in artificial intelligence by 2035. Deep neural networks are being trained on China's ever-growing volume of data. Chinese tech giant Baidu has become a leader in machine translation and natural language processing, while Tencent sits on a wealth of data gathered through WeChat and its video gaming platforms. From health care to smart cities, education to social control, the Chinese state's priority under its current leadership is to implement, if not to perfect, its vision of global governance. The country now enjoys a level of confidence it did not have for two centuries. China is no longer trying to catch up to anyone—except the future it sees for itself.

There is a growing sense that China must now go its own way, having spent more than two centuries following the ways of the West, a path it believes it has exhausted. Through the technological revolution of the Chinese script, China got its cultural confidence back. Yet an underdog mentality remains strong. The country came close to losing its written language but was saved, time and again, by its own language devotees and people. But there are no ready believers in the world beyond China and the Chinese language, where, despite the progress and determination China has made in the past forty years, the new global power has to renegotiate with the world it is trying to reshape in order to host a different world order than the one it has learned. The Chinese state is cognizant of the importance of crafting its own image in the world. To tell China's story well, as Xi Jinping reminded the Chinese people at the Nineteenth National Congress of the Communist Party of China in October 2017, is to build the country's cultural soft power. Millennia of acculturating and surviving the intrusion of outsiders has led to the return of a deep-rooted belief in the ultimately correct path of sinicization. With the country's most ambitious scientific and technological plans to date now under way, the China story no doubt aims for a triumphant narrative. But China will not be the only author. There are no easy converts in the world the way there were native champions of the Chinese language, and the opinions of others will determine the new global power's success and failure. Still unfolding, history will overtake China's story.

ACKNOWLEDGMENTS

For a book about Chinese information technology and language revolution, a shout-out must go to librarians all over the world. Michael Meng's assistance over the years at the Yale library has facilitated much of my work and research. As a literary scholar and humanist, my foray into writing a book about science and technology would not have been possible without the generous support of the New Directions Fellowship from the Andrew W. Mellon Foundation. I thank the Institute for Advanced Study at Princeton for a fellowship in 2014, which allowed me to put first thoughts on paper, as well as the John Simon Guggenheim Foundation for further supporting the later phase of the writing of this book. Elias Altman has been a tireless agent and interlocutor, a comrade in arms from the early days of this project. I have had the good fortune of finding the brilliant editor Courtney Young at Riverhead, whose extraordinary patience and meticulous eye and editing have made the book what it is. She and the dynamic team at Riverhead took a chance on this project, and I am grateful for their faith in me. My thanks to my colleagues and deans at Yale for supporting and tolerating my ever-itinerant path and, in particular, to

Frances Rosenbluth and Ian Shapiro, Barry Nalebuff and Helen Kauder, and Ann-ping Chin and Jonathan Spence for their kindness, advice, and humor. I am also thankful for the generosity of colleagues elsewhere in the world—from Oxford to Singapore—for inviting me to speak on the subject and offering invaluable feedback along the way, especially David Wang, Benjamin Elman, Liu Hong, Alan K. L. Chan, K. K. Luke, Joachim Kurtz, Iwo Amelung, Eugenia Lean, Nicola Di Cosmo, and Margaret Hillenbrand. My early Google Tech Talk on the project in Mountain View steered the book in important ways, as did the honor of a Tan Lark Sye Professorship at the Nanyang Technological University. That there are still too many others to name here (see Chapter Notes) bespeaks the indebtedness of this project to the different communities and conversations I have been lucky enough to participate in, as is always the case with any idea. As for personal debts and friendship, there are the usual suspects in Los Angeles, Cambridge, Hong Kong, Mountain View, Ithaca, and Chicago: Ming Tsu and Lorenz Gamma, Alina Huo and Florian Knothe, Thor Olsson and Wai-Kwok Chong, Dan Russell, Paul Ginsparg, Andy Strominger, and Neil Brenner; and the newer suspects in New York: Colin Moran, Emily Tepe, Ben de Menil, Nitsan Chorev, Andreas Wimmer, Marshall Meyer, and James Leitner. Elsa Walsh made a vital suggestion that made the final manuscript complete. I've had the gift and support of David Cohen's wise counsel over the past thirty years. As with before, this book could not have been written without Cassandra and her eternal Yam Garden.

NOTES

Except where Chinese-language sources are more important, the following bibliographical summaries provide primarily English-language sources for the reader's reference. Specific original sources are cited in the chapter notes.

INTRODUCTION

The study of Chinese script, or characters, has a long tradition. Distinct from philology and etymology, script study has to do with the shape, sound, and meaning in characters and extends to styles of inscription on different surfaces, from bone to bronze, bamboo to paper. Apart from a third century B.C.E. glossary or word list—one of the thirteen Confucian canonical texts—Xu Shen's *Shuowen jiezi*, written during the Han dynasty, is considered the oldest example of such a study. In it are six principles that categorize and classify basic patterns for why and when a given ancient character's shape, sound, and meaning change—as the three often go together. The six features I outline in this chapter do not have to do with this tradition but instead focus on what a modern, non-Chinese reader might need to know in order to understand the Chinese writing system's great transformation in the twentieth century. For those who are interested in the premodern tradition, there are a number of useful references: David N. Keightley, *Sources of Shang History: The Oracle-Bone Inscriptions of Bronze Age China* (Berkeley: University of California Press, 1978); Mark E. Lewis, *Writing and Authority in Early China* (Albany: State University of New York, 1999); Qiu Xigui, *Chinese Writing* (Berkeley, CA: Society for the Study of Early China, Institute of East Asian Studies, 2000). Pinyin.info, founded and maintained by Victor Mair, is a valuable website for past and present debates on the Chinese language. There is also the PRC's own official website on the Chinese script, overseen by the Ministry of Education: http://www.china-language.edu.cn.

xi **Mao's calligraphy still:** "Gangda xuezhe faxian Xi Jinping qianming de 'xi' zi jinggen Maoti 'xi' zi yige muyang," Radio France Internationale (July 1, 2019), https://www.rfi .fr/tw/; Yan Yuehping, *Calligraphy and Power in Contemporary Chinese Society* (London: Routledge, 2012), pp. 15–32, esp. 15–18; Richard Curt Krauss, *Brushes with Power: Modern Politics and the Chinese Art of Calligraphy* (Berkeley: University of California Press, 1991), pp. 65–70, 123–138; Simon Leys, "One More Art," *The New York Review* (April 18, 1996): https://www.nybooks.com/articles/1996/04/18/one-more-art/.

xii **Kings, clerics, adventurers:** Athanasius Kircher, *China monumentis, qvà sacris quà profanis: Nec non variis naturæ & artis spectaculis, aliarumque rerum memorabilium argumentis illustrata, auspiciis Leopoldi Primi roman* (Amsterdam: Joannem Janssonium à Waesberge & Elizeum Weyerstraet, 1667); Christian Mentzel and Clavis Sinica, *Ad Chinesium scripturam et pronunciationem mandarinicam, centum & viginti quatuor Tabuli accuraté Scriptis praesentata* (Berlin: n.p., 1698); Joshua Marshman, *Clavis sinica: Containing a dissertation, I, on the Chinese characters, II, on the colloquial medium of the Chinese, and III, elements of Chinese grammar* (Serampore: Mission Press, 1813); Knud Lundbaek, *The Traditional History of the Chinese Script: From a Seventeenth Century Jesuit Manuscript* (Aarhus: Aarhus University Press, 1988).

xii **Sixteenth-century Jesuit missionaries:** D. E. Mungello, *Curious Land: Jesuit Accommodation and the Origins of Sinology* (Stuttgart: Franz Steiner, 1985); David Porter, *Ideographia: The Chinese Cipher in Early Modern Europe* (Stanford, CA: Stanford University Press, 2001); Cécile Leung, *Etienne Fourmont, 1683–1745: Oriental and Chinese Languages in Eighteenth-Century France* (Leuven: Leuven University Press, Ferdinand Verbiest Foundation, 2002).

xiii **Joseph Needham, a renowned:** Manuel Castells, *The Rise of the Network Society* (Malden, MA: Blackwell Publishers, 1996), pp. 355–56; Eric Havelock, *The Literate Revolution in Greece and Its Cultural Consequences* (Princeton, NJ: Princeton University Press, 1982), pp. 6–7; Joseph Needham, *Science and Civilization in China*, vol. 2, *History of Scientific Thought* (Cambridge: Cambridge University Press, 1956), p. 77.

ONE: A MANDARIN IN REVOLUTION (1900)

The source material for this chapter falls into four categories. The first is Western missionary linguistics, which includes the earliest compilations of Chinese-European dictionaries and Jesuit translation activities in the sixteenth century, separated by a long hiatus from the second, and much larger, footprint of Protestant and other missionaries in the nineteenth century. Sources include original dictionaries and studies of grammar, which are scattered across libraries around the world. The most complete collection of the Jesuit efforts is at the Vatican Library (especially the Borgia Chinese collection) and several of the smaller libraries in Rome, including the Biblioteca Angelica and the Historical Archives of the Jesuits (Archivum Romanum Societatis Iesu). Studies by Federico Masini are useful guides to and studies of missionary linguistics and translations, as are the two volumes edited by Nicolas Standaert, *Handbook of Christianity in China* (Leiden, Boston: Brill, 2001–2010), for a historical background not limited to linguistics. Henning Klöter's *The Language of the Sangleys: A Chinese Vernacular in Missionary Sources of the Seventeenth Century* (Leiden, Boston: Brill, 2011) gives a valuable account of the translation of the southern dialect, Min, by Spanish Dominican missionaries.

The second is China's own long-standing and technical history of philology and phonological change, including how the translation of Buddhist scriptures from Sanskrit in the seventh century introduced the cross-cut phonetic method, as well as the sound shift during the Manchu dynasty that created a different premise for notating and analyzing the sounds of Mandarin. Medieval Chinese phonology can be quite technical. There are a few standard works and dozens of articles in English that provide an excellent overview, with in-depth treatments of rime tables, rhyming dictionaries, and phonological reconstructions—including those that built on early missionary linguistics. See Bernhard Karlgren's classic *Sound & Symbol in Chinese* (London: Oxford University Press, 1929); David Prager Branner, ed., *The Chinese Rime Tables: Linguistic Philosophy and Historical-Comparative Phonology* (Amsterdam, Philadelphia: John Benjamins, 2006); W. Coblin South and Joseph A. Levi, eds., *Francisco Varo's Grammar of the Mandarin Language, 1703: An English Translation of "Arte de la lengua Mandarina"* (Amsterdam, Philadelphia: John Benjamins, 2000); Jerry Norman, *Chinese* (Cambridge, New York: Cambridge University Press, 1988); William G. Boltz, *The Origin and Early Development of the Chinese Writing System* (New Haven, CT: American Oriental Society, 2003). For the larger intellectual context, see Benjamin A. Elman, *From Philosophy to Philology: Intellectual and Social Aspects of Change in Late Imperial China* (Leiden, Boston: Brill, 1984).

Third are works documenting late nineteenth-century Chinese script reform, which often carried a direct link to the missionary dictionary activities of the nineteenth century. Many of the Chinese script reformers were first recruited as young native assistants for dictionary compilation or translation projects but grew dissatisfied with the results and hence embarked on building their own phonetic schemes. The phonetization movement inside China has been authoritatively documented by Ni Haishu, and many of the original phonetic schemes were reprinted under the auspices of the Committee on Script Reform in the PRC between 1956 and 1958, as part of the committee's work to devise modern-day pinyin (see chapter 5). A selection of phonetic schemes from the late nineteenth century includes Wang Zhao's own *Guanhua hesheng zimu* (Beijing: Wenzi gaige, 1956) and *Duibing shuohua* (Beijing: Pinyin guanhua shubaoshe, 1904); Cai Xiyong, *Chuanyin kuaizi* (Beijing: Wenzi gaige, 1956); Shen Xue, *Shengshi yuanyin* (Beijing: Wenzi gaige, 1956); Lao Naixuan, *Jianzi pulu: Wuzhong* (Jinling: Lao Shi self-published, 1906–7); Li Jiesan, *Minqiang kuaizi* (Beijing: Wenzi gaige, 1956); Wang Bingyao, *Pinyin zipu* (Beijing: Wenzi gaige, 1956). For a list of extant schemes, see Ni Haishu, *Qingmo Hanyu pinyin yundong biannianshi* (Shanghai: Shanghai renmin, 1959), pp. 9–12. See also Ni's *Zhongguo pinyin wenzi yundongshi jianbian* (Shanghai: Shidai shubao, 1948) and *Zhongguo zi Ladinghua yundong nianbiao: 1605–1940*

(Shanghai: Zhongguo Ladinghua shudian, 1941). Reports and introductions to the various phonetic schemes in the late nineteenth century can also be found in newspaper sources from the time: (in Chinese) *Wanguo gongbao, Dagongbao, Shenbao;* (in English) *The Chinese Recorder, North China Herald.* For Wang Zhao's biography and writings, see chapter notes. Li Jinxi, in particular, reveals unusual details about his life in "Wang Zhao zhuan," *Guoyu zhoukan* 129 (1934): 51–52.

The above three historical developments came to a head in the early twentieth century with the fall of the last dynasty in 1911 and were decisive in the way the modern sounds of Chinese, or Mandarin (and later Putonghua), came to be notated for the first time in a national phonetic system, concomitant with the founding of the modern Chinese nation. Wang Zhao's biography and accounts of his exile, return, incarceration, and release are reconstructed from his own memoir and poetry, as well as verified through newspapers of his time. Li Jinxi's memoir remains the most comprehensive account of the national language reform movement from the early decades of the twentieth century. There has been a resurgence in scholarship on Chinese language history since 2010, extending the field to include questions of language, philology, and regional and global Chinese diaspora. See Jing Tsu, *Sound and Script in Chinese Diaspora* (Cambridge, MA: Harvard University Press, 2010); David Moser, *A Billion Voices: China's Search for a Common Language* (Scorsby, Victoria: Penguin, 2016); Peter Kornicki, *Languages, Texts, and Chinese Scripts in East Asia* (Oxford: Oxford University Press, 2018); Zev Handel, *Sinography: The Borrowing and Adaptation of the Chinese Script* (Leiden, Boston: Brill, 2019); Gina Tam, *Dialect and Nationalism in China, 1860–1960* (Cambridge: Cambridge University Press, 2020); Li Yu, *The Chinese Writing System in Asia: An Interdisciplinary Perspective* (Abingdon, New York, NY: Routledge, 2020); Marten Saarela, *The Early Modern Travels of Manchu: A Script and Its Study in East Asia and Europe* (Philadelphia: University of Pennsylvania Press, 2020). The illustration, *The Situation in the Far East,* is taken from and discussed in detail in Rudolf G. Wagner, "China 'Asleep' and 'Awakening': A Study in Conceptualizing Asymmetry and Coping with It," *Transcultural Studies* 1 (2011): 4–139.

5 **It had been said:** Quoted in Paul A. Cohen, *China and Christianity: The Missionary Movement and the Growth of Chinese Anti-Foreignism, 1860–1870* (Cambridge, MA: Harvard University Press, 1963), pp. 144, 291.

9 **"the nature of the written language":** Quoted in Joseph Needham and Christoph Harbsmeier, *Science and Civilization in China,* vol. 7, part 1 (Cambridge: Cambridge University Press, 1998), p. 25.

9 **"Their teeth are placed":** Thomas Percy, ed., *Miscellaneous Pieces Relating to the Chinese* (London: Printed for R. and J. Dodsley in Pall-Mall, 1762), pp. 20–21.

11 **"No amount of change":** Wu Zhihui, "Bianzao Zhongguo xinyu fanli," *Xin Shiji* 40 (March 1908): 2–3.

11 **Born in 1859:** Wang Zhao's family background and biography: Wang Zhao, *Xiaohang wencun,* 4 vols., in *Qingmo mingjia zizhu congshu chubian: Shuidong quanji* (Taipei: Yiwen,

1964); Wu Rulun, "Gaoshou wuxian jiangjun zongbingxian jingcheng zuoying youji Wang gong mubei," in *Tongcheng Wu xiansheng wenshiji*, in *Jindai Zhongguo shiliao congkan*, vol. 365, part 2 (Taipei: Wenhai, 1969), pp. 667–72; Li Jinxi, "Wang Zhao zhuan," *Guoyu zhoubao* 5 (1933): 1–2; Li Jinxi, "Guanyu 'Wang Zhao zhuan,'" *Guoyu zhoukan* 6 (1934): 18; Duan Heshou, Lun Ming, and Li Jinxi, "Guanyu 'Wang Zhao zhuan' de tongxin," *Guoyu zhoukan* 6 (1934): 6; Chen Guangyao, "Lao xindang Wang Xiaohang xiansheng," *Guowen zhoubao* 10 (1933): 1–6; Yi Shi, "Tan Wang Xiaohang," *Guowen zhoubao* 10 (1933): 1–4.

12 **"In grief I passed":** Wang Zhao, "Xingjiao Shandong ji," in *Xiaohang wencun* (Taipei: Yiwen, 1964), p. 53.

12 **As he traveled through:** Wang Zhao's travels, role in 1898 reform, and meeting with Timothy Richard: Wang, "Xingjiao Shandong ji," pp. 47–76; Wang Zhao, "Guanyu Wuxu zhengbian zhi xin shiliao," in Zhongguo shixuehui, ed., *Wuxu bianfa*, vol. 4 (Shanghai: Shenzhou Guoguang, 1953), p. 333; Timothy Richard, *Forty-Five Years in China* (London: T. Fisher Unwin Ltd., 1916), p. 268.

18 **Sympathetic to the 1898 reform:** Timothy Richard, "Non-phonetic and Phonetic Systems of Writing Chinese," *The Chinese Recorder* 39, no. 11 (November 1898): 545.

18 **Just to make his feelings clear:** Wang Zhao, "Guanyu wuxu zhengbian zhi xin shiliao," *Dagongbao* (Tianjin) (July 24, 1936).

20 **"Awful sights were witnessed":** In a letter from Protestant missionary Robert Morrison to *The Times* on October 15, 1900. Quoted in Marshall Broomhall, *Martyred Missionaries of the China Inland Mission: With a Record of the Perils & Sufferings of Some Who Escaped* (London: Morgan & Scott, 1901), p. 260.

22 **Wang later recalled:** Ni Haishu, *Zhongguo pinyin wenzi yundongshi* (Zhengzhou: Henan renmin, 2016), pp. 44–46.

22 **"The greatest disadvantage":** Ni Haishu, "Wang Zhao he tade 'Guanhua zimu,'" *Yuwen zhishi* 53 (1956): 18; 54 (1956): 25; 55 (1956): 17.

24 **There had been others:** A total of twenty-six proposals have survived and were republished after the mid-1950s by the Committee on Script Reform. See Ni Haishu, *Qingmo Hanyu pinyin yundong biannianshi* (Shanghai: Shanghai renmin, 1959), pp. 9–12.

27 **"the conquered race":** In James Dyer Ball, *Things Chinese: Being Notes on Various Subjects Connected with China* (London: S. Low, Marston, and Co., 1892), p. 240.

28 **"I couldn't help myself":** He Mo, "Ji yuyan xuejia Wang Xiaohang," *Gujin* 5 (1942): 19.

30 **"I suddenly realized":** Wang Zhao, "Fuji yu touyu shi," in *Fangjiayuan zayong jishi*, ed. Shen Yunlong, *Jindai Zhongguo shiliao congkan*, vol. 27 (Taipei: Wenhai, 1968), pp. 683–84.

30 **In early March 1904:** Concerning Wang's imprisonment and release: Wang, "Fuji yu touyu shi," pp. 680–86; "Wang Zhao beibu, Wang Zhao beishe," *Xin baihua bao* 3 (1904), in *Xinhai geming xijian wenxian huibian*, vol. 8, ed. Sang Bing (Beijing: Guojia tushuguan; Hong Kong: Zhonghe; Taipei: Wanjuanlou, 2011), p. 301; "Yuan Wang Zhao gongzui," *Shenbao* (April 10, 1900); "Wang Zhao meng'en shifang," *Shibao* (July 3,

1904); "Wang Zhao baike," *Shibao* (July 10, 1904); "Wang Zhao zishou chengqing dai zou yuangao," *Dagongbao* 662 (May 1, 1904); "Wang Zhao an zhi kaiyan," *Dagongbao* 662 (May 1, 1904).

31 **Natong's journal entries:** *Natong riji*, ed. Beijing shi dangan guan (Beijing: Xinhua, 2006), p. 501.

32 **Despite the outpouring of sympathy:** "Wang Zhao an zhi kaiyan," *Dagongbao* (May 1, 1904).

33 **"The morning breeze grazes":** "Jiachen sanyue yuzhong zuo," *Xiaohang wencun*, p. 680.

33 **Two months later:** Reports on Wang's release: "Jiwen," *Xin baihua bao* 3 (1904): 1; "Wang Zhao meng'en shifang," *Shibao* (July 3, 1904).

34 **Recent research shows that:** Wang's letter to Natong, quoted in Ma Zhongwen, "Weixin zhishi Wang Zhao de 'zishou' wenti,'" *Jindai shi yanjiu* (Beijing) 3 (2014): 32–46.

38 **To prove his point:** He Mo, "Ji yuyanxue jia Wang Xiaohang," *Gujin* 5 (1942): 22.

39 **To Wang's Mandarin ear:** Li Jinxi, "Min er duyin tongyi dahui shimoji" (Wang Zhao Guanhua Zimu zhi tuotai huangu xu), *Guoyu zhoukan* 6 (1934): 10.

41 **Some sung his deeds:** Lai Lun, "Ku Wang Xiaohang xiansheng (Zhao)," *Guangzhi guan xingqi bao* 264 (1934): 5–7; Shang Hongkui, "Tan Wang Xiaohang," *Renjianshi* 36 (1935): 12–13.

41 **People who remembered his feisty years:** Lingxiao Yishi, "Suibi," *Guowen zhoubao* 32 (1933): 2.

41 **"Most people suffer":** Quoted in Chen, "Lao xindang Wang Xiaohang xiansheng," p. 2.

TWO: CHINESE TYPEWRITERS AND AMERICA (1912)

The discussion of world exhibitions and fairs is drawn from archival sources in the Victoria and Albert Museum, the British Library, and the Department of Records at the City of Philadelphia. Primary sources on China's process of industrialization from the early twentieth century, including detailed accounts of exportable domestic and competing foreign goods, are mostly in Chinese. See Chen Zhen, *Zhongguo jindai gongyeshi ziliao*, 4 vols. (Beijing: Sanlian, 1957); Shanghai shi gongshang xingzheng guanliju, Shanghai shi diyi jidian gongyeju jiqi gongye shiliao zu, eds., *Shanghai minzu jiqi gongye* (Beijing: Zhonghua, 1979).

Zhou Houkun's student records are kept in the MIT archives and summarized here: http://chinacomestomit.org/chou-houkun#:~:text=Hou%2DKun%20chow%20(1891%2D%3F). Zhou's personal background and life in China before studying abroad are gleaned from his father Zhou Tongyu's writings, which Zhou Houkun collected and privately published in 1935 as *Shanting wenji* (Wuxi: Wuxi Zhou self-published, 1935). His experience at the Commercial Press is drawn from the diary of the press's director, Zhang Yuanji (see notes). Records on Qi Xuan before his arrival in America are scant, but Chinese-language sources link him to the revolutionary movement at home. The best primary sources on the Chinese students who studied abroad in places like the United States, Japan, and France are in the articles they themselves wrote and published, expressing their views and perspectives on world politics in relationship to China. Important journals, many of which were founded by these students, include *Tianyi bao* (founded in 1907 in Tokyo and influenced by Russian anarchism), *La Novaj Tempoj* (established in 1907 in Paris and associated with the Chinese anarchists and supporters of Esperanto), and *The Chinese Students' Monthly* (founded by the Chinese Students' Alliance in 1906 in New York, in English). *New Youth,* or *La Jeunesse* (established in 1915 in Shanghai), remains indispensable for understanding the nationalistic ideas these students brought back during this period. These views tend to be Western in outlook—and best consulted alongside the dozen or so more politically extreme student journals in China such as *Zhejiang Chao* and *Jiangsu* for a fuller grasp of the revolutionary landscape. For a general history of this period, *The Cambridge History of China,* vol. 12, *Republican China, 1912–1949,* part 1 (New York: Cambridge University Press, 1983) remains a standard reference. I thank the Huntington Library in Pasadena, especially Li Wei Yang, curator of the Pacific Rim Collections, for allowing me to use the photograph of Shu Zhendong's Chinese typewriter.

43 **A six-cylinder Silent Knight:** *Boston Post* (March 4, 1912), p. 11, https://newspaper archive.com/boston-post-mar-04-1912-p-11/; "A Six-Cylinder 'Silent Knight,'" "New Flavors in Show Dish at Boston," *Automobile Topics* 25 (March 9, 1912): 193–200.

44 **"sat in front of a keyboard":** Zhou Houkun [H. K. Chow], "The Problem of a Typewriter for the Chinese Language," *The Chinese Students' Monthly* (April 1, 1915), pp. 435–43.

46 **For any Chinese watching:** "China's Iron and Steel Industry," *The Chinese Students' Monthly* (February 10, 1914), p. 288.

47 **Or from fabricating a firsthand report:** Henry Sutherland Edwards, *An Authentic Account of the Chinese Commission, Which Was Sent to Report on the Great Exhibition Wherein the Opinion of China Is Shown as Not Corresponding at All with Our Own* (London: Printed at 15 and 16 Gough Square by H. Vizetelly, 1851).

49 **At President Grant's invitation:** Li Gui, *A Journey to the East: Li Gui's A New Account of a Trip Around the Globe*, trans. Charles Desnoyers (Ann Arbor: University of Michigan Press, 2004).

49 **China's total imports:** Wolfgang Keller, Ben Li, and Carol H. Shiue, "China's Foreign Trade: Perspectives from the Past 150 Years," *The World Economy* (2011), pp. 853–91, esp. 864–66.

49 **In 1911, in contrast:** Albert Feuerwerker, *China's Early Industrialization* (Cambridge, MA: Harvard University Press, 1958), pp. 1–30; Anne Reinhardt, *Navigating Semi-Colonialism: Shipping, Sovereignty, and Nation-Building in China, 1860–1937* (Cambridge, MA: Harvard University Asia Center, 2018), pp. 21–93.

50 **At the 1873 Vienna World's Fair:** Susan R. Fernsebner, "Material Modernities: China's Participation in World's Fairs and Expositions, 1876–1955" (Ph.D. dissertation, University of California, San Diego, 2002), pp. 20–21.

50 **By the 1870s, Chinese laborers:** Alexander Saxton, *The Indispensable Enemy: Labor and the Anti-Chinese Movement in California* (Berkeley: University of California Press, 1971), p. 10.

51 **They made up 90 percent:** "Forgotten Workers: Chinese Migrants and the Building of the Transcontinental Railroad," online exhibition at the Natural Museum of American History, https://www.si.edu/exhibitions/forgotten-workers-chinese-migrants-and-building -transcontinental-railroad-event-exhib-6332.

51 **The carnivalesque Joy Zone:** *Panama-Pacific International Exposition 1915 Souvenir Guide* (San Francisco: Souvenir Guide Publishers, ca. 1915), p. 15.

52 **Zhou senior turned his focus:** Zhou Tongyu, "Banshuo shi Kun'er," in *Shanting wenji* (Wuxi: Zhou Houkun self-published, 1935), p. 11.

54 **"where want and pain":** F. L. Chang, "Innocents Abroad," *The Chinese Students' Monthly* (February 10, 1914), p. 300.

56 **"For a country to lack":** Hu Shi, "Guoli daxue zhi zhongyao," in *Hu Shi quanji,* vol. 28 (Hefei: Anhui jiaoyu, 2003), p. 57.

57 **He graduated that spring:** Zhou Houkun [H. K. Chow], "The Strength of Bamboo," *The Chinese Students' Monthly* (February 2015), pp. 291–94.

58 **"serve momentarily one character":** Zhou, "The Problem of a Typewriter for the Chinese Language," p. 438.

58 **Whether it was a Royal No. 5:** "Machine for the Brain Worker," *The Chinese Students' Monthly* (April 1915), pp. vi, xv.

58 **"Any such idea":** Zhou, "The Problem of a Typewriter for the Chinese Language."

59 **Some of the machines:** Bruce Bliven, *The Wonderful Writing Machine* (New York: Random House, 1954), p. 63; Tony Allan, *Typewriter: The History, the Machines, the Writers* (New York: Shelter Harbor Press, 2015), pp. 14, 16–18.

59 **An early 1856 John H. Cooper Writing Machine:** *The Typewriter: An Illustrated History* (Mineola, NY: Dover, 2000), p. 12.

59 **An American Presbyterian missionary:** Devello Zelotes Sheffield, "The Chinese Type-writer, Its Practicability and Value," in *Actes du onzième Congrès International des Orientalistes,* vol. 2 (Paris: Imprimerie Nationale, 1897).

60 **"an irresolvable individual":** Sheffield, "The Chinese Type-writer," p. 51.

62 **"master of his own thoughts":** Sheffield, "The Chinese Type-writer," p. 63.

63 **After consulting with friends:** Zhou Houkun, "A Chinese Typewriter," *The National Review* (May 20, 1916), p. 429.

64 **He unveiled it:** Zhou, "A Chinese Typewriter," p. 428.

64 **In his article for *The Chinese Students' Monthly*:** Zhou Houkun, "Chuangzhi Zhongguo daziji tushuo," trans. Wang Ruding, *Xuesheng zazhi* 2, no. 9 (1915): 113–18; 2, no. 11 (1915): 95–104.

66 **In three steps:** "4,200 Characters on New Typewriter: Chinese Machine Has Only Three Keys, but There Are 50,000 Combinations; 100 Words in Two Hours; Heuen Chi, New York University Student, Patents Device Called the First of Its Kind," *The New York Times* (March 23, 1915), p. 6.

66 **If you treat radicals:** Heuen Chi [Qi Xuan], "Chinese Typewriter," *The Square Deal* 16 (1915): 340–41.

66 **You can generate more words:** Heuen Chi, "Apparatus for Writing Chinese," U.S. Patent 1260753 (Filed April 17, 1915), p. 8.

67 **Soon he and Qi:** "Typewriters in Chinese," *The Washington Post* (March 28, 1915), p. B2; "4,200 Characters on New Typewriter," *The New York Times* (March 23, 1915).

70 **"as I have already succeeded":** Heuen Chi, "The Principle of My Chinese Typewriter," *The Chinese Students' Monthly* (May 1915), pp. 513-14.

74 **His presentation was to be followed:** For a transcription of the lecture, see Tang Zhansheng and Shen Chenglie, "Zhou Houkun xiansheng jiangyan Zhongguo daziji jilu (July 22, 1916)," *Linshi kanbu* 11 (1916): 7-13.

75 **"The Chinese people loathe":** Tang and Shen, "Zhou Houkun xiansheng jiangyan Zhongguo dazjii," p. 7.

78 **Soon, China began to export:** Xu Guoqi, *Strangers on the Western Front* (Cambridge, MA: Harvard University Press, 2011), pp. 126-51.

79 **Members of the Chinese Students' Alliance:** "Japanese Demands Arouse Indignation," *The Chinese Students' Monthly* (March 1915), pp. 400-401.

80 **"We at once awoke":** Quoted in Zhou Cezong [Tse-tsung Chow], *The May Fourth Movement: Intellectual Revolution in Modern China* (Cambridge, MA: Harvard University Press, 1960), p. 93.

80 **"It sickened and disheartened me":** Quoted in Zhou, *The May Fourth Movement*, p. 94.

81 **As with world affairs:** Hu Suh, "The Problem of the Chinese Language," *The Chinese Students' Monthly* (June 1916), pp. 567-72; Y. T. Chang, "The Chinese Written Language and the Education of the Masses," *The Chinese Students' Monthly* (December 1915), pp. 118-21.

82 **Speaking before a Chinese audience:** Zhou, "A Chinese Typewriter," p. 428.

82 **The Commercial Press had hired:** For details on Zhou and the Commercial Press, see *Zhang Yuanji riji*, vol. 6 (Beijing: Shangwu, 2007), pp. 19-20, 56.

84 **Zhou wanted the press:** *Zhang Yuanji riji*, p. 141.

85 **On the third try:** Zheng Yimei, "Shouchuang Zhongwen daziji de Zhou Houkun," in *Zheng Yimei xuanji*, vol. 2 (Ha'erbin: Heilongjiang renmin, 1991), pp. 66-67.

85 **At the Philadelphia Sesquicentennial International Exhibition:** *Descriptions of the Commercial Press Exhibit* (Shanghai: The Commercial Press, ca. 1926). The honor was also reported in China; see "Zhu Mei zong lingshi hangao Feicheng saihui qingxing," *Shenbao* (January 14, 1927), p. 9.

86 **Glued to the very back:** Zhou, "Banshuo shi Kun'er." The insert is included in the original at the Archive and Special Collections, School of Oriental and Asiatic Studies, London, England.

THREE: TIPPING THE SCALE OF TELEGRAPHY (1925)

Materials on the Great Northern Telegraph Company's exploits in East Asia, including personal correspondence between the various parties involved and discussed in the chapter, can be found in the special collection at Rigsarkivet (National Archives), Copenhagen, Denmark. I thank archivist Simon Gjeroe for assisting me with the Danish-English translations of the original letters between Carl Frederik Tietgen and Hans Schjellerup (the professor of astronomy who devised the first draft of the Chinese telegraphic code), Edouard Suenson and Septime Auguste Viguier. Minutes from the 1925 International Telegraphic Union's meeting in Paris—as well as all those from past ITU conferences, starting with the first in 1865—are available online: https://www.itu.int/en/history/Pages/ConferencesCollection .aspx. Rigsarkivet also has a number of Chinese telegraphic codebooks, though most of them can be found in a number of university libraries in the United States as well. A complementary source to consult is the report of the U.S. Delegation to the International Radiotelegraph Conference in Washington, D.C., in 1927. See William Frederick Friedman's *Report on the History of the Use of Codes and Code Language, the International Telegraph Regulations Pertaining Thereto, and Bearing of the History on the Cortina Report* (Washington, D.C.: United States Government Printing Office, 1928). Individual Chinese perspectives and descriptions of the diplomatic missions can be found in the diaries of the various emissaries and their team members, collected in a ten-volume series, Zhong Shuhe, ed., *Zouxiang shijie congshu* (Changsha: Yuelu shushe, 2008), its fifty-five-volume sequel *Zouxiang shijie congshu xubian* (Changsha: Yuelu shushe, 2017), as well as contemporaneous reports in newspapers like *Shenbao*. Also important is the *Haifang dang* (Archives of Maritime Defense), published by the Institute of Modern History, Academia Sinica, Taiwan, especially vol. 4, parts 1 and 2, "Telegraphy." Strategies undertaken by the Qing court to counter the advances of telegraphic technology can be found there. For studies of Chinese telegraphy in the English language, see Jorma Ahvenainen, *The Far Eastern Telegraphs: The History of Telegraphic Communications between the Far East, Europe and America before the First World War* (Helsinki: Suomalainen Tiedeakatemia, 1981); Erik Baark, *Lightning Wires: The Telegraph and China's Technological Modernization, 1860–1890* (London: Greenwood Press, 1997); Erik Baark, "Wires, Codes and People: The Great Northern Telegraph Company in China 1870–90," in Kjeld Erik Brødsgaard and Mads Kirkebæk, eds., *China and Denmark: Relations since 1674* (Copenhagen: Nordic Institute of Asian Studies, 2000), pp. 119–52; Zhou Yongming, *Historicizing Online Politics: Telegraphy, the Internet and Political Participation in China* (Stanford, CA: Stanford University Press, 2006); Thomas S. Mullaney, "Semiotic Sovereignty: The 1871 Chinese Telegraph Code in Historical Perspective," in Jing Tsu and Benjamin A. Elman, eds., *Science and Technology in Modern China, 1880s–1940s* (Leiden, Boston: Brill, 2014), pp. 153–83; Wook Yoon, "Dashed Expectations: Limitations of the Telegraphic Service in the Late Qing," *Modern Asian Studies* 3 (May 2015): 832–57; Saundra P. Sturdevant, "A Question of Sovereignty: Railways and Telegraphs in China; 1861–1878" (Ph.D. dissertation, University of Chicago, 1975). For an understanding of the state of China's infrastructure during the Republican period more generally, see Zhu Jianhua (Chu Chia-hua), *China's Postal and Other Communications Services* (Shanghai: China United Press, 1937).

For personal accounts by Septime Auguste Viguier and Pierre Henri Stanislas d'Escayrac de Lauture, see Viguier, *Mémoire sur l'établissement de lignes télégraphiques en Chine* (Shanghai:

Imprimerie Carvalho & Cie., 1875); Pierre Henri Stanislas d'Escayrac, *Mémoires sur la Chine* (Paris: Librarie du Magazin pittoresque, 1865); Pierre Henri Stanislas d'Escayrac, *De la transmission télégraphique et de la transcription littérale des caractères chinois* (Paris: Typographie de J. Best, 1862); Pierre Henri Stanislas d'Escayrac de Lauture, *Short Explanation of the Sketch of the Analytic Universal Nautical Code of Signs* (London: John Camden Hotten, 1863); Pierre Henri Stanislas d'Escayrac [P. H. Stanislas], "Telegraph Signal," U.S. Patent no. 39,016 (June 23, 1863). For biographical sketches of Viguier and d'Escayrac, see Henri Cordier, "S. A. Viguier 威基谒," in *T'oung Pao* 10, no. 5 (1899): 488–89; Richard Leslie Hill, "Escayrac de Lauture, Pierre Henri Stanislas d', Count," *A Biographical Dictionary of the Sudan* (London: Cass, 1967), pp. 120–21; Gérard Siary, "Escayrac de Lauture (Pierre Henri Stanislas, comte d'), 1826–1868," *Dictionnaire illustré des explorateurs et grands voyageurs français du XIXe siècle.* vol. 2, *Asie* (Paris: Editions du C.T.H.S., 1992). There have been a number of Chinese telegraphic codebooks since the versions designed by Viguier and Zhang Deyi, mostly modern adaptations of the four-number code format. I thank John McVey for meeting with me in Cambridge, Massachusetts, in 2014 and for sharing his private collection of telegraphic codebooks, some of which (including d'Escayrac's system) are posted and discussed on his website: https://www.jmcvey.net/index.htm.

For Wang Jingchun's writings in English, including his studies of the Western railway system and the political views that inform his work on telegraphy, see his "Why the Chinese Oppose Foreign Railway Loans," *The American Political Science Review* 4, no. 3 (August 1910): 365–73; "The Hankow-Szechuan Railway Loan," *The American Journal of International Law* 5, no. 3 (July 1911): 653–64; "The Effect of the Revolution upon the Relationship between China and the United States," *The Journal of Race Development* 3, no. 3 (January 1913): 268–85; "Legislation of Railway Finance in England" (Ph.D. dissertation, University of Illinois, 1918); "Hsinhanzyx (Phonetic Chinese)," *Chinese Social and Political Science Review* 24, no. 4 (December 1940): 263–90A; "A Solution of the Chinese Eastern Railway Conflict," *Foreign Affairs* 8, no. 2 (January 1930): 294–96; "How China Recovered Tariff Autonomy," *The Annals of the American Academy of Political and Social Science* 152 (November 1932): 266–77; "China Still Waits the End of Extraterritoriality," *Foreign Affairs* 15, no. 4 (July 1937): 745–49; "Manchuria at the Crossroads," *The Annals of the American Academy of Political and Social Science* 168 (July 1933): 64–77; "The Sale of the Chinese Eastern Railway," *Foreign Affairs* 12 (October 1933): 57–70.

90 **"instantaneous highway of thought"**: Quoted in Tom Standage, *The Remarkable Story of the Telegraph and the Nineteenth Century's On-line Pioneers* (New York: Walker and Co., 1998), p. 74.

92 **The most frequently used letter**: http://letterfrequency.org/letter-frequency-by-language/.

92 **Every Chinese character was transmitted**: Wang Jingchun, "Phonetic System of Writing Chinese Characters," *Chinese Social and Political Science Review* 12 (1929): 147.

93 **But when the young nation**: Shuge Wei, "Circuits of Power: China's Quest for Cable Telegraph Rights," *Journal of Chinese History* 3 (2019): 113–35.

96 **In one article:** Wang Jingchun, "The Hankow-Szechuan Railway Loan," *The American Journal of International Law* 5, no. 3 (July 1911): 653.

97 **"With us," he once advised:** Wang Ching-chun, "Memorandum on the Unification of Railway Accounts and Statistics" (Beijing: n.p., 1913), pp. 4–5.

98 **"The new China will be":** "Dr. Ching-Chun Wang, Yale Graduate, Associate Director Pekin-Mukden Railway and Prominent among Chinese Progressives, Declares That China Wants to Deal with Straightforward American Business Men Who Don't Mix Business with Politics," *The New York Times* (November 10, 1912).

101 **It stipulated that if China granted:** C. C. Wang (Wang Jingchun), "How China Recovered Tariff Autonomy," *The Annals of the American Academy of Political and Social Science* 152 (November 1930): 266–77.

102 **On a cloudless moonlit night:** Erik Baark, *Lightning Wires: The Telegraph and China's Technological Modernization, 1860–1890* (Westport, CT, London: Greenwood Press, 1997), p. 81.

102 **The job was completed:** Baark, *Lightning Wires,* p. 75.

102 **"The foreigners know of God":** Yang Jialuo, ed., *Yangwu yundong wenxian huibian,* vol. 6 (Taipei: Shijie shuju, 1963), p. 330.

104 **Its funky script was lifted:** Knud Lundbaek, "Imaginary Ancient Chinese Characters," *China Mission Studies 1550–1800* 5 (1983): 5–22.

104 **Instead, d'Escayrac set out:** Stanislas d'Escayrac de Lauture, *Mémoires sur la Chine* (Paris, Librairie du Magazin pittoresque, 1865), pp. 74–75.

105 **The professor had learned Chinese:** "Hans Carl Frederik Christian Schjellerup," *Monthly Notices of the Royal Astronomical Society* 48 (February 10, 1888): 171–74.

108 **He recommended using numbers:** S. A. Viguier, *Mémoire sur l'etablissement de lignes télégraphiques en Chine* (Shanghai: Imprimerie Carvalho & Cie., 1875).

108 **By June 1870:** Letter from Schjellerup to Tietgen (April 19, 1870); Kurt Jacobsen, "Danish Watchmaker Created the Chinese Morse System," *NIASnytt* (Nordic Institute of Asian Studies) *Nordic Newsletter* 2 (July 2001): 15, 17–21.

110 **A quiet young Chinese translator:** Zhang Deyi, *Suishi Faguo ji* (Changsha: Hunan renmin, 1982), pp. 534–35.

114 **Two generations of Western scholars:** Baark, *Lightning Wires,* p. 85; Thomas S. Mullaney, *The Chinese Typewriter: A History* (Cambridge, MA: The MIT Press, 2017), p. 354, n. 70.

115 **Given that telegrams were priced:** "Ocean Telegraphy," *The Telegraphist* 7 (June 2, 1884): 87.

115 **A telegram, recorded in 1854:** "Short Letters," *Yankee-notions* 3 (1854): 363, https://babel.hathitrust.org/cgi/pt?id=hvd.32044092738434&view=1up&seq=369.

116 **They came up with shorter spellings:** *Telegraph Age* (October 16, 1906), p. 526.

116 **An 1884 manual:** Anglo-American Telegraphic Code and Cypher Co., *Anglo-American Telegraphic Code to Cheapen Telegraphy and to Furnish a Complete Cypher* (New York: Tyrrel, 1891), pp. 70, 111.

116 **"Wires being down":** As cited in Steven M. Bellovin, "Compression, Correction, Confidentiality, and Comprehension: A Look at Telegraph Codes," paper presented at the Crytologic History Symposium, 2009, Laurel, MD.

116 **Telegraphic companies grew weary:** "Orthography and Telegraphy," *The Electrical Review* 59 (September 1906): 482.

117 **Plain language, reaffirms Article 8:** William F. Friedman, *The History of the Use of Codes and Code Language, International Telegraph Regulations Pertaining Thereto, and the Bearing of This History on the Cortina Report* (Washington, D.C.: United States Government Printing Office, 1928), pp. 2–5.

117 **Consider the incomparable economy:** A. C. Baldwin, *The Traveler's Vade Mecum; or, Instantaneous Letter Writer by Mail or Telegraph, for the Convenience of Persons Traveling on Business or for Pleasure, and for Others, Whereby a Vast Amount of Time, Labor, and Trouble Is Saved* (New York: A. S. Barnes and Co., 1853), p. 268.

119 **When there was a call:** *Documents de la Conférence télégraphique internationale de Paris*, vol. 2 (Berne: Bureau International de l'Union, 1925), pp. 218–19.

120 **On October 9:** *Documents de la Conférence télégraphique internationale de Paris*, vol. 2, pp. 44–55.

120 **"Whereas the foreign public":** *Documents de la Conférence télégraphique internationale de Paris*, vol. 1 (Berne: Bureau International de l'Union, 1925), pp. 426–27.

FOUR: THE LIBRARIAN'S CARD CATALOG (1938)

Character indexing, or a way of classifying Chinese for logical storage and retrieval, has its modern origin in library cataloging. Lin Yutang and others were drawn to the efforts made by a number of earlier indexers, including foreigners who had tried their hand at compiling bilingual Chinese dictionaries but never got beyond single attempts. Lin cites several that had experimented with the radical heading: the *kanji* table of Latvia-born Russian Buddhologist Otto Ottonovich Rosenberg, P. Poletti's *A Chinese and English Dictionary, Arranged According to Radicals and Sub-radicals* (Shanghai: American Presbyterian Press, 1896), and Joseph-Marie Callery's two-volume *Systema phoneticum scripturae sinicae* (Macau: n.p., 1841). There are several available biographical accounts of Lin in English and Chinese. Information about his Chinese typewriter, however, has been pieced together from nonliterary sources, such as records of his personal and professional relationship with Richard Walsh and Pearl Buck, as well as his business dealings with the Mergenthaler Company. His correspondences with Buck and Walsh, as well as draft schematics of the principles behind his eventual typewriter, are stored in the archives of the John Day Company at Princeton University. Records of his dealings with Mergenthaler are held at the Mergenthaler Linotype Company records at the National Museum of American History in Washington, D.C. See also his daughter Lin Taiyi's biography and memoir of him, *Lin Yutang zhuan* (Taipei: Lianjing, 1989), as well as Lin's autobiography, *Bashi zixu* (Taipei: Fengyun shidai, 1989), for details about the typewriter. His writings on philology and linguistics are found in *Yuyanxue luncong* (Shanghai: Shanghai shudian, 1989); Jing Tsu, "Lin Yutang's Typewriter," in *Sound and Script in Chinese Diaspora* (Cambridge, MA: Harvard University Press, 2010), pp. 49–79.

Du Dingyou's complete writings have been published as the twenty-two-volume *Du Dingyou wenji* (Guangzhou: Guangdong jiaoyu, 2012), but an earlier collection of his essays on library science remains useful: *Du Dingyou tushuguanxue lunwen xuanji* (Beijing: Shumu wenxian, 1988). Wang Yunwu left ample writings, including his various highly publicized autobiographies, the most relevant of which is *Xiulu bashi zixu* (Taipei: Shangwu, 1967). These self-narratives can be checked against the numerous reports on the character index race from the 1920s to the late 1940s in dozens of Chinese-language journals, including *Minguo ribao, Jiaoyu zhoukan, Shenbao, Dagongbao*, and various provincial-level library journals. Most of these journals can be found in the Shanghai Municipal Archives.

128 **"If the Chinese script is not abolished":** Ni Haishu, ed., *Lu Xun lun yuwen gaige* (Shanghai: Shidai, 1949), p. 10.

134 **He chose a seemingly innocuous, dry topic:** Lin Yutang, "Hanzi suoyin zhi shuoming," *Xin Qingnian* 4 (1918): 128–35.

140 **"To 'order' is to find":** Hu Shi, "Sijiao haoma jianzi fa xu," in *Hu Shi quanji*, vol. 3 (Hefei: Anhui jiaoyu, 2003), pp. 847–48.

142 **Even a laundryman:** Lin Yutang, *From Pagan to Christian* (Cleveland: World Publication Co., 1959), p. 35.

146 **Someone took notice:** Wan Guoding, "Gejia xin jianzifa shuping," *Tushuguanxue jikan* 2, no. 4 (1928): 46–79.

146 **Another collated list:** Jiang Yiqian, *Zhongguo jianzifa yange shilüe ji qishiqi zhong xin jianzifa biao* (n.p.: Zhongguo suoyin she, 1933); Ma Ying, "Zonghe jianzifa xuyan," *Zhejiang sheng tushuguan guankan* 3, no. 5 (1934): 29–54; "Zonghe jianzifa paizi liyan," *Zhejiang sheng tushuguan guankan* 3, no. 6 (1934): 1–17.

147 **Leveraging his position:** Shen Youqian, "'Hanzi paijian' wenti tanhua," *Shuren yuekan* 1, no. 1 (1937): 37–40.

147 **Its influence spread:** "Sijiao haoma jianzi fa caiyong jiguan ji chuban wu," *Tongzhou* 3, no. 9 (1935): 7.

147 **Whenever anyone asked how:** Wang Yunwu, "Wode shenghuo yu dushu," in *Wode shenghuo yu dushu* (Taipei: Jinxue, 1970), pp. 143–49, esp. 143.

147 **This early autodidacticism:** Wang Yunwu, "Haoma jianzi fa (fubiao)," *Dongfang zazhi* 22, no. 12 (1925): 82–98, esp. 86–87.

148 **An elementary school that compared:** Huang Dalun, "Bushou jianzifa yu sijiao haoma jianzifa de bijiao shiyan baogao," *Jiaoyu zhoukan* 177 (1933): 27–43.

148 **In 1928, a hapless:** Wen Zichuan, "Zhang Feng de mianxiandian," in *Wenren de ling yimian* (Guilin: Guangxi shifan daxue, 2004), pp. 18–20.

148 **He had clearly thought:** Zhang Feng, "Zhang Feng xingshu jianzifa," *Minduo zazhi* 9, no. 5 (1928): 1–11; Qi Feng, "Zhang Feng xingshu jianzifa," *Minguo ribao* (September 3, 1928), p. 1.

149 **"Zhang Feng may perish"**: Zhang, "Zhang Feng xingshu jianzifa," pp. 1–2. During a public speech, Wang called himself a "stink bug" (*chouchong*) because his home telephone number shared the four-corner numerical values of the Chinese character for "stink." See Shi Yanye, "Shuqi yanjiu suo zhi chigua dahui," *Shenbao* (August 6, 1928), p. 17.

149 **Zhang could only promote**: Wen, "Zhang Feng de mianxiandian," p. 19.

149 **Back in 1917**: Wang Yunwu, "Wo suo renshi de Gao Mengdan xiansheng," *Tongzhou* 4, no. 12 (1936): 78–84.

149 **According to its terms, Lin**: Wang Yunwu, "Jianzi fa yu fenlei fa," in *Xiulu bashi zixu* (Taipei: Shangwu, 1967), pp. 85–96, esp. 91–92.

150 **Wang later maintained he**: Wang, "Jianzi fa yu fenlei fa," pp. 85–96, esp. 91–92.

150 **He acknowledged Lin's research**: Cf. Wang Yunwu, *Wong's System of Chinese Lexicography: The Four-Corner Numeral System in Arranging Chinese Characters* (Shanghai: The Commercial Press, 1926), pp. 7–8; *Wong's System for Arranging Chinese Characters* (Shanghai: The Commercial Press, 1928).

150 **It was not until decades later**: Lin Yutang, "Invention of a Chinese Typewriter," *Asia and the Americas* 46 (1946): 58–61, esp. 60.

151 **Even a textile factory worker**: Li Jingsan, "Bianyan haoma jianzifa," *Tushu zhanwang* 6 (1948): 8–12.

153 **For the next seventy-two hours**: Du Dingyou, "Tushu yu taoming," in *Guonan zazuo* (Guangzhou: n.p., 1938), p. 2.

153 **Surely, others pleaded**: Du, "Tushu yu taoming," p. 2.

154 **In a treatise on using Chinese script**: Du Dingyou, *Hanzi xingwei paijianfa* (Shanghai: Zhonghua shuju, 1932).

154 **Treating each character**: Du Dongfang, *Tan "Liushu" wenti* (Shanghai: Dongfang, 1956).

159 **Each person had to cram**: Du Yan, "Cifu Du Dingyou huiyilu," in *Du Dingyou wenji*, vol. 22 (Guangzhou: Guangdong jiaoyu, 2012), pp. 385–86.

160 **So Du designed**: Ding U Doo [Du Dingyou], "A Librarian in Wartime," *American Library Association Bulletin* 38, no. 1 (1944): 5.

160 **and was convertible into**: Ding, "A Librarian in Wartime," p. 5.

160 **"Use your intelligence for good"**: Du Dingyou, "Yeyu yishu," in *Du Dingyou wenji*, vol. 11 (Guangzhou: Guangdong jiaoyu, 2012), p. 299.

161 **Library science was a pilot**: Charles Knowles Bolton, *American Library History* (Chicago: American Library Association Publishing Board, 1911), p. 6.

161 **He wrote about the amorous affair**: Du Dingyou, "Wo yu tuan," in *Du Dingyou wenji*, vol. 21 (Guangzhou: Guangdong jiaoyu, 2012), pp. 151–59.

167 **The USAF handed Lin's keyboard**: W. John Hutchins, ed., *Early Years in Machine Translation: Memoirs and Biographies of Pioneers* (Amsterdam, Philadelphia: J. Benjamins, 2000), pp. 21–72, 171–76.

FIVE: WHEN "PEKING" BECAME "BEIJING" (1958)

An abundance of materials, from personal accounts to official CCP documents, exists on the 1950s language policies regarding character simplification and pinyin Romanization. A still underutilized source is the KMT (Guomindang) Archives at the party archives in Taiwan, which has a duplicate (in microfilm) housed at the Hoover Institution, Stanford University. It contains Wu Yuzhang's manuscripts and handwritten notes on devising Romanization systems for Chinese, including draft schemes of his own. Important series published by the Committee on Script Reform include the Historical Sources of Phonetic Scripts Series (Pinyin wenzi shiliao congshu). The battle between National Romanization and Latin New Script is well documented but also scattered or embedded in different sources, from journals to pamphlets, party-sponsored surveys, government circulars, local official reports, memoirs of the different language reformers, literature, etc. The complete works of Zhou Youguang, *Zhou Youguang wenji*, 15 vols. (Beijing: Zhongyang bianyi, 2013), provides a useful window into this landscape, as do the writings of key people like Qu Qiubai, Wu Yuzhang, Zhao Yuanren, Li Jinxi, and Qian Xuantong, which are available in complete works or selections. Perspectives from two sides of the Taiwan Strait after 1949, in particular, capture the hardening of this history along political and ideological lines. For a representative view of the Nationalist side, see Wei Jiangong, *Wei Jiangong wenji*, 5 vols. (Nanjing: Jiangsu jiaoyu, 2001). A recent dissertation on the topic of Chinese Latinization and Soviet Turkish illiteracy campaigns provides new insight from a Eurasian-oriented perspective. See Ulug Kuzuoglu, "Codes of Modernity: Infrastructures of Language and Chinese Scripts in an Age of Global Information Revolution" (Ph.D. dissertation, Columbia University, 2018). Context for the Latinization of Chinese in Soviet language policy can be gleaned from Terry Martin, *Affirmative Action Empire: Nations and Nationalism in the Soviet Union, 1923–1939* (Ithaca, London: Cornell University Press, 2001); Michael G. Smith, *Language and Power in the Creation of the U.S.S.R., 1917–1953* (Berlin, New York: Mouton de Gruyter, 1998); A. G. Shprintsin, "From the History of the New Chinese Alphabet," in D. A. Olderogge, V. Maretin, and B. A. Valskaya, eds., *The Countries and Peoples of the East: Selected Articles* (Moscow: Nauka Publishing House, 1974); M. Mobin Shorish, "Planning by Decree: The Soviet Language Policy in Central Asia," *Language Problems and Language Planning* 8, no. 1 (Spring 1984): 35–49. For a useful bibliography of the teaching texts on Latin New Script published in the Soviet Union during the important years of 1930 to 1937, see Shi Pingqing, "1930 nian dao 1937 nian zai Sulian chuban de beifanghua ladinghua xin wenzi duwu de mulu," *Wenzi gaige* 21 (1959): 10. Essential studies of Dunganese include Mantaro Hashimoto, "Current Development in Zhunyanese (Soviet Dunganese) Studies," *Journal of Chinese Linguistics* 6, no. 2 (June 1978): 243–67; Svetlana Rimsky-Korsakoff Dyer, V. Tsibuzgin, and A. Shmakov, "Karakunuz: An Early Settlement of the Chinese Muslims in Russia," *Asian Folklore Studies* 51, no. 2 (1992): 243–78. On the life of Iasyr Shivaza, Rimsky-Korsakoff Dyer's study remains the primary account in English: *Iasyr Shivaza: The Life and Works of a Soviet Dungan Poet* (Frankfurt am Main, New York: P. Lang, 1991). See also Jing Tsu, "Romanization without Rome: China's Latin New Script and Soviet Central Asia," in Eric Tagliacozzo, Helen F. Siu, and Peter C. Perdue, eds., *Asia Inside Out: Connected Places* (Cambridge, MA: Harvard University Press, 2015), pp. 321-53.

Events of the Anti-Rightist Campaign and its ideological impact on character reform discussions—and persecutions of those who criticized Mao's language policies—can be assessed from articles published in the newspaper *Guangming ribao* and in the two journals it spawned during this period: *Xin Yuwen* and *Wenzi Gaige*. The newspaper reprint was published in Japan: *"Kōmyō nippo" senkan shigaku bungaku monji kaikaku: shigaku bungaku dai 101-ki—dai 200-ki, monji kaikaku dai 1-ki—dai 146-ki* (Kyoto: Hoyu Shoten, 1981). For a summary of the national language reform in English, see John DeFrancis, *Nationalism and Language Reform in China* (Princeton, NJ: Princeton University Press, 1950); *The Chinese Language: Fact and Fantasy* (Honolulu: University of Hawaii Press, 1984); *In the Steps of Genghis Kahn* (Honolulu: University of Hawaii Press, 1993). As is evident in his scholarship, the late DeFrancis was a staunch supporter of Romanizing Chinese. I am grateful for the conversations I had with him in his home at Uluwehi Place, Honolulu, in 2008, the year before he passed away.

172 **The first concrete proposal:** "Our sole goal is to reduce the number of strokes in characters, so it matters not whether the examples are taken from ancient script, vernacular script, original characters, borrowed cognates, regulated calligraphy, or cursive writing—as long as they fulfill this one criterion." From Qian Xuantong, "Jiansheng hanzi bihua de tiyi" ("Proposal to Reduce the Strokes in the Han script"), *Xin Qingnian* 7, no. 3 (1920): 114.

174 **The use of these characters:** "Guanyu Hanzi jianhua gongzuo de baogao" ("Report on the Work on Character Simplification"), collected in *Diyici quanguo wenzi gaige huiyi wenjian huibian* (Beijing: Wenzi gaige, 1957), pp. 20-37.

175 **One linguist recalled that:** Yin Huanxian, "Relie huanying Hanzi jianhua fang'an cao'an," in Wu Yuzhang, *Jianhua Hanzi wenti* (Beijing: Zhonghua shuju, 1956).

176 **After the release:** "Paizi gongren shi wenzi gaige de cujinpai," in *Gongnongbing shi wenzi gaige de zhulijun* (Beijing: Wenzi gaige, 1975), pp. 1-8.

177 **By 1982, the literacy rate:** http://uis.unesco.org/en/country/cn.

177 **The character for "love":** https://web.shobserver.com/wx/detail.do?id=114364.

178 **They argue that simplified "love":** https://zhuanlan.zhihu.com/p/26480178.

183 **"I was told that":** Quoted in David Porter, *Ideographia: The Chinese Cipher in Early Modern Europe* (Stanford, CA: Stanford University Press, 1991), p. 77.

184 **The story is vividly conveyed:** For translation and commentary in English, see Wolfgang Behr, "In the Interstices of Representation: Lucid Writing and the Locus of Polysemy in the Chinese Sign," in Alex de Voogt and Irving Finkel, eds., *The Idea of Writing: Play and Complexity* (Leiden, Boston: Brill, 2010), pp. 283-36.

190 **As a Soviet Tajik poet explained:** "When the Latin letters adorned the new alphabet / Soon the demand became slow for the Arab alphabet / In the scientific era the new

alphabet is like a plane / The Arabic alphabet is like a weak donkey in pain." As quoted in M. Mobin Shorish, "Planning by Decree: The Soviet Language Policy in Central Asia," *Language Problems and Language Planning* 8, no. 1 (Spring 1984): 39.

191 **Between 1931 and 1936:** Nie Gannu, *Cong baihuawen dao xin wenzi* (Beijing: Beijing zhongxiantuofang keji fazhan youxiangongsi, 2007).

193 **In this regard, the Russians:** See Ulug Kuzuoglu, "Codes of Modernity: Infrastructures of Language and Chinese Scripts in an Age of Global Information Revolution" (Ph.D. dissertation, Columbia University, 2018), pp. 241–89, 292–324.

195 **"There is no such difficulty":** Quoted in A. G. Shprintsin, "From the History of the New Chinese Alphabet," in D. A. Olderogge, V. Maretin, and B. A. Valskaya, eds., *The Countries and Peoples of the East: Selected Articles* (Moscow: Nauka Publishing House, 1974), p. 335.

195 **Already in the 1929 draft:** Qu Qiubai, "Zhongguo ladinghua de zimu," in *Qu Qiubai wenji,* vol. 3 (Beijing: Renmin wenxue, 1989), p. 354.

196 **Within a year of being reintroduced:** Ni Haishu, *Zhongguo pinyin wenzi yundongshi jianbian* (Shanghai: Xiandai shubao, 1948), pp. 150–72.

199 **It was necessary, they argued:** Terry Martin, *The Affirmative Action Empire: Nations and Nationalism in the Soviet Union, 1923–1939* (Ithaca, London: Cornell University Press, 2001), pp. 199–200.

203 **One member, Ma Xulun:** Fei Jinchang and Wang Fan, *Zhongguo yuwen xiandaihua bainian jishi (1892–1995)* (Beijing: Yuwen, 1997), p. 171.

204 **As this was a language campaign:** "Zhongguo wenzi gaige yanjiuhui mishuchu pinyin fang'an gongzuozu," in *Gedi renshi jilai Hanyu pinyin wenzi fang'an huibian*, 2 vols. (Beijing: Zhongguo wenzi gaige yanjiuhui mishuchu pinyin fang'an gongzuozu, 1955).

208 **In the first year alone:** "Pinyin zimu wei saomang he tuiguang Putonghua kaipile jiejing," *Renmin ribao* (April 5, 1959).

SIX: ENTERING INTO THE COMPUTER (1979)

Zhi Bingyi's experience during imprisonment and details on his "On-Sight" input method can be pieced together from newspaper reports and his own essays, interviews, and articles: "Hanzi jinrule jisuanji: Ji Zhi Bingyi chuangzao 'jianzi shima' fa de shiji," *Wenhui bao* (July 19, 1978); Zhi Bingyi and Qian Feng, "'Jianzi shima' hanzi bianma fangfa jiqi jisuanji shixian," in Zhongguo yuwen bianjibu, ed., *Hanzi xinxi chuli* (Beijing: Xinhua, 1979), pp. 28–53; Zhi Bingyi and Qian Feng, "Jiantan 'jianzi shima,'" *Ziran zazhi* 1, no. 6 (1978): 350–53, 367; Zhi Bingyi, "Hanzi bianma wenti," *Kexue* 3 (1981): 7–9. Information on Project 748—and on the Chinese computing industry—in the English language is scant. A chapter on Founder Group can be found in Qiwen Lu, *China's Leap into the Information Age: Innovation and Organization in the Computer Industry* (New York, Oxford: Oxford University Press, 2000). My reconstruction draws from a collection of firsthand testimonies from those who participated in either the design or execution of Project 748: Jinian qisiba gongcheng ershi zhounian gongzuozu, ed., *748 gongcheng ershi zhounian jinian wenji* (Beijing: n.p., 1994). Held in the Beijing University Library, this collection was put together to commemorate the twentieth anniversary of the founding of the Founder Group. It contains personal accounts from approximately fifty people who were directly involved in the project as engineers, policy makers, managers, or scientists. An important complementary source is the numerous published proceedings of Chinese-language information processing conferences that began to appear in the late 1970s through the late 1980s, starting with the first one held in December 1978 in Qingdao. I thank Bo An, a doctoral candidate at Yale who is writing the first English-language dissertation on the history of Chinese computing, for his conversations and help with these materials. Pertaining to the automation of print technology, a useful resource is the Xinhua News Agency's account of the different print technologies it was trying to acquire and develop: Sun Baochuan, *Chachi feixiang: Xinhua she tongxin jishu fazhan jishi* (Beijing: Xinhua, 2015). The dozen or so trip reports from the various academic or industrial scientific exchanges between the United States and China in the 1970s, which are in English, offer invaluable witness accounts of what China's state of science and technology was like on the inside, after the long period of isolation during the Cultural Revolution. They include: F. E. Allen and J. T. Schwartz, "Computing in China: A Trip Report" (July 1973), unpublished; "Computing in China: A Second Trip Report" (October 1977), unpublished; H. Chang, Y. Chu, and H. C. Lin, "Report of a Visit to People's Republic of China" (April 14, 1975), unpublished; T. E. Cheatham, W. A. Clark, A. W. Holt et al., "Computing in China: A Travel Report," *Science* 182 (October 12, 1973): 134–40; B. J. Culliton, "China's 'Four Modernizations' Lead to Closer Sino-U.S. Science Ties," *Science* 201 (August 11, 1978): 512–13; H. L. Garner, Y. L. Garner et al., eds., "Report of the IEE Computer Society Delegation to China" (January 1979), unpublished; H. L. Garner, "1978: Computing in China," *Computer* (March 1979): 81–96; R. L. Garwin, "Trip Report of a Visit to China" (1974), unpublished.

Multiple biographies of Wang Xuan have been published in Chinese, and this chapter draws from his own memoir as well as his more technical scholarly papers. Though he was prolific in Chinese, very little of his research is available in English, as is the case with most scientific research in the PRC from the time. For a rare example, see Wang Xuan et al., "A High Resolution Chinese Character Generator," *Journal of Computer Science and Technology* 1, no. 2 (1986): 1–14. His Chinese-language writings are available at http://www.wangxuan .net/.

For the details on Francis F. Lee's life, I thank Charles Bagnoschi, Lee's former associate, for helping me track down his daughter, Gloria Lee, in Austin, Texas. I am grateful to Gloria for generously sharing her father's private letters and her family memories with me. Documents related to the Sinotype invention—its genesis, development, construction, marketing, technical specifications, circumstances, etc.—are collected in the Graphic Arts Research Foundation archives at MIT Special Collections. Some records concerning the Sinotype's subsequent adaptation by RCA (as the Chinese Ideographic Photocomposer), under contract to the U.S. Army Natick Research Laboratories, are available at the Hagley Library, Wilmington, Delaware. Internal memos of the Pentagon working group and its—in the end—unexecuted plan to use the Sinotype to preempt China in the area of Chinese print technology are collected in the White House Office, National Security Council Staff Papers, 1948–1961, held at the Dwight D. Eisenhower Presidential Library in Abilene, Kansas. Details concerning GARF's early sponsorship by the Carnegie Corporation of New York are stored at the Rare Book and Manuscript Library, Columbia University. I thank archivist Jennifer S. Comins for her extraordinary, beyond-the-call-of-duty assistance.

211 **He had been branded:** The following treatment of Zhi Bingyi is pieced together from his recollections in newspapers and interviews. See "Hanzi jinrule jisuanji," *Wenhui bao* (July 19, 1978); Zhi Bingyi and Qian Feng, "Qiantan 'jianzi shima,'" *Ziran zazhi* 1, no. 9 (1978): 350–53, 367; Zhi Bingyi, "Hanzi bianma wenti," *Kexue* 3 (1981): 7–9.

234 **He needed a succinct way:** Wang Xuan, Lu Zhimin, Tang Yuhai, and Xiang Yang, "Gao fenbianlu Hanzi zixing zai jisuanji zhongde yasuo biaoshi ji zixing dianzhen de fuyuanshebei," in *Proceedings of 1983 International Conference on Chinese Information Processing*, cosponsored by CIPSC and UNESCO, Beijing, October 12–14, 1983, vol. 2, pp. 71–92.

240 **Within a few months, Lee wrote:** Francis F. Lee, "A Chinese Typesetting Machine," Quarterly Progress Report, Research Laboratory of Electronics (April 15, 1953), pp. 69–70.

242 **"Since the conclusion":** Letter from W. W. Garth to Vannevar Bush, dated November 2, 1960, Manuscript Library, Columbia University.

242 **"symbolic manipulation is not":** Francis F. Lee's private correspondence with his daughter, Gloria Lee, dated February 28, 2018.

245 **Beijing University and its various units:** Jiang Zemin's letter, dated February 22, 1980, collected in Jinian qisiba gongcheng ershi zhounian gongzuozu, ed., *748 gongcheng ershi zhounian jinian wenji* (Beijing: n.p., 1994).

SEVEN: THE DIGITAL SINOSPHERE (2020)

This chapter is based almost entirely on interviews and fieldwork and draws on the recollections of some of the original East Asian participants in the preliminary conversation in the 1970s. For Taiwan's perspective, see Xie Qingjun and Huang Kedong, *Guozi zhengli xiaozu shinian* (Taipei: Zixun yingyong guozi zhengli xiaozu, 1989). For Japan's perspective, see Tatsuo Kobayashi, *Yunikōdo senki: moji fugō no kokusai hyōjunka batoru* (Tokyo: Denki Daigaku Shuppankyoku, 2011). I am indebted to the representatives from the Unicode Consortium and IRG who provided helpful pointers: Lu Qin, Ken Lunde, Michel Suignard, Lee Collins, Joe Becker, Eiso Chan, Wang Yifan, Tao Yang, Tseng Shih-Shyeng, Selena Wei, and Ngô Thanh Nhàn. I thank Mr. Tseng for sharing his private files with me, documenting the early days of Taiwan's encoding work on the Chinese Character Code for Information Interchange. My deepest thanks to Lu Qin and Lee Collins for their generosity and introduction to key people in the project, as well as Eiso Chan and Tao Yang for the helpful follow-up conversations. IRG allowed me to participate in their meetings in Hanoi in 2018 and Shenzhen in 2020. For general information about Unicode, see https://home.unicode .org/. For the website for specialists that posts information on the tech updates and participation process: https://www.unicode.org/main.html. For Han unification history, see "Appendix E: Han Unification History," http://www.unicode.org/versions/Unicode13.0.0/appE .pdf. Also widely referenced is Ken Lunde's standard work, *CJKV Information Processing*, 2nd ed. (Sebastopol, CA: O'Reilly, 2008), which is written for computer programmers but contains useful information for nonspecialists as well. Also useful are Huang Kedong et al., *An Introduction to Chinese, Japanese and Korean Computing* (Singapore, Teaneck, NJ: World Scientific, 1989); William C. Hannas, *Asia's Orthographic Dilemma* (Honolulu: University of Hawaii Press, 1997); Viniti Vaish, ed., *Globalization of Language and Culture in Asia: The Impact of Globalization Processes on Language* (London, New York: Continuum, 2010); Daniel Pargman and Jacob Palme, "ASCII Imperialism," in Martha Lampland and Susan Leigh Star, eds., *Standards and Their Stories: How Quantifying, Classifying, and Formalizing Practices Shape Everyday Life* (Ithaca, NY: Cornell University Press, 2009). I thank Karen Smith-Yoshimura and John W. Haeger for sharing their personal recollections about the early days of RLG. Original documents of the organization can be found in the RLG Records at Special Collections at Stanford University. A complete history of the founding of Unicode and its earlier battles with ISO is connected to but ultimately lies beyond the scope of this chapter. Unicode's fascinating history, especially in the early days preceding the formation of the Unicode Consortium, remains to be written. I was unable to use all the insights that experts in the Chinese font design industry—Chris Wu, Caspar Lam, and Eric Liu—took the time to share with me and I remain in admiration of their ongoing commitment to the Chinese font.

Continual experimentations with and cultural reverence for the Chinese script form can be found in Chinese diasporic communities around the world. Malaysian Chinese literary writers and intellectuals, for whom questioning the Chinese script heritage is a way of challenging a pan-Chinese identity, have been especially prolific in recent times. See the works of Zhang Guixing and Huang Jinshu (Kim Chew Ng). Novel reinventions of the written Chinese character in contemporary Chinese art include those by artists of Chinese descent outside of China, such as Cuba-born Flora Fong, whose works like *Chino en las Américas* (2010) and *Cucú, baja, Cucú, baja* (2019) play on the pictographic quality of characters to tell a diasporic story. I thank her for receiving me in her home and studio in Havana, Cuba, in September 2019. Contemporary artistic reinventions of the Chinese script should also be compared with the historical precedents of appropriating the Chinese writing system by non-Chinese people (see chapter 1 notes), which have been no less creative.

For controversies concerning Confucius Institutes, see Marshall Sahlins, "China U," *The Nation* (October 29, 2013); "McCaul Statement on the Biden Administration's Withdrawal of a Proposed Rule on Confucius Institutes" (February 9, 2021); "China Task Force Report,"

U.S. House of Representatives (September 2020), https://gop-foreignaffairs.house.gov/wp
-content/uploads/2020/09/CHINA-TASK-FORCE-REPORT-FINAL-9.30.20.pdf; Jan Pet-
ter Myklebust, "Confucius Institutes Close as China Relations Deteriorate" (May 16, 2020),
https://www.universityworldnews.com/post.php?story=20200513092025679, and China's response, https://sverigesradio.se/artikel/7449665.

250 **Someone from Taiwan:** http://www.newhua.com/2020/0714/351298.shtml.

252 **The first encoding standard:** Control codes, some of which were inherited from the
      typewriting era, had command functions like moving the paper carriage so the device
      can start at the beginning of a new line.

256 **In the 1960s alone:** *East Asian Libraries—Problems and Prospects: A Report and Recom-
      mendations* (ACLA, 1977), p. 5.

256 **Digitizing these collections:** *Library of Congress Information Bulletin 1982*, appendix,
      p. 95; Chi Wang, *Building a Better Chinese Collection for the Library of Congress* (Lanham,
      MD: The Scarecrow Press, 2012), p. 98.

257 **"solved the problem":** *Automation, Cooperation and Scholarship: East Asian Libraries in
      the 1980's: Final Report of the Joint Advisory Committee to the East Asian Library Program*
      (Washington, D.C.: The American Council of Learned Societies, 1981), p. 24.

259 **Long established in Chinese lexicology:** Shen Kecheng, *Shutongwen: Xiandai Hanzi
      lungao* (Shanghai: Jinxiu wenzhang, 2008).

260 **They wished to engage:** Weiying Wan et al., "Libraries and Institutions," *Journal of
      East Asian Libraries* 63 (1980): 17–18.

265 **"soaring dragon in the sky":** "Mingzi yong shengpizi '69' ziku dabuchu minjing ji-
      anyi yong changyongzi," www.anfone.com; "Zongzai zhengming 'woshiwo' shengpizi
      tongyi ziku daodi you duonan?," http://xinhuanet.com/politics/2017-05/12/c_11209
      58591.htm.

267 **The attitude in Vietnam:** Alexander Woodside, "Conceptions of Change and Human
      Responsibility for Change in Late Traditional Vietnam," in D. K. Wyatt and A. B. Wood-
      side, eds., *Moral Order and the Question of Change: Essays on Southeast Asian Thought* (New
      Haven, CT: Yale University Press, 1982), p. 104.

267 **"The last time the Chinese came":** Declassified Pentagon Papers, https://en.wikisource
      .org/wiki/Page:Pentagon-Papers-Part_I.djvu/170.

270 **In the original 1988 Unicode:** Joe Becker, *Unicode 88* (Palo Alto, CA: Xerox Corpo-
      ration, 1988), p. 5.

276 **"Dear Beloved Chairman Xi":** "Dear Beloved Chairman Xi," letter from Peng
      Hongqing of Chongqing, dated October 8, 2016. I thank Tao Yang for this informa-
      tion.

278 **It learned the critical importance:** https://www.wsj.com/articles/from-lightbulbs
      -to-5g-china-battles-west-for-control-of-vital-technology-standards-11612722698.

278 **Instead of laying down:** Jonathan E. Hillman, *The Emperor's New Road: China and the
      Project of the Century* (New Haven, CT; London: Yale University Press, 2020), p. 24.

INDEX